THE AGE OF PARODY

THE AGE
OF PARODY

Dispatches from The Eighties

Philip Norman

HAMISH HAMILTON · LONDON

To Liz Jobey

HAMISH HAMILTON BOOKS
Published by the Penguin Group
27 Wrights Lane, London w8 5tz, England
Viking Penguin Inc., 40 West 23rd Street, New York, New York 10010, USA
Penguin Books Australia Ltd, Ringwood, Victoria, Australia
Penguin Books Canada Ltd, 2801 John Street, Markham, Ontario, Canada l3r 1b4
Penguin Books (N.Z.) Ltd, 182–190 Wairau Road, Auckland 10, New Zealand

Penguin Books Ltd, Registered Offices: Harmondsworth, Middlesex, England

First published in Great Britain 1990 by
Hamish Hamilton Ltd
Copyright © 1990 by Philip Norman
1 3 5 7 9 10 8 6 4 2

British Library Cataloguing in Publication Data
CIP data for this book is available from the British Library

Printed in Great Britain by Richard Clay Ltd, Bungay, Suffolk
ISBN 0–241–12845–5

Author's Note

A shorter version of the title essay first appeared in *the Guardian*. The rest have appeared variously in *The Times*, *The Sunday Times*, *the Sunday Times Magazine*, the *Observer*, the *Independent*, the *Guardian* and the *London Daily News*

P.N.

Contents

Contents

The Age of Parody

For me, the whole character of Britain in the Eighties is summed up by what has been done to the pubs. It is the process which a great English novelist, Patrick Hamilton, called 'ye-olde-ing'. In Hamilton's day, the style was mock-Tudor; today, it is mock-imperial Victorian. The look is standard to every brewing conglomerate: a dark green, scarlet or black exterior, covered with gold copperplate phrases intended to evoke Dickensian comfort, plenty and lavishness. *Choice Old Ales in Keg & Bottle . . . Rare Imported Wines & Brandies . . . Splendid Home-Cooked Dishes . . . Sumptuous Cold Collations Always Available.*

Not that Britain's drinkers seriously imagine themselves transported en masse back to the era of Pickwick, stagecoaches and posthorn gallops. A weary common faculty automatically translates the flowery 19th century promise into late 20th century fact. The Fine Old Ales will more likely be brand-new lagers, the Rare Imported Wines delivered by tanker and dispensed by tap. The Splendid Home-Cooked Dishes swelter as usual under Gestapo interrogation-lights next to a Cold Collation far from Sumptuous, never mind Always Available. The whole tariff of ludicrous make-believe is swallowed without protest or dissent.

For this is the Age of Parody. In British life at the decade's end, little remains that does not wear the cosmetic mask of something else considered happier, more desirable, romantic or glamorous. The country through the Eighties has increasingly reminded me of the never-never land in that old American TV show, where people could live out their dreams, however absurd, babyish or perversely unsuited to the environment. Britain truly has turned into Fantasy Island.

The Eighties were never forecast as such. Difficult though it be to remember now, their original profile was of chaste realism. After the enervated whimsy and dragged-out nostalgia of the Seventies, our chance finally had come to get to grips with the modern world. Whereas the Sixties took almost a full decade to expire, the Seventies were pillow-stifled and the Eighties instantly determined out of that widespread euphoria and hope. Science, mocked for 10 post-hippy years, suddenly glowed with alluring chic. 'High Tech' became the fashionable rage. Computers ceased to be the butt of ill-natured jokes and transformed themselves into 'user-friendly' household pets. On New Year's Eve, 1979, one felt palpable impatience to cross over into that bright new vista of soft-bumpered cars, house-trained robots and cosy red indicator-lights.

Who could have dreamed that in two years the 1980s would have leapt back to the 1880s, with Britain embroiled in a gunboat war containing as much jingoistic pantomime as the 'Grand Tableau' which used to conclude Victorian Music Hall? Who could have imagined all reasonable argument, all pertinent inquiry overwhelmed by a Prime Minister whose sole masterstroke was to rifle the dressing-up box for cast-offs from Churchill, Boadicea and Good Queen Bess? Who, at the height of burlesque, could have conceived a military communiqué beginning 'Be pleased to inform Her Majesty . . .' or the sky over St Paul's screaming with jet fighters as if Hitler, Boney and the Armada had been trounced together? From the Falklands on, we knew what the Eighties *really* were to be. It was Kate Carney's Circus all the way.

Eight years later, 'Falklands Spirit', as first bottled by Messrs. Saatchi & Saatchi, is confirmed as the decade's major merchandising force. *Campaign*, the admen's magazine, recently announced that the quickest way to sell anything in Britain nowadays is to link it – however implausibly – with our regained imperial apotheosis. Hence 'Mrs Bridges'' jams and chutneys, after 'or-

iginal' recipes of a cook, who never was, in a kitchen more real
than a TV drama-set. Hence 'Royal Yacht' after-shave, warranted
to contain 'The Essence of Edwardian England'. Hence the
'Lark Rise to Candleford' range of toiletries, purveying talc and
soap-on-a-rope in the name of villagers who for their ablutions
used tin baths and garden privies. Campaign subsequently
devoted a long, admiring feature to the trouble taken by one
soft drinks manufacturer to put its ginger beer into bottles
parodying the brown earthenware of old-fashioned 'stone
ginger'. Each mass-produced container was to be given a
specially 'aged' look as if it had not just been apathetically
hooked from a parody Victorian pub's cold shelf but, rather,
found in an E. Nesbit attic or dredged from the bottom of a
lake.

The most successful elements in Britain's new pedestrian
precincts are Victorian parody shops, with artificially archaic
names like 'Crabtree & Evelyn' – lavendar-reeking labyrinths of
soap, 'Edwardian lady' bath sachets, herb-pillows, reproduction
samplers and mustard bath foot-soak, all packaged with that odd
calligraphic mixture ('This *Famous* SOAP . . .') that gives provenance to the daftest anachronism. 'Traditional' and 'Original' are
retailing buzz words, used to shift the mundanest stock from
supermarket shelves: whether chocolate chip cookies 'baked
according to an old family recipe by villagers in the Yorkshire
Dales' or 'Real Cornish ice cream, made in the heart of Shakespeare country in Henley-in-Arden.' A shop can increase its
business a hundred-fold by restyling itself an 'emporium'. Taking
a gold leaf from parody pubs, the most faceless supermarket
chains bill themselves as 'Purveyors of Fine Food & Wines'.
Oh, the late Eighties revival of the ampersand!

Nostalgic craving for books and films about British rule
in India effortlessly added itself to the marketing mix. Repining
those verandahs and servants and Simla hill-stations long ago
ceased to be the perquisite of dispossessed memsahibs only.
Classes whose forbears were no more than cannon-fodder to the
Raj now flock as eagerly, with the same poignant memories, to
Indian restaurants named The Far Pavilions, The Jewel in the

Crown or (I'm quite serious) Gandhi's. Raj-mania having become somewhat exhausted, African Safari-mania took its place, with Anne Diamond presenting her breakfast TV show in 'Out of Africa' jodhpurs and pith helmet. Even the TV ad for a Wall's ice lolly now features a Karen Blixenish female, locked in passionate embrace before an African sunset.

Costume drama and historical myth have spelled instant box-office, no matter how dodgy the premise or brain-shrivellingly awful the script. The quintessential line of Eighties movie-dialogue, for me, came in The Draughtsman's Contract, a film about Jacobean nobility – highly critically praised – when one peri-wigged gentleman broke off from the Prithee-ing and By Your Leave-ing to exclaim 'There is no *way*, Sir, I'm going to do that!'

One musical piece has dominated the psyche of the decade. It is Vangellis's theme for Chariots of Fire, a film about heroic 1920s athletes, widely interpreted as a parable of Mrs Thatcher's heroism over The Falklands. Its machine-made chords could, indeed, be a Saatchi & Saatchi slogan rendered into melody – dramatic, portentous, muzzily suggestive of green fields and great deeds; of limitless victory forged by a single, indomitable will.

Hence the patriotism which, after pot noodles, must rank as the Eighties' great synthetic triumph. You can shut your eyes, think of Chariots of Fire and feel proud you're British, no matter what beastly things you happen to be doing. Even the football thugs who smash up Europe carry Union Jacks and evidently believe, in some addled part of their brains, that they are 'an army . . . doin' it like Maggie done it in The Falklands'.

The great myth about the British is that we are a nation rooted in tradition and continuity. Can you imagine the French, the Germans, even the Americans, tolerating the devastation that has happened here, not just over the last 10 years but over the last 40? The tearing of hearts from our cities. The idiotic redrawing and renaming of our counties. The temporary facades, plastered one over another like layers of cheap wallpaper. Despite far greater historical interruptions, the French, the German, even the American way of life goes on much as it has for the past 100 years. For all our roast beef and Royalty, we have no way of life beyond that reflected in our feckless, covetous eyes.

Britain's Age of Parody thus works on two separate, schizophrenic levels. First, and most obvious, there is *self*-parody – the officially-sanctioned drive to earn money from tourists by presenting ourselves in every possible ridiculous historical cliché and stereotype. This is the so-called Museum Culture which, through the Eighties, has been busily remodelling a thousand-year heritage in celluloid, Polystyrene and acrid hamburger meat. Poor benighted London shows what the whole country is intended soon to become: a wasteland of plastic Beefeaters, imitation 1920s open-top buses and the uncontrolled imposture of bureaux de 'change'.

Then again there is parody as escapism, the device of a people increasingly unsure about their own place in the world and afraid of the present, let alone the future. Once, mimicry and masquerade were the prerogative of a few, aesthetes, bohemians or hippies. In late Eighties Britain, virtually every man, woman and child is, consciously or unconsciously, playing a role, striking a pose or acting out a daydream.

The best guide to current mass fantasy – better even than TV commercials – are the lengthy advertising films which unscrupulous cinema-chains now show instead of a second feature. Whether the product on offer be shampoo, beer, banks or employment agencies, two dream worlds tend to predominate. One is Fifties America, with drape suits, pink Cadillacs, drive-ins and acappella singing. The other is downtown New York loft life, with stripped wood floors, industrial walls, Venetian blinds and giant ceiling fans (though, naturally, not muggers, rotting garbage or all-night police-sirens). Thus are young Britons most easily persuaded to engage as temps in solicitors' offices with one-bar electric fires, or deposit savings with what used to be the plain old Woolwich.

Though America has always fed its idylls and illusions to Britain, this used to be at second hand, via Hollywood or pop music. In the Eighties, cut-price transatlantic air fares allow millions to visit every dream landscape ever pined for over a choc-ice in the one-and-nines. Even for stay-at-homes, the American dream can be instantly assembled complete, with baseball on TV, American fast food, American six-packs, popcorn and '57 Flavor' ice cream. The world of soda fountains, High School hops and bobby-pins is seen to possess, not only more glamour and excitement but also more resilience – more dependable solidarity – than all our heaped up, disposable images of Olde England.

Wholesale imitation of a culture founded on wholesale imitation naturally produces some paradox. The 'Yuppie' style favoured by young bankers and brokers in Mrs Thatcher's economic Wonderland is believed the epitome of hard-nosed, thrusting, fingerpopping New York. It is actually New York's rather confused parody of English 'classic elegance'. Francophobes for ever, we have nonetheless managed to take on New York's naive awe of all things French – witness the absurd little runabout styled Le Car. I hear even that former bastion of true British culture The Hammersmith Palais has renamed itself 'Le Palais'.

Parody Americanisms assail us from all sides even of mundane everyday life. The telephone-user, pursuing a service slower and more dilatory than ever, now hears a recorded voice say 'Thank you for calling Directory Inquiries'. The Southern Region commuter, as his train limps finally to base, sees a sign reading 'Welcome to London Waterloo'. The Police wear letters on their fronts spelling POLICE. London taxi-passengers, shrinking from driver-contact, as likely as not encounter a placard 'Thank you for not smoking'. Corporations which plainly don't have to give a toss for anyone spend ever more millions on public relations campaigns emphasising how much they 'care'.

As America's runway-in-the-Atlantic, we have lived under the thrall of a President himself unarguably the greatest concatenation of parody, burlesque and outright slapstick ever seen on the world stage. This is the President who, after what even his own administration concedes was a 'show' invasion, of territory even more inconsequential than the Falklands, awarded 1000 decora-

tions for bravery. Against Ronald Reagan, even Margaret Thatcher is reduced to the role of bespangled assistant, performing
obedient bunny-dips and shouting 'Houpla!'

The terrible power of both has lain in their mutual inability to
descry any element of the ludicrous, fatuous or fantastic in the
constantly-changing charades their image-machines devise for
them. They simply read the script, whatever it may say, however
it may promise to make the collective sphincter of future generations cringe in embarrassment. Presidential pseudo-folksiness
will never surpass that quavery post-surgical voice over the
world's networks, saying 'Nancy . . . are ya doin' anything
tonight?' Mock-Swiftian parliamentary epigram will never again,
thank God, descend to the nadir of 'The Lady's not for turning.'

The two leaders have presented an interesting contrast in
styles of utter bogusness. While Reagan's matured over
long years in Hollywood, Mrs Thatcher came upon hers almost
by accident. She began the decade as a shrilling harriden,
unable to control the emphasis in her words or prevent her eyes
from glaring as madly as Miss Havisham's. Then came the
famous night when she appeared on television to explain
something messy in Belfast, coincidentally suffering from an
attack of laryngitis. The result was 'gentle and low – an excellent
thing in woman'. In the Universal surprise and delight, that
messy something in Belfast simply melted away.

Since then, we have seen Mrs Thatcher put on ad hoc
burlesques and discard them with the fretful insensibility of
some house wife trying on hats at C and A. Barbie herself does
not possess more perfectly cosmeticised golden hair or so many
wildly different and contradictory disguises. There has been the
Lady with the Lamp, dabbing Kleenex for poor boys maimed in
designer war. There has been the stern upholder of Victorian
'values' (all except compassion and charity), turning aside any
cavil or query with that cry of 'Rejoice'. Especially at Election
time, there has been the friendly housewife shopper, and lover
of animals and little children. There has been the 'committed
Christian', signing the Channel Tunnel's dingy deal in the
Chapter House at Canterbury Cathedral. With no inkling of

incongruity or amazing volte-face, there has been the Earth Mother guardian of the environment and the Cossack-hatted guardian of union freedom in Poland.

At some point it was suggested to an evidently surprised Mrs Thatcher that her attitude to the electorate did not markedly seem to differ from that of China's Deng Xaoping. Since then, every Prime Ministerial utterance, however insensately cold or crass, has been couched in a thrill-laden 'caring' contralto. In recent years, as a series of awful transport disasters has chronicled Britain's infrastructural disintegration, Gloriana has changed into the mother of all Her People, hastening to the wrecks of boats and planes to occupy the foreground, hog the camera and, at a dramatically advantageous point, be seen to be 'in tears'.

She has had the profoundest effect on British politics, demonstrating to all of every party that nothing works so well as the cheap PR con-trick. Thus did Labour use its vast electoral opportunity in designing itself a droopy Dickins & Jones rose. Thus did the SDP deploy its massed intellects in coming up with yellow for the rosettes.

Neil Kinnock is the saddest case in his eternal confusion about which parody his followers wish him to be. Latterly, not even President Reagan has looked so bewildered by the contradictory promptings of cue-cards. Least fortunate was the parody chosen for Labour's 1987 Election campaign – Kinnock walking with wife amid wild, honest coastal scenery, like that famous picture of J. F. Kennedy and Jackie at Hyannis Port.

There is a crucial difference, of course. Kennedy walked beside the surf. He did not fall headlong into it.

It might be thought that, with such a motley of fakers, poseurs and cack-handed card-tricksters thronging their public life, the Eighties would have seen ordinary British people become steadily more worldly, knowing, perspicacious and cynical. How is it that, on the contrary, we seem to have grown – and be manifestly still growing – more gullible, suggestible and infantile?

Basic evidence of this comes from a source that should know.

In the early Sixties, the advertising industry, led by such gurus as the late Sir Misha Black, decided there must be an end to the little cartoon brand-emblems with which old-fashioned manufacturers like Tate and Lyle sugar had built up recognition and goodwill since Victorian times. Early Sixties consumers had grown much too sophisticated to be influenced by such things. So, with due regret, it was goodbye to Tate and Lyle's 'Mr Cube', the Bisto Kids, the Guinness toucan, the Bird's Custard chicks et al.

Twenty years on, what do we find? Mr Cube is back, as genial and villainously bare-legged as ever. So are the Bisto Kids, albeit redrawn in sub-punk pastels like cast-offs from Wham. Television ads are swamped with talking, singing and dancing potato crisps, detergent bottles, breadknives, butter-pats and gravyboats. Not only food manufacturers but faceless public utilities employ Disneyesque little animals and birds to communicate their essential whimsy and warmth of heart. From British Telecom's 'Buzby' to the Listening Bank's friendly griffin, a world of predatory commerce addresses us in the idiom of prewar nursery walls. Little children and their cute little sayings promulgate the fraud of privatization. I see there is even a condom-by-post firm which warns against AIDS with a humanoid sheath, one hand upraised in the stern attitude of a spermicidal Mr Plod.

The fecklessness and irresponsibilty that were youth's prerogative in the Sixties have spread to all age-groups in the Eighties. Desite the facade of busy business – the mania for Filofaxing effiency and self-organisation – it is difficult to find anyone in the length and breadth of Fanatasy Island willing to do a hand's turn. For this, above all, has been the decade of Leisure – pale, spirit-sinking Eighties word! – and its concomitant mass self-delusion, Lifestyle.

Everyone on Fantasy Island, whether employed or not, claims a right to limitless and continually-expanding Leisure. Everyone has a Lifestyle, modelled in most essentials on the silvery-haired, soft-focused, barely animate beings who inhabit American TV soap operas. Lifestyle is what turns every High Street into useless labyrinths of video-game shops and every pub not Pick-wickised into a pseudo cocktail bar named 'Bogart's or 'Visions'. It is what has put virtually the entire population into the same perpetual weekend attire of stone-washed denim and sickly pastel turquoise, yellow and pink. It is what causes the air of a Dynasty swingers party or South Fork barbecue to hover grotesquely over inner city slums, secondary picketing, even that public, televised butchering of the two Army corporals in Belfast.

On Fantasy Island, work of whatever kind, is seen as no more than a short, painful vigil between pleasure and partying. Post-men make their rounds dressed as postmen no longer, but Miami Vice gigolos. Dustmen empty our bins in shades and Bermuda shorts. The very building sites are scaffolded discos where tattooed Travoltas disport themselves in garments one would think too perversely tight for the simplest lifting work. A minor Eighties environmental curse is that macho Monday Morning Fever display of low-rise denim trouser-seat and high-rising anal crack.

Pop music is the universal placebo, wooshing and tishing in the earpieces of a million Walkmen, soothing the awful exertion of having to walk or catch a bus or train. Eighties pop has been chiefly parody, a witless synthesised stream of Fifties and Sixties revivals cashing in on what seems inexhaustible nostalgia for those far distant, thrice blessed times. Greater still is the parody of youth's rebel music having been hijacked by TV ads to sell detergent, cat food, even Sanatogen tonic for the elderly. In America – where the concept of parody is unknown – they now use Hip-Hop music to promote the Army. Even that symbol of despair, the job centre, has been given a disco-ish relaunch as a 'Job Club'.

Central to every lifestyle is a pop-induced parody of eternal adolescence. The decade's great heroine is Joan Collins, for playing sex kitten roles in TV soap opera to the point where she qualifies for a bus pass. Ageing men are scarcely less blindly narcissistic than women, stuffing their wizened buttocks into form-fitting Levis, their brewer's goitres into pink woollens with little lambs gambolling across the chest. Last summer I crossed to the Isle of Wight with a gruesomely pastel-attired cloud of what used to be London day-trippers. Near me on the ferry was a Cockney paterfamilias who, 20 years ago, would have been decently attired in brown chalkstripe suit with braces and sun-bonnet made from knotted handkerchief. Today he wore a Tour-de-France cap, Rififi-style blouson, collarless aquamarine shirt, white trousers with mock-punk knee-zippers and grey pearlised pointed shoes. Needless to add, he looked as comfortable as someone in an Iron Maiden.

Our leaders have been nothing if not skilful in recognizing and exploiting this sybaritic myopia. Alongside real, troubled, neurotic and divided Britain there has come to exist a parallel Leisure 'n' Lifestyle Britain, suffused with all the lip-glossed hyper-reality of the American soaps. This is the Britain shown in Government pre-privatization TV ads, where men, women and children gather in naive wonder to witness mass share-ownership descend from above in the form of an irradiant Stephen Spielberg spacecraft. It is the Britain where services that are every taxpayer's normal right, like post, telephones and water-supply are re-invented as soul-stirring dramas of impossible privilege and good fortune. It is the Britain where – also for pre-privatization purposes – the discovery has just been made that electricity is a marvellous thing, used for illuminating homes, factories and cities all over the place. 'The electric guitar . . .' you doubtless have heard the slogan. 'Powered by electricity.'

Lifestyle Britain might alternatively be called Telecom Britain after its most active exponent. It is characterized by relentless substitution of the cosmetic for the material, the superfluous for the desperately needful. Deprived of an efficient telephone system we may nonetheless call up any number of Lifestyle lines to hear a pop tune, receive a betting tip or engage in subpornographic party talk. At Piccadilly Underground station the traveller can now watch continuous pop videos and commercials on giant TV monitors slung above the platform. Nearby is the station clock, broken these many months.

There is seemingly no end to our willingness to be wooed by bright new names for bad old things ('Network South-East!') by

paint-jobs and catchphrases as substitutes for reliability and service. Shiny logos entrance us as did missionary beads the primitive African savage. The power of graphics in the Eighties, has
rivalled the totem pole or juju stick. Redesign it and it *must* be
better. That is why even so modest a magazine as *The Listener*
has undergone as many fruitless facelifts as some poodle-toting
Palm Beach hag. The supposedly intelligent, literate *Guardian* is
the latest willing sacrifice to rampant designer self-abuse.

In general, where graphics become exciting, quality of life pro-
portionately diminishes. For decades London buses have carried
on their sides the plain, explicit phrase 'London Transport'.
Now the phrase, within a jolly yellow stripe, is 'London Buses'.
Reinforcing the unmistakable nuance, drivers and conductors
have been secretly kitted out in leisure blousons and anoraks.
Lifestyle is at its deadly work again.

Journalists – all but for a subversive and threatened handful –
follow the official line of make-believe. It has become normal to
see banner headlines in mass-circulation dailies, announcing
some imminent plot change in Dallas or EastEnders. Black-face
editorials thunder fearlessly against the villainy of Alexis in
Dynasty. With the parody news comes parody sentiment, pumping up public indignation at the minuscule and inconsequential;
while most true, aching issues about Kate Carney's Britain are
determinedly ignored. In an epoch unparalleled for human suffering, what have been the great issues of British tabloid journalism?
There was Who Shot J.R.? There was the mercy dash to Blackie,
the Spanish donkey. There was the drawn-out agonizing su-
spense over the naming of Anne Diamond's baby.

The decline of half our national papers to a cross between
TV company handout, bingo-card and masturbation-aid is generally agreed to have started with Rupert Murdoch's *Sun*. Yet
this at its birth – or, rather-rebirth – was no more than parody,
consciously apeing the populist clout of Hugh Cudlipp's *Daily
Mirror* at its apogee in the Forties and Fifties.

The differences scarcely need enumerating. The old *Mirror*
was a wholly original voice produced by a brilliant team dedi-

cated to widening the bounds of mass journalism and moving its readership ever upward. However brash and vulgar, it always had a powerful underlying morality. The *Sun* and *its* parodies, by contrast, are produced by the lowest forms of journalistic life among whose many demerits the foremost is pure laziness. Put simply, it is far easier to make up stories about artificial celebrities than obtain genuine scoops about real ones.

Headline-writers do their duty for Fantasy Island, refusing to embrace any topic that does not already have provenance as a Hollywood movie or TV soap. Hence the 'Star Wars' option that may blow the planet apart accompanied by unheard John Williams music. Hence the 'French Connection' that car-chases drugs to our children, and the 'godfathers' of Belfast and Lebanon, slaughtering with a faint fragrance of Brando and de Niro.

In almost all its garish Eighties forms, British tabloid journalism parodies earlier times. The breathless, empty gossip columns of *Mail* and *Express* burlesque a form considered redundant and discontinued 20 years ago. Coverage of Royalty reaches back even further, being for the most part couched in glutinous sloppiness that would make Nannie Crawford turn in her grave. My front-page headline of the decade occurred after the 'fairy tale' Princess of Wales attended her first Royal Film Premiere. It was in the once-proud, irreverent *Daily Mirror*: DI WEEPS FOR E.T.

Most stupendously archaic and amnesiac are the periodic bursts of Nonconformist self-righteousness evinced by papers whose Page Three girls give such constant stimulus to the rape statistics. The 1963 Profumo Affair – with a government's future and national security at stake – scarcely unleashed tabloid mock-morality like the sad, dingy little Eighties matter of Cecil Parkinson, Sara Keays and the illegitimate baby. Equally convincing zeal for international justice subjected that silly but hapless Royal also-ran Princess Michael to a racist witch-hunt that wouldn't have been out of place in Der Stermer's Berlin.

Imaginary news has inevitably led to imaginary newspapers. Along with the several new titles created out of computer technology and the print unions' defeat, other wholly formless and fantastical titles have floated like ectoplasm overhead, serv-

ing the inscrutable fiscal plan of Eighties press barons passing
all Northcliffian parody. Most notably there was Rupert Murdoch's *London Post*, mooted as a propaganda weapon in his
parody-Colditz Wapping war. The great disgrace was the *London
Evening News*, a good paper unregretfully murdered 20 years ago
and 'revived' in feeble *Sun*-parody form as a spoiling tactic
against Robert Maxwell's worthy *London Daily News*. 'The *Evening News* is here to stay', its management chorused. When the
Daily News went under, the *Evening News* was quietly throttled
all over again.

A decade willing to spend £22 million on a single joke would
appear to have held humour in high regard. The joke was
'Remember to tell Sid about British Gas shares'. Its humour lies
in the name 'Sid', connoting a type of proletarian individual,
probably in cloth cap, that ad-executives find amusing, especially
after lunch. On that addled four-second parody of a creative
brainwave, British Gas's flotation budget was committed. Water
privatisation has since gone one better, investing £25m in such
stunners as 'Water Floats' and 'Be an H2-Owner'.

We certainly are a nation of avid comedians. Almost every
Briton now possesses a T-shirt with an amusing slogan, carries
an amusing sticker on the back window of his car and, on the
side window, an amusing toy animal fixed by suction. Almost
everyone has perfected an imitation of Michael Caine saying
'Not many people know that' and, for powerful, though inexplic-
able reasons, laughs at any mention of the word 'ferret'. In
headlines, ad-slogans, even governmental announcements, the
commonest idiom is the obstinately humourless pun, 'Wedgewood – would you?' Cue Perrier bottle and birdsong. Caption:
'Swalleau'. God that's *brill*, Jeremy. Take a £10,000-a-year rise.

Gales of strained laughter have floated over some of the least
funny movie and TV comedies ever contrived by man, from
BBC 1's ''Allo 'Allo' (The Gestapo – funny?) to John Cleese's
world-mesmerising masterpiece, 'A Fish Named Wanda'. The
blight on Cleese's talent, indeed, is a perfect microcosm. In the
Seventies, he was Basil Fawlty. In the Eighties, he wrote hand-

books on psychotherapy. Elsewhere, British humour has swung back to a simple footing of racism. The turnip-headed kraut. The laughable little Jap. The joke Jewish mother. They are all to be found, unchallenged, in British TV commercials.

Spitting Image has been almost the sole benefit from television, otherwise a glass eye trained uncritically on Lifestyle Britain, the gruesome knitwear of sport and weather forecasters and the highlights in Noel Edmonds' beard. Technically miraculous, it remains, as a means of understanding and interpretation, naive to the point of idiocy; simple Plasticine to any con-artist in or out of politics. If politicians have learned anything, indeed, it has been from the gigantic TV followings of self-evident dummies like Roland Rat or Miss Piggy. Hence Neil Kinnock in his comedy sketch with Tracey Ullman and David Steel pontificating about disco music at Stringfellow's. Hence the mind-numbing tedium of Sir Geoffrey Howe lately transferred from Parliament to Wogan.

To watch television is to be reassured that nothing in this whole unspeakable car-bombing, hostage-taking, child-slaughtering world *really* need be taken seriously. Main news bulletins are now presented as light entertainment with disco beat, shiny logos spinning like Star Wars craft, reference pictures, even of the most ghastly things, unpeeling and cheerily floating away, just to show what graphics can do. On Doomsday itself, no doubt, the last item on the very last bulletin will be such as to allow the newscaster to put away his pen with an ingratiating smirk.

Television – despite its elaborate pantomime of 'ratings' and 'seasons' – is merely inertia-selling by other means, its only life force the relentless peddling of mediocrity like so much unwanted yoghurt left on the nation's doorstep. It is the essence of Fantasy Island that we should consider Melvyn Bragg an important novelist, Terry Wogan a charming conversationalist, Derek Jameson a rollicksome and lovable Renaissance Man. Media fame outran all previously known unreality with Russell Harty, in life merely a rather inadequate TV interviewer but on his death mourned as an intellectual Colossus on the scale of Leavis or Alvaraz.

Television's chief contribution to Eighties culture has been a proliferation of game shows, each one more technologically elaborate and flashingly futile, palliating a vast, unseen audience of have-nots much as Hollywood musicals did in the slumps of 50 years ago. Out of the game show subcontinent have developed spectacular displays of mass ego and exhibitionism when thousands in pale pink and turquoise receive their Warhol-prescribed five minutes' fame by 'doing crazy things for charity'. What profit might accrue from doing *sensible* things for charity is a notion which has yet to strike the telethon industry.

The most spaced-out fantasist could scarcely have conceived Royal It's a Knockout, wherein Royals dressed as jerks mingled with jerks dressed as Royals in democratic tomfoolery. The subsequent decision of the Queen's third son to quit the Royal Marines and work for Andrew Lloyd-Webber seemed a natural, if not inevitable step. For what else is our Princess of Wales but living testimony to the magic of Phantom of the Opera? And how utterly that huge, empty symphonic meringue expresses Fantasy Island. Each spellbound West End night, hundreds stream forth, convinced that what they have just seen was a musical, and trying to remember a tune.

Least affected by Fantasy Island are the young of what can no longer be accurately termed the 'working' class. Born into vistas of unemployment and decay, what basis can they have for self-blinding nostalgia? From them has come the healthy backlash of 'street' culture and 'anti-fashion', crying scorn on parental Dynasty shoulder-pads and senescent teen-age. The virtue they set most store by is authenticity, re-named Street-Cred. Their whole generation's message might be summed up as Cut the Crap.

Not so the young of what is once more unabashedly termed the 'upper' class, licensed by Kate Carney's Circus to a millennium of born-again snobbery, elitism and braying noise. To open *Tatler* or *Harper's & Queen* magazine is to enter a world of parody debs, chinless wonders and competitively pompous Young Fogies; barely surpassed in Wodehouse or Waugh. Sense literally boggles at the futile puns; the brutishly witless writing, on subjects like 'sexy people with facial scars' or 'sexy gynaecologists'; the frenzied sucking up to any nob, however tedious or inert. Thus did *Tatler* recently summarize the compulsive characteristics of the Cecil family: 'Love of political intrigue . . . Tendency to talk in a high-pitched way . . . Strong C of E-ism, viz trouble over Lord Cranborne's marriage to Catholic Harriet Stirling . . .'

Piling parody on parody, the Tatlerite speaks in the accent of late Sixties hippies, flattening the 'ou' vowel as through a love-and-peace smile: 'Thank yee'. Or rather, Screw yee. Our decade's great swashbuckler, indeed, is a parody flower child whose first act, on arriving at this or that mega-buck press conference, is to flip back his hair like some faux naive roadie with Deep Purple. His inevitable ennoblement can hardly stretch the farce further: Lord Branson of Reelly-Groovy?

A curious by-product of stripe-shirted Hoorays in the ascendant is a music-hall Cockney voice, assumed – one can only suppose – as a last two fingers to East End communities obliterated by Dockland 'redevelopment'. Cries of 'Gorblimey!' and 'Leave it aht!' ring through the winebars and money-pits as if all therein truly are as honest and plain-spoken as Pearly Kings on Ampstead Eath. Stage Cockney is increasingly becoming the pink-socked ad man's nervous tic. Following God knows what managerial brainstorm, the Victoria and Albert Museum lately advertised itself as 'An ace caff with quite a nice museum attached.'

Restaurants are mostly pastiches of Paris brasseries, routed via New York, where, supposedly, one can linger, sipping coffee and reading newspapers; just try it in most places. Mock cafe society has reached almost every provincial High Street, garbed in the wishful Madison Avenue chic of the Next chain. As the Sixties had hippies, the Eighties have 'Nexties'. How nearly animated they look, sipping their *ersatz* cocktails over plates of razor-sliced Kiwi fruit and butterflied radish. What else is Nouvelle Cuisine but graphics on a plate?

Sex itself is turning into parody, and likely to continue so as

AIDS phobia takes hold. The great male sex object of the Eighties is Rambo, a musclebound half-wit beyond all macho burlesque. The great sex goddess Joan Collins, is a parody vamp who would have been laughed out of even the silent-screen Twenties. The girls who began the decade in parody Princess Di hacking jackets end it in parody Alexis frills, flounces and naughty little hats with veils. Most of the Seventies' hard-won notions about female dignity and equality are – with Kate Carney's strong approval – thrown back into the closet again.

Here and there, the national trance has been disturbed. The ash-haired, blandly-smiling waxwork show has wobbled with un-foreseen movement. A voice has defied every convention and profit-incentive by stubbornly ringing true.

There was the voice of Bob Geldof in 1985 as he rubbed Fleet Street's – perhaps even Kate Carney's – nose in some truth. There was the voice of Terry Waite, God help him, a true old-fashioned hero as compared with the Eighties Richard Branson million-dollar powerboat kind. There was the voice of Doctor Cutting from the Beirut refugee camp, and of the man whose daughter was blown-up at Enniskillen. There were the voices of the parents whose children were so disgracefully abducted by 'social workers'. Latterly, there has been the voice of Mikhail Gorbachev, more forceful and inspiriting than the entire cue-carded, back-lit, photo-opportunistic White House Medicine Show. Affording various degrees of stimulation and amusement, there have been the voices of Rik Mayall, Jeremy Isaacs, Jasper Carrot, Geoff Boycott, Brian Redhead and Ruby Wax.

I myself gave an inward cheer to an anonymous Sussex clergyman who was present on the day when Mrs Thatcher signed the Channel Tunnel deal in the Chapter House at Canter-bury Cathedral.

The feisty voice of that clergyman deserves to ring down the ages.

'One can only think of Christ casting the moneychangers from the temple. But He didn't say "On your way out, stop off in the Chapter House and ruin the economy."'

Nor let us forget a figure whom the Eighties have mocked for his earnest efforts to grapple with non-Dallas matters like inner city decay and hospice-care, and to evolve a genuine thought before speaking. To hear Prince Charles is to feel a glimmer of hope, if not for the Nineties, then perhaps the Two-Thousands. The future King of Fantasy Island – against all odds – is for real.

Le Patron Ne Mange Pas Ici*

Peter Langan is lying low. For days at a time no sightings are reported in Stratton St. W1. The Brasserie pianist tinkles his melodies with ever-increasing confidence. The girls at the reservations desk are less apt to flinch at a sudden bump of the revolving door. Diners at the celebrity tables along the window no longer glance nervously round like tail-gunners sweeping the horizon for kamikazes.

The word goes out, and returns its answering swell of ballpoint annotations on the page under the shaded light. If you book at Langan's Brasserie you can almost depend on it. Peter Langan won't be there.

Where Langan is would surprise that large public which cannot imagine him anywhere, vertical and coherent, before noon. He is standing in broad daylight at the lonely railway halt of Kelvedon, near Colchester. Though dressed in full table-divebombing regalia of white suit, striped shirt and asymmetric kipper tie, he is at present offering no disturbance to the tranquil rural scene.

The look on his smudgy face is not bellicose but wry, sidelong and insinuating. Taken with his much-enlarged girth it gives him somewhat the air of a younger, more vanilla Alfred Hitchcock. Indeed there are those who would say he had shown them the gastronomic equivalent of 'Psycho.'

* Written a few weeks before Peter Langan suffered fatal burns in a fire at his Essex home.

Even for Langan this has been a turbulent year. Seldom in two checkered decades has he so comprehensively overstepped marks, blurted out what were best kept in, got on the right side of the wrong people and the wrong side of people who can do him most good. The public row with his business partner Michael Caine confirmed a widespread view that his prime motive as a restaurateur is hara-kiri with a blunt cheese knife. He has had major problems over cash flow, tax, extra-mural partners and − least surprisingly − his health. There also has been the drawn-out saga of the first Langan's restaurant in Los Angeles, which finally opened last June with Langan removed from any influence on its running beyond his name on the marquee.

Hence his retreat to rural Essex, avowedly on a diet, off the booze and given to recurrent flights of Irish melancholy. 'I wanted to see,' he says piteously, 'one last lovely spring.'

The quiet village of Coggeshall never expected to find the French pastel green frontage of a restaurant named Langan's just off its bijou main square. 'It's all because of the landlord of the pub,' Langan explains. 'The f-er threw me out a few months ago. I thought, "Right, you . . . I'll open up a place of my own, where I can at least get a drink in peace."'

For what crime was he ejected from the pub?

'Sleeping,' he replies aggrievedly.

Langan's of Coggeshall, until recently a video shop, is the London Brasserie miniaturised under a conservatory roof. As in all Langan restaurants, every wall is covered with paintings, not infrequently of the restaurateur himself. An outsize canvas by Guy Gladwell represents what some might think the ultimate eating-out nightmare. It shows Langan in white suit and turquoise shirt, reproduced seven or eight times, brandishing champagne bottle and glass like the elements of some collapsible trench-mortar.

On the menu card is a portrait by Patrick Procktor, whose fine brush has been so unexpected an accompaniment to Langan's broadly-slapping life. Tumbled locks awry, he leans on his arms, blinking up muzzily as if interrupted at sad, beautiful thoughts.

'Bedad, it's a powerful hard world,' seems the implicit sentiment.

Lunch is a somewhat symbolic affair with Langan on his diet
and off the Bollinger which formerly served him as rocket-fuel,
whether soaring or plummeting to earth. He is under stern
orders to reduce from his present 17 stone to 14½. The prescrip-
tion, of doubtful efficacy, is Grolsch beer mixed with alcohol-
reduced Klaustenthaler.

Dabbing at some carrot soup and goujons of sole, he recounts
painful tales of his 10-year effort to set up Langan's, Los
Angeles. David Puttnam's recent West Coast mauling sounds
almost cosy by comparison.

'I got mugged twice. Once was outside the Park Sunset.
These three black guys shoved a .38 down my throat, kicked me
in the balls and stuck a hypo through my hand. So on top of
everything else I'd to go for an Aids test. The other time was in
le Toque after hours. I was there alone with the owner when
this guy came from the back and held us up. It was the time I'd
got my bet on with Michael Parkinson that I could stay dry for a
month. I remember lying on the floor with this gun on me,
thinking, 'If he *does* kill me, no one will believe the f-ing
autopsy.'

Lunchers at adjacent tables glance in our direction, clearly
wondering whether the Langan of metropolitan legend operates
similarly in Coggeshall. Will he at any moment approach that
ringleted female and indistinctly ask her to open her blouse?
Will he take a dive, as from the top board, into that older lady's
seasonal salad? Or, possibly, crawl over and bite that business-
man in the leg, ending with his chin stuck on an avocado shell
like some ghastly reincarnation of Pharaoh Rameses?

Langan maintains such stories have mostly been invented by
journalists, usually with his connivance over the champagne he
unstintingly lavishes on the most indifferent gossip hack.

'That one about me throwing up in the pool of The Cipriani
in Venice was pure invention by Nigel Dempster. A complete
load of cock. All I did was walk up to the pool while he was

swimming in it and say "Hello, Nigel." I remember the look of horror that came into his face.'

'Then Angela Levin wrote in *The Mail on Sunday* that when she interviewed me I vomited over the table. What I did was spit a piece of food, that had got caught in my throat, into a napkin. It was only that big! I'd *never* vomit. I'm *particular* about my table manners.'

Real enough was the verbal chundering over Michael Caine, which caused Langan's third partner, Richard Shepherd, urgently to impress on him the charms of country life. He continues to simmer about it as Grolsch rises in the glass, now defiantly minus its low-alcohol mixer.

The trouble was Caine's failure, as Langan thought, to recruit investors in Langan's, Los Angeles, from among his Hollywood movie mogul friends. Langan's response was to give what might be termed the old Brasserie one-two to those of Caine's mogul friends he felt had slighted him. For example, Irwin Winkler, producer of the 'Rocky' pictures and one of the most powerful men in Hollywood. On declining to join its subscription list, Winkler received a hand-delivered copy of the restaurant's prospectus with its specially-drawn David Hockney cover. On it was written 'F-you s-head. I do my job better than you do yours. Langan.'

Caine ordered Langan out of his house and vowed never again to eat at the Brasserie. Langan then summoned the gossip writers to announce Caine was banned – a point he underlined by picking up the star's special window-side table and hurling it across the room. He added that Caine had a 'council-house mind' and was 'a mediocrity with halitosis'.

The story made headlines in *The Sun*, a paper not normally known for interest in the catering world. Whatever Langan may have done for or to his profession, no one can deny he has given it a nationwide audience.

Twelve years ago, as *The Sunday Times'* Atticus columnist, I sat in the half-open Brasserie, listening to a youthful and, it now

seems, slim and fresh-faced Peter Langan outline his plan for a
totally new kind of London restaurant. The idea was a place like
La Coupole and the best Paris brasseries where one went not
only to eat but to drink coffee, socialize, even read from a
double shelf of old books set into the fireplace. 'What I want is
one big f-ing Lyons Corner House,' was how Langan himself
eloquently phrased it.

He was never a likely reincarnation of Joe Lyons. Born in
County Clare in 1941, he comes from a background he describes
as Bourgeois Nouveau. His father, an ex-Irish rugby international, was head of Texico Oil in Eire. He went to school at
Castleknock College, near Dublin, a Joycean establishment
where he earned the nickname 'Slapey Pater' for an already
chronic predisposition to nod off. His first job – which brought
him across to Sunderland in the early Sixties – was teaching
garage forecourt staff how to operate petrol pumps.

Lodged in a Wearside boarding house where the landlady
topped and tailed bananas for the pudding with her teeth, he
would escape as often as possible down to London for nights of
dedicated solitary eating out. It is how he claims he learned
everything he knows about food and cooking.

In April 1966 he happened to walk into a restaurant named
Odins in Devonshire Street, Marylebone. The owner was a
Danish woman, Kirsten Bo Anderson, then not long widowed.
Irish persuasiveness went into overdrive. Within a few weeks
Langan had moved in with Kirsten and taken over the cooking
at Odins.

The rather gloomy Swinging London decor was revamped in
what would become typical Langaon style. In place of *faux naif*
Victoriana, paintings blossomed round the walls, under a ceiling
crowded with inverted white umbrellas. Fussy, over-sauced
Sixties food yielded to no-nonsense Langan family dishes like
his mother's pre-war recipe for chocolate pudding. A further
innovation was the rather truculent young man in chef's whites
who periodically emerged from the kitchen to talk to customers,
not in the spirit of host so much as inquisitor.

Kirsten's upstairs neighbour was Patrick Procktor, an immensely tall youth with an anxious, daffodil face, currently gaining recognition in a dazzling new generation of British painters. Procktor became a regular at Odins, as did his friend David Hockney and others, such as Francis Bacon, Lucian Freud and R. B. Kitaj, attracted by the new chef's insatiable hunger for paintings and his willingness to provide meals ad lib by way of exchange. In Paris such relationships have always been commonplace. In London the only known precedent was old Signor Bertorelli's largesse to Aubrey Beardsley in return for the odd Salomé on his menu-card.

Odins quickly expanded into larger next-door premises, retaining the umbrella-cloud place as Langan's Bistro. New Odins went for silver plus opulence in a post-hippy era still not quite comfortable with unabashed hedonism. David Hockney's half-guilty coinage for it was 'piss-elegant'.

Langan gave up cooking in the early Seventies, after flinging a kitchen knife at an employee. 'He let my soufflés go down. The blade stuck in the wall only a couple of inches from his back. I've often thought about it – and decided that, if it were to happen today, I'd do exactly the same.'

His impetuous ways very nearly scuppered the Brasserie project, which was originally to have been backed by a firm of caviar-importers. 'There were two brothers,' Langan says. 'They pulled out after I picked a fight with the older one at The Ritz over whether Roederer's Cristal champagne ought to have declared a vintage that year.'

Substitute partners had to be quickly found. One was Richard Shepherd, a young chef who had trained under Silvino Trompetto at The Savoy. The other was Michael Caine, a frequent customer at Odins. Caine, in fact, was as zealous about the idea as Langan. 'I was sick of all the clique restaurants you had then – actors at The Ivy, fashion people at San Lorenzo, politicians at The Gay Hussar. I loved the idea of a place where *everyone* went. You walked in – you were a celebrity. You sat there – you were a voyeur. The restaurant was better than a floor-show.'

It's odd to remember what a stylistic departure the Brasserie was for 1976, with its huge concourse, carved out of the old

Coq d'Or restaurant's five separate rooms, its soft Art Déco lights, its Hockney paintings both on walls and menu-cards, its cheese trolley designed by Anthony Caro, its Patrick Procktor mural of Venice in what would evolve as the less fashionable upstairs. This was the expiring Callaghan era: recession and repression. If you had it, you took care *not* to flaunt it.

Its instant colossal success, indeed, seemed born of every unlikely reason: noise, confusion, long inter-course vigils and a complement of waiters generally as tactful and soothing as Gibraltar's monkeys on the rock. Langan himself quickly decided they were way beyond his control. 'I remember one old waiter saying to me, "Ah Mr Langan, they're robbing you blind, you know. I'm reasonable. I just take six or seven hundred a week. But some of those greedy buggers are taking twelve and thirteen hundred."'

Here, amid orange tulip lights and plethoric stars, grew up the legend of Peter Langan as cuisine's answer to Brendan Behan. Those who previously thought it rather an honour to be joined at their table by the restaurateur, drastically thought again after being joined by Langan. Often the first intimation of his joining one would be his forehead striking the tablecloth. The scandalous tales multiplied: how he would offer female customers unlimited champagne to strip off; how he swallowed a cockroach and bit a dog; how he took off his shoes and dumped them on Lady Falkender's plate before coyly settling himself in her lap.

He portrayed the restaurateur as semi-vagrant, passing out each night after the 12th bottle of Bollinger, uncertain whether he would awake in bed, in a Shepherd Market doorway or in police custody. The one-time gourmet confessed to a reporter that on mornings-after, which meant every one, the only dish able to stir his poleaxed taste buds was a meat pie covered in HP sauce.

He cherishes the multifarious memory of places that have thrown him out, rather as other people hoard up old valentines. 'Once they wouldn't even let me *in* to Vine Street nick. I'd gone there asking for a bed for the night. I've even been thrown out of a jail, as a matter of fact. It was in Tuscany, a few years ago. They couldn't stand me singing "The Wild Colonial Boy."'

With all that went prodigal generosity, especially to the hacks who flocked to chronicle his excesses. It became the staple of any slow news day to dispatch a girl reporter to do a piece about being revolted by Peter Langan. (The latest one, from the *London Evening Standard*, spent four hours there, being revolted.) No scribbler ever found a softer touch. When *The Sunday Times*, under former management, shut down in 1979, Langan gave over the entire Brasserie to the wake, allowing the grieving scribes to drink 900 bottles of new Beaujolais and did not pass on the bill of £1000 for cleaning the floor after them.

Twelve years on, for good or ill, his influence on restaurant style can be seen to be massive. The brasserie is perhaps the most vital component of late-Eighties yuppiedom. Even poor old pubs are now being forced to join in the universal parody of Stratton Street. In London scarcely a restaurant remains undisturbed by the piffling ego of some wishfully Langanesque owner or chef. There is genuine need for a new Michelin category: the No-Star Restaurant.

On Langan's Brasserie menu-card David Hockney's crayon sketch of its three presiding deities unconsciously captures the unrest that has occurred. Langan's face is suspiciously bland. Michael Caine looks across at him as if in disbelief. Richard Shepherd has the air of one poised to move in and separate them.

Shepherd is the invisible man of Langan's Brasserie. He merely keeps the place running, tidies up what has been disarranged, pacifies what has been affronted, replaces what has been smashed and keeps the ledger healthy. He is a thickset man of 43 with a West Country accent and the air of a not unkindly plain-clothes policeman.

As a restaurateur his style is noticeably unlike Peter Langan's. Dressed in his neat charcoal CID suit, he moves round the cocktail bar, making sure all the bowls of peanuts are at the required level. He smiles at incoming customers, greeting some by name, shaking others' hands.

Mention of Langan has a profound effect on Richard Shepherd. One can compare it only to the passionate eruption of a dessert soufflé when the hot liqueur is poured inside.

'I can do 400 covers a day here, but *he* makes me more nervous than all of them put together. When he walks in through that door, you never know *what* he's going to do. Like when he smashed up the piano. Just went over and smashed it, because he didn't like what the pianist was playing.

'It started as an act that could be quite funny, but it's long gone beyond a joke. Now he just insults people. What's the point in that? I mean, I know Dudley Moore isn't tall, but that's no reason to call him a f-ing dwarf, is it?

'I must love the guy, else I wouldn't waste all the time I do just patching up the havoc he causes . . . telling staff he's fired for no reason that it's all right really. Like yesterday. I had to go down to Oxfordshire, have lunch with Michael Caine and try to sort all *that* out. I can't *quantify* the benefit Michael's been to this place over the years with all the big stars he's brought in here.'

Shepherd has taken the strain at Langan's since he arrived from the Capital Hotel in 1977, fondly imagining his role was simply to be that of chef. 'I had to go into management because no one else was doing it. In fact, the place was going broke. I had to do deals with the suppliers, the VAT, the Income Tax. We traded insolvently for 18 months. At one point I was on eight Valium a day.

'Peter's a great front man. He's fine on concept, he knows how to buy paintings. But he's never done a day's work in his life, if you want the truth. Someone else has always got to be there to deal with the headaches. Someone else has always got to be behind him, watching his arse.'

We adjourn to a table just across the gangway from Michael Caine's, now restored and reconsecrated. Shepherd takes a roundabout route in order to greet Ian McShane the actor, Roger Moore's agent and the bass-player in the Bootleg Beatles. His manner is that of some groundsman, guarding newly-planted bulbs from vandals in hobnail boots.

The notion of Langan off the booze brings a dry, hollow meringue of a laugh from Richard Shepherd.

'When I rang him the other *morning*, he was assholed. And last week he was on the loose with Francis Bacon, and I can tell you what they were drinking then. Port and red wine!'

He beckons over Dick, the oldest Brasserie waiter, one of the original Coq d'Or staff. 'Here's someone who can tell you all about Peter Langan. Seen it all, over the years, haven't you, Dick?'

The old waiter winces elaborately and raises both hands as if to ward off several imaginary Langans.

'Remember what he did to Olga Deterding on the table?'

'In the *window*,' the old waiter murmurs discreetly along the back of one hand.

'Licked her . . . didn't he?'

'And another one . . . on the floor,' the old waiter half-whispers up his sleeve.

'Over by the front door, wasn't it? While there was a big party going on.'

The Brasserie, run by Shepherd free of interruption, reflects his solid virtues. The 500-item menu, beneath the wistful idylls of Hockney, has evolved from mainly French to mainly traditional English dishes. With brasserie mania raging everywhere, Stratton Street has a dignified establishmentarian look, rather like Rules of old. Far from being the tourist magnet generally supposed, Shepherd says its business is 70 per cent regular.

After so long in the white suit's shadow, he himself is finally starting to emerge as a culinary star. In 1984 he was Restaurateur of the Year. He has appeared to good effect on television programmes like 'Take Six Cooks' and 'In at the Deep End.'

For rest and recreation, as it were, he has two restaurants of his own in Portugal. 'And shall I tell you what's marvellous about that? It's having partners who discuss *my* problems. All the time I've been here, no one's ever sat down with me and said, "Richard, how are tricks?" I need that. *I've* got an ego, *too*!'

*

Back in Coggeshall, Langan sits under the Guy Gladwell portrait of multiple Langans, interviewing a possible new manager for his country place. The candidate is young and Next-suited, with a fresh, open and resolutely smiling, optimistic face.

'On a good day I'm good enough,' Langan tells him. 'But on a bad day . . .' He narrows his eyes, as if the young man were something to be sprinkled on a side-salad. 'I can make the fillings rattle in your teeth and your brain sweat . . .'

He sends for a sixth Grolsch and muses on the restaurant now trading in Los Angeles under his name but unconnected with him in all but his $400,000 stake. He spent two million dollars – not necessarily his own money – on different attempts to launch an LA restaurant, in the process encountering putative partners who sometimes reduced even Peter Langan to the role of bemused onlooker. 'There was this Greek named Alex, who used to eat his entire cigar in the course of luncheon. And Eddie Dracula Dharma, an Indonesian Chinese who drank snake's blood. He used to have it made up into cocktails. Flavoured with a little vermouth.

'I'm a great restaurateur,' he says, turning back to the mesmerized young man. 'But business-wise, you may as well know, I'm shit. I always say that if Joan Collins and I were to go into a room where there were 1000 people and four bums, she'd unerringly find two of the bums as husbands and I'd find the other two as business partners.'

In his Essex retreat he has contracted to write an autobiography. He isn't sure yet if it will give the candid low-down on Pamela Stephenson's stripteasing, Keith Waterhouse's varicosey legs, Molly Parkin's strong right hand or Terry Wogan's slowness to lift a tab. Work thus far has progressed little beyond reading Strachey's 'Eminent Victorians' as a first shaky press-up for the mind.

He lives outside the village of Bures, in a house deep among flowers, fields and ponies, with the most surprising background detail of all. This is his wife Susan, a neat, brisk, clear-spoken woman, discovered at the ironing-board. So far as his life can be organized, Susan has organized it. On the sofa is a cardboard sign, 'Langan is at . . .' followed by the address of the house in outsize capitals, as if to warn low-flying aircraft.

As Langan checks in, Susan is preparing to drive off in tracksuit and running shoes.

'You and your f-ing keep-fit class,' her vanilla-clad spouse observes.

'Don't mutter, there's a good chap,' Susan says crisply. 'I've switched on the oven and set the video. So, Peter, there's absolutely *no need* to go anywhere tonight.'

So Stratton Street breathes again. But is, perhaps, just a teensy bit disappointed.

Home Styles From Abroad

Interpreting the British character has always been prone to spectacular mishap. In the second world war, Germany decided to create a super-spy, able to pass undetected through Britain's subtlest social echelons. Alas, the method Hitler's spy-masters chose to penetrate our national psyche was a methodical reading of P. G. Wodehouse. As a consequence, the spy was parachuted into East Anglia wearing spats and pince-nez with orders to go straight to the Drones Club.

That unfortunate operative came frequently to my mind at the Designer Menswear collections in London last week. Almost everything on show laboured to be so mutedly, understatedly, ineffably English. The result was as alien as addled thinking and wonky PR prose could contrive. 'Ach, so! Ze English country-side . . . Ve scrag Pongo Twistleton and throw bread at ze game pie, yes?'

The dominant look next winter is to be something called 'the urban forester'. Men will put aside their Big Bang suits and stripey shirts and, instead, hanker for the sylvan lifestyle of a late-20th century Robin Hood. They will walk the mean streets in Stock Exchange uniformity no longer, but in Norfolk jackets, Morris-dancer breeches and little green hats with feathers sticking up. Their accessories will change from briefcase and Filofax to knobby sticks, hunting horns, bird warblers and whistles that only labradors can hear.

Watching this purported 'classic English' look parade in half a dozen variants, I tried to think of any classic Englishmen who would be caught dead in such dire sub-Tyrolean gunk. I came up only with Rudolf Rassendyll in *The Prisoner of Zenda* and Basil Rathbone in those Hollywood Sherlock Holmes films where someone walks into a pub and orders a whisky sour on the rocks.

The difference nowadays is that such anachronisms do not come from foreigners as much as from the English themselves. The supreme irony of our destruction as a country and culture is that 'Englishness' has become a commodity mass-produced throughout Europe, America, even Asia, and ricocheted back at us in a thousand awkward approximations and disguises. All British fashion can do in a cut-throat market is try to out-parody the parody.

With the offerings of a company called Artwork, parody verged on the surreal. 'Edward and Wallace take a bracing weekend stroll', my programme note said as some truculent-looking youths appeared on the catwalk (should it be puppy-walk?) in cheese-nightmare versions of the woollens Michael Fish wears to read the weather forecast. I assume 'Wallace' was not a misprint and did in fact refer to the youth on the right, glancing rather prematurely at his watch. Or perhaps they felt 'Wallis' sounded too downmarket.

More than once did the programme copy hark back to that luckless German spy, trying to pass himself off as Bertie Wooster in a hostile, unsuitable environment. Waterland's collection was said to be 'full of romantic baroque out of long-flown times, inspired by nomadic folklore and the english [sic] nobility . . .' Drugstyle opera's offering – of which I can recall only something like a skating skirt worn over trousers – presented 'fabrics in jewelled colourways' and 'an extreme sculptured look which allows the fabric to perform the unexpected function'.

Metaphors came in a profusion of shades and startling mixtures. Ally Capellino, for instance, rejected the urban forester in favour of the urban mariner with 'sea town tweeds', 'shore suits' and 'covert cloth battle jacket' . . . 'accessories kept to a minimum for dock-siding and fastnet lifestyles'.

For me, almost the whole pleasure in clothes is their precise relevance to place or moment. What pleasure, I wonder, will

accrue to wearers of these balloon-skin fantasies – urban foresters
in their unverdant wine bars, urban mariners on seas of concrete,
'eccentrics' all looking exactly alike. Significant of such a word-
blind occasion was its sub-genre 'literati', involving things like
loose scarves and gamin hats that would instantly fall off any
man attempting to read, let alone write, a book.

I think I understood the problem. Men's clothes, unlike
women's, have so doggedly few essential components. Men
wear suits, jackets, trousers, shirts, pullovers: that's it. True
innovations of recent years, such as frocks or ratty feather boas
for men, have all failed utterly. The presence here of a grey
anorak – albeit lined in Delft china blue – revealed the designer's
pitiably small turning circle.

Hence the desperate ingenuity one could practically hear
short-circuiting behind each successive Ruritanian mixed metaphor. Hence the brutal torment of the few permissible colours
into terms such as 'mole', 'arctic', 'lichen' and 'buttermilk' that
cannot be uttered beyond the wholesale stage, save with a fully
merited blush.

Hence the maze of new directions, invariably leading up their
own backsides. Stephen King, labouring on his 'executive
Stress-less' look of the Eighties, finally succeeded in reproducing
Burton's bronze lovat circa 1959. Soap Studio's manic juggling
of buttons and lapels on an innocent black suit ended up as near-
perfect garb for a British Rail porter.

The few designers to stray from the consensus cliché merely
vied with each other in degrees of discomfort. I could visualize
nobody wearing Emilio Cavallini's bobble hat and red body
yoke, except perhaps one of the nastier stallholders at Goblin
Market. John Flett's dank-looking grey frock coat and culottes
aroused still less fragrant associations. I remembered the school
play in which I had to wear a teacher's wife's skirt, and realized
she was not a woman of outstanding personal hygiene.

The fashion show over, I toured the individual designers'
display stands, seeking what further illumination might be there.
At one I saw Jasper Conran and – even more marvellous – some
of his clothes hanging on a nearby rail. Master Conran designs

self-evidently wonderful clothes: the problem is getting hold of the damn things. In every season of the year I've visited his shop and been told they're sorry but his new garments haven't arrived yet.

Another stand was completely occupied by the hats that will be worn by urban foresters, 'new Navals' and 'literati'. Most resembled bowlers, left too long in a Turkish bath. Some were encrusted with gilt medallions, others rimmed or banded with halves of zip-fasteners. A mysterious few had tiny pockets containing handkerchiefs. For sopping up water on the brain?

The heart of this whole caper seemed to be a shop called English Eccentrics, on whose stand I finally hunted down its essential motif. To show you are an eccentric, classic and English (if anyone truly doubts that) next winter, your attire must exhibit ducks. Shirts, jacket-linings, scarves, braces, even the ledger where you record your Docklands penthouse dinner-parties, must carry the same pattern of lifeless-looking mallard and widgeon. A total dead duck, in other words.

A Typical English Wedding

There are, we know, two separate worlds in modern Britain. There is the real world, and that which is brought to us, morning, noon and night, by television news. Its eye is all-seeing and all-believing, its self-esteem stupendous, its brain smaller than that of a Diplodocus. TV Newsland is where Margaret Thatcher and Neil Kinnock could simultaneously restore their respective political images merely by test-driving new Rover cars, a blue one for her, a red for him.

These past three months, all preparations for the Wedding have reached us via TV Newsland. It was a gruesome vigil. Towards the end, film-sequences came tagged with invitation-card script and pink ribbon. Commentaries were spoken against a disco beat version of The Wedding March. Grown-up reporters were compelled to utter lines like 'The silkworms that worked for Diana are working for Sarah now.' The ultimate flourish came from Thames Television. 'Reporting the great day will be our *own* Andrew and Sarah ... Andrew Gardner and Sarah Kennedy.'

And the merchandising! O Mammon! Radio commercial land is not far behind TV Newsland in rendering us down to a nation of half-wits. 'Do you hope your *Prints* will come?' 'I do!' 'Then take them to your Colourama shop ...' 'Don't miss the marriage of real cheddar cheese with sauteed onions in the Burger King Double Onion Cheddarburger ...'

So it continued, Thatcher Britain at the apotheosis, Naff speaking unto Naff, till the Wedding morn.

*

Myself, I worried less about the young couple's ordeal than about poor old London's. Laid waste by tourist trade, its streets and open spaces filthy, the very walls of its Monarch's palace used as a coach-stop urinal, would London still rise to the occasion imperially, as of old?

There had been – unremarked by TV Newsland – the most God Almighty clean-up. From Apsley House all along Constitution Hill, not so much as a chewing gum wrapper remained. Under a dishmop sky traversed by joke airships, the wedding eve afternoon was tranquil. Lamps burned eerily along the Palace front. The crowd at the gates included several women in full wedding rig, hats, even veils, 24 hours early (unless they were late leavers from the last Garden Party).

To the east, TV Newsland massed its pantechnicons. Boarded up with grey wood camera-steps, the Victoria Memorial seemed enclosed in a primitive armoured car. Heraldic lions steadied Antipodean knapsacks under their paws. Below, the first spectators waited in deck chairs, Nike shoes propped along the barrier, ears muffed by Walkman sets. Some had already covered their heads and, lulled by the traffic roar, gone peacefully to sleep.

Home to watch the joint BBC–ITV interview of young couple, and hear the answer to TV Newsland's perennial question: 'How do you feel?'

They are thoroughly engaging, and bright enough to speed the ordeal by having fun themselves. At one point, Prince Andrew playfully cuffs his bride-to-be, almost knocking her off the wall where they are sitting. (Foreplay here ought to be fairly brisk.) Down at Portland, where he is stationed, she says she has found a good fish and chip shop. 'Oh!' the Prince exclaims. 'So you've already been skiting abite.'

Most Interesting Insight: she intends to learn to fly a helicopter in order to be able to talk to him about his work.

A pity Sir Alistair Burnet wasn't interviewing. These things don't seem the same without the Wizard of Ooze.

Preparatory reading-list
Queen Victoria by Lytton Strachey; Edward VII by Philip
Magnus; George V by Harold Nicolson; Queen Mary by James
Pope-Hennessy. Of little use in present assignment, but perennially
enjoyable.

I week's supply *Daily Express, Daily Mail, Mirror, Sun, Star*.
Reading abandoned midway, owing to sincere desire to retch.

Best Buy in Wedding literature: official souvenir, £2.25, pro-
ceeds in aid of Royal Jubilee Trusts, written by Alan Hamilton
of *The Times*. Antidote to tabloid sick-making and *Guardian*
snootiness, reminding us that what's going forward is, after all,
really rather pleasant.

Investigative research
Ring up friend of friend who is good friend of bride. She
confirms suspicion that Fergie is awfully nice, friendly, warm,
down to earth etc. Says she is marrying Prince 'for all the right
reasons'. Adds by now familiar observation that he is 'no great
brain . . . But they make each other laugh. And don't forget
she's older than he is.' Doesn't see how bride can carry on in
publishing after marriage. Thinks that press discussion in re size
of bottom cruel and unnecessary. I agree.

Chat at lunch to member of Royal Household and tentatively
raise subject of Wedding breakfast. RH man thinks it's to be
'something lobstery, followed by lamb . . .' Reflect this must be
discreetest member of Royal Household ever. Then he tells
story of Prince Philip's video camera.

It seems that at a recent equestrian event, Prince Philip asked
one of his detectives to film him taking part in the four-in-hand
class. What the detective didn't realize, however, was that the
camera had a sound facility. Filming his Royal master, he
uttered a stream of exasperated and satirical comments sotto
voce, as well as making intermittent attempts to get off with a
young woman standing next to him.

No one looked at the film until some time later, when Prince
Philip himself showed it to a gathering of carriage-driving enthusiasts.

As the stately equipage moved round the ring with its Royal driver, a voice over could be heard saying things like 'Gawd, how do you work this thing? . . . All right for later, are we darling? . . . Oh, blimey, where's the old sod got to now?'

Final check-list

1 avocado and blue admittance card to Westminster Abbey, North Transept Aisle Lower, bearing warranted signatures of Dean and Lord Chamberlain. (Will there be Royal Wedding touts?) Doors open 10 a.m., congregation to be seated by 10.40. July 23 not a 'Collar Day', therefore orders and decorations to be worn only by officers in uniform.

1 Moss Bros morning suit, Richmond grey, as near as possible to unstructured. Soft-collar shirt, sans any form of link, stud or metal protruberance. Quite nice Art Nouveauish tie. Top hat dispensed with to facilitate use of notebook (and likely motorcycle journey back to office).

1 *Sunday Times Magazine* pass, not good for crossing picket-lines.

1 set passport photos, just in case.

1 packet Polo.

Strange how empty London seems on Royal Wedding days. Except for the pavements, of course.

Just what made this particular Wedding crowd so effervescent is still not quite clear. As the 1981 crowd took their cue from sober, serious Charles and his Dresden-dream bride, this one clearly felt the licence to be far saucier. The most constant refrain, behind the barriers, was 'All the nice girls love a sailor'. As with the best music hall version, the second 'Ship ahoy' in the chorus was altered to 'Naughty boy!'

Intermittent showers did not dampen their ebullience. Fortunately, a good many – outside the Abbey, at least – seemed to be golfers. They cheered the white-gloved police and dark khaki boy soldiers, with an extra burst for the odd, hopelessly-lost cyclist. They cheered the sweeping machine, giving the road a final buff.

More than an hour early, I wandered along Millbank, past a House of Commons looking positively sullen in its total eclipse. As I returned, a policeman approached me. I have just spent two years living in a city where, when they approach you, policemen say 'Okay Mac', where's your ID?'

'Excuse me, Sir,' this policeman said. 'Who exactly *are* you?'

When I returned, the crowd were cheering a Council workman obliterating the Zebra crossing with sand.

By 9.30, I had been joined by about a dozen female journalists, all fancifully-dressed, all steadying their hats in the funny way women at weddings always steady their hats. Some represented publications in Germany and Scandinavia. 'I hear the Azores is a red herring,' someone said. 'So it's Marbella, is it?' her neighbour replied. Deep agitation among the Scandinavians. 'Vat are you telling?' their spokesperson demanded. 'Zey are not going to ze Azores? Vy?'

Spoke to Jilly Cooper, vamping every pc in sight with her gap-toothed smile. 'Isn't it fabulous?' she said. 'They're cheering the dust-carts.'

'Well, they don't often see them,' I said.

To my amazement, Ms Cooper noted this down.

Last stroke of Big Ben dies away. In through tiny aperture in North Door, directed by RAF officer to right of indeterminate statue and up scaffolding via steps like those in funfair helter-skelter. At first level, greeted by headmasterly man in medals, Queen's Scholar in white cravat and PR lady, who hands me sealed Buckingham Palace envelope containing embargoed details of The Dress.

Not at all bad vantage-point. Bridegroom's and bride's red kneeling-stools in plain view, below right, and chairs of almost entire Royal Family. Queen's and Prince Philip's chairs naturally nicest. Queen Mother's slightly different, almost as nice. Remainder, uniform gilt. Behind them, a tapestry and what looks like family silver.

Congregation, below smaller than expected. Preponderance of

men with broad red stripes down their trousers, carrying thin, highly-polished sticks evidently precious beyond price. Statues, all around, like extra, solicitous ushers. Flowers, a disappointment. Peach and pink do not go with medieval stone.

Above me: monitors displaying TV Newsland's Royal Wedding logo, unfortunately entwining initial letters of South Africa.

In front of me, Paul Callan, Joycean stylist of *Mirror*, Walkman plug in Old Etonian ear. Further down, Jennifer of Jennifer's Diary, almost too pink for the eye to bear. Beside me, charming woman from *Dundee Courier*. 'What's your deadline?' I ask her. 'I don't have one,' she replies. 'They know it worries me. They just say "Send it in when you can."'

Action starting on monitors. Cars leaving Palace, Horse Guards in mime. Neil Kinnock, smiling. At least he can't mess *this* up, Mrs Thatcher in some kind of steep choir-stall that, for an instant, resembles a cage. Suppress thought it may be augury of impending confinement in Tower.

Outside, wedding bells, renewed cheers and strains – can it really be so? – of 'What Shall We Do with the Drunken Sailor?'

As Dr Runcie and every quasi-ecclesiastic on Radio 2 has been urging for the past fortnight, I now spare a thought for the young people and what they must be going through.

What is he feeling now, our playboy Prince, as he shuts his service locker for the last time on the bevy of curvaceous lovelies and sultry starlets with whom he has made such right Royal whoopee?

(Royal tabloidese, as can be seen from the above specimen, is an eerie confection of Fifties voyeurism in aspic; the breathless prurience of the Aly Khan era, topped off with vintage *Woman's Weekly* moon gush. The Queen, especially, must feel an overpowering *deja vu*. When Whitaker of the *Mirror* speaks, Nannie Crawford walks the earth once more.)

It need be no disrespect to say that Prince Andrew isn't *that* big a dreamboat. His looks are classic Windsor, seen at their best on slightly eroded Coronation ware. Clap a moustache on him and he could take his place instantly among the Berties and

Nickys in any Victorian family group under the guns of a Dreadnought.

Several of Fergie's friends, I am told, find him insipid and unappealing, not least in his fondness for jokes lacking the element of humour. One girl in a weekend party where he was present awoke to find the Prince standing by her bed, about to squirt a soda-siphon at her. As with his great-great grandfather, Edward VII, he seems to veer between wanting to be one of the boys and standing on Royal dignity. Another girl remembers playing Sardines in the version beloved of Prince Andrew and his set, where females are blindfolded, then have to identify the males by feeling their anatomy. Pursuing someone under a table, the girl put out her hand and felt a large, tweedy bottom. 'Steady on . . .' she heard a voice say. 'HRH here . . .'

Different indeed has been the testimony of the Naval types endlessly questioned on camera this past fortnight. Prince Andrew, his shipmates say, is 'thoroughly professional . . .' 'He mucks in with everyone, gets on with the job . . .' 'Being Royal, he always has to set himself a standard twice as high as the rest of us . . .' Naval virtues are still, somehow, believable. They almost entirely directed the reigns of two outstanding Kings, George V and George VI – both, originally, second sons, as Prince Andrew is, and of comparably limited intellectual power.

Do not let us ever underestimate the benefits of a Royal serving officer. It is what allows us the secure belief that military coups are things which happen only abroad, that every British soldier, sailor and airman automatically loves the Queen. The insurance policy is woven into our national consciousness. We scarcely notice that every Royal son enters one, if not more, armed service, that every Royal wardrobe includes every possible uniform, that the Queen spends her official birthday in uniform reviewing troops, that even the cuddly Queen Mother is 'Colonel-in-Chief' of certain crack operational regiments.

For the nice, strapping, freckly girl, at the brink of her terrifying metamorphosis, I spare more than a thought. Were I beside her at this moment, I should ask, as Prince Philip is said to have asked the African president at his independence ceremony, 'Are you *sure* you want to go through with this?'

Only one other person in this gathering knows what lies in front of Sarah Ferguson. That person knows what it is to be a Royal princess in TV Newsland, to live trapped in unwanted fame like an Iron Maiden, to have one's whole body mapped and ticketed like something on a butcher-chart, one's face stolen and misappropriated a hundred times a day. The only possible analogy is with the Beatles during Beatlemania at its most consuming, when each of them felt he was ageing at twice the normal rate.

Remember the pretty young girl caught by gang-banging camera-shutters six years ago? This one is infinitely more confident and streetwise. The immediate benefit of today, they're all saying is that, at long last, Princess Diana will have a friend.

The coup is breathtaking. About to set off for his wedding, Randy Andy is, quite simply, abolished. In his place comes the Duke of York, namesake of all in his line that has been steady, solid and serious. Where but in British Royalty can a black sheep be so totally disinvented, a new image bestowed with such incredible, instant shine?

Golly, what an operator that woman is! I refer, in all deference and respect, to Queen Elizabeth II, now present, dressed in a shade of blue as visible yet mollifying as a night-light. How is it that, through three decades of ever-multiplying chaos, she has contrived never to put a foot wrong, to stay above all mundane matters as well as inextricably part of them, to still appear spotless, timeless, ageless and – most amazing – defenceless? Genius as she is at deploying power and people, she remains the shy girl whom everyone wanted to protect on her Coronation Day.

Beside Prince Philip, the Queen Mother, an ambulatory smile, winks with as many sparkly bits as he has decorations. She is chatting to Prince Charles, her favourite. Princess Anne, in yellow, sits just like the Queen, comfortably, as if watching horses. Princess Diana leans forward, to see if her new friend is coming. Wonderfully long, pretty legs. Turquoise with black polka-dots. Try to forget someone's recent remark that Princess Diana's arrival in the Royal Family was like that of plastic toys in the nursery. Everything became more vivid and more vacuous.

Climactic mime on overhead monitor. Bride's conveyance has arrived at Abbey Great West Door. Bride alights with noticeable briskness that momentarily disconcerts postillion. Cheers filter in. Herald trumpets shout. Blood undeniably stirred.

We had at long last come to the part outside TV Newsland.

TV's joke archbishop became a real archbishop, not mouthing Thought for the Day platitudes but speaking words unsurpassable in their beauty, explicitness and comprehensive demands upon the character. Words that stir in their listeners the same awe and resolution as through the past three centuries. Offices which, in their stern practicality, link us with our earliest ancestors. The bridegroom's kin apart from the bride's, so that no fighting can start. Tributes of gold. Loving pity, in total strangers, for the white-veiled, willing sacrifice. Woe to the hacks and revisionists who would change a syllable or semitone.

There were moments which even TV Newsland's hundred eyes and ten thousand avid eavesdroppers could not catch. When Andrew said 'I do', an almost psychic cheer came through the Abbey walls. When Sarah made her response, it came through even louder.

There was the Tati-esque confusion among us media people about whether to stand when the congregation did. Half of us would rise, a third sit confusedly down again, then a fifth struggle to their feet. The Queen must have thought we were trying out a Mexican Wave.

There was the sense that, in an understandable spirit of ecumenical oneupmanship, Cardinal Hume, in his Blessing, went completely over the top.

My friend on *The Guardian* thought it all disappointingly

inferior to 1981. 'We're leaving,' he said, 'And they've hardly even started Crown Imperial.'

Myself, I thought it a perfect example of its kind. The bride looked beautiful. The bridegroom looked happy. His mother looked nice. Women steadied hats, and everyone watched the children.

Despite BBC, ITV, NBC, ABC, CBS, Burger King and even Thames's own Andrew and Sarah, it was a pleasant English wedding.

Thank God.

Hells Teeth

From the age of 10 to 39, my overruling personal neurosis was my hair. In childhood, there was the effort getting it to lie flat. In adolescence, there were the fights over getting it cut. Finally, there was the realization that I hadn't nearly as much of it as I would like. I used to be the sort of person who'd walk backwards rather than let you see the height of my forehead.

The ghastly, humiliating saga of my hair ended three years ago when I started having it cut by a woman. Her name is Sharon and what she does is, simply, cut it too short to be a bother, even walking through the tailstream of a jet. She also trims my eyebrows and makes me laugh. I do not have to walk backwards any more.

But you know how it is with personal neuroses. As one door shuts, another opens. My new preoccupation – exceeding any old hair fetish – is my teeth.

Up to the age of 39, my relationship with my teeth was fairly relaxed. I knew they were not great, but they sufficed. Twice a year, I took them to be looked over by an amiable man in Bloomsbury who plays Radio 2 as he works, and whose strongest term of dental disapprobation is 'Oh dear'. The sense he has always conveyed, loading each consignment of ironwork into my mouth, is that all seemed to be chugging along just fine.

Not that I was complacent, you understand. I gave up mint humbugs and keeping biscuits beside the bed. I took to floss, the oral equivalent of jogging. My dentist even commended me once for becoming 'more hygiene-conscious'.

This cosy state of affairs ended in New York last summer

when my tongue tripped and fell into a hollow among my right
lower teeth – a mislaid filling, so I thought. Since I would not
be returning to London for a month, I decided I must get it
fixed locally. A friend recommended her dentist, Eugene P.
Lasota at Rockefeller Center.

Two days later, I found myself sitting in a chair that seemed
more electrical than dental, in a room dismally lacking Radio 2
or the silver dangly thing with which my London dentist
beguiles the tense mind. Eugene P. Lasota had not yet deigned
to appear. A Hispanic nurse X-rayed my tooth, then murmured
'Ho boy.' It appeared the whole back portion had gone mysteri-
ously awol.

Then Mr Lasota came in. He wore a sky blue smock buttoned
over to one shoulder, and had that pleasanter kind of New York
face that is a cross between General Patton and Jimmy Durante.

New York healer that he was, he got straight down to
essentials. The depleted tooth would have to be filed down, then
crowned. There would be the cost of 'root canal work' with
another man, as well as his fees for making and fitting the
crown. We were talking about something around 1200 bucks.

'I don't live in the States,' I said. 'I'm going back to London
next month.'

'In that case, why spend the dough,' Mr Lasota said, surprisingly. 'The tooth is asymptomatic. It's not going to hurt you. It
can wait till you go home. Do you trust your man in London?'

'I trust him.'

Mr Lasota looked round my mouth again, then he stepped
back and fixed me with a General Pattonesque eye.

'Do you know,' he inquired sternly, 'how most people lose
their teeth?'

'Receding gums?' I had learned that much.

'Right. And shall I tell you what makes them recede? Your
gums are the same way you are. If you didn't like a place, you
wouldn't stay there. It's the same with your gums when deposits
of plaque build up around your teeth. They don't like it. So they
go away.' He made gums sound like fastidious maiden aunts,
catching up their skirts and hurriedly leaving the room.

'There's orthodontal decay here,' he went on. 'And what looks like chronic gingivitis.'

Wordsmith that I am, I'd never heard of gingivitis. It sounded like something made by McVitie & Price.

'Here's a toothbrush,' Mr Lasota said, breaking through its Cellophane like Patton through Panzers. 'Show me the way you brush your teeth.'

I showed him.

'That's the wrong way,' Mr Lasota said. 'Watch me. You're not watching! Okay. You hold the toothbrush at an angle of 45 degrees. Most people just brush the fronts of their teeth, and get a minty taste. Those parts of your teeth clean themselves. You gotta get right up under the gum. Keep the brush at 45 degrees. Attack those deposits. Each tooth individually. Not just the area. Not two at a time. Each individual tooth. Back and front. Right?'

'Right.'

'Okay. Now, here's a piece of floss. Show me the way you floss.'

I showed him.

'That's the wrong way. Watch me now. You aren't watching.'

'I am.'

'Okay. Take the floss. Work it up gently between your teeth and round a little way under the gum. Use a to-and-fro motion with a little pressure from behind, as if you're planing wood with an old-fashioned plane.'

I rose from the chair, a little dazed. But the Primal Tooth Therapy wasn't over. 'Come look here,' Mr Lasota said. On a table by the door lay what looked like some fragments of Neanderthal skulls. They were casts of the teeth of wealthy New Yorkers. Mr Lasota picked one up and studied its ghastly, snaggled grin. 'That guy . . .' he murmured. 'Ah, Jeez, *that* guy . . .

'Dentures,' he exclaimed, rounding on me, 'are an *abortion*! Never forget that. A good top set might give you 45 per cent efficiency. But a bottom set! Forget it! A colleague of mine said to me the other day "Which would you rather lose, your sight or your bottom teeth?" I said "My bottom teeth" – but I really hesitated.'

'I didn't realize,' I said. 'Teeth are a full-time job, aren't they?'

'No!' Mr Lasota cried passionately. 'They're a battle! If you wanna keep them you've got to fight for them and keep on fighting for them every day of your life.'

He held out his warm, dry dentist hand.

'Safe home.'

That is why, today, I begin cleaning my teeth at least half an hour before bed and why, if you were to pass my bathroom at almost any hour, you would probably hear shrill screams. The battle goes on, amid bombardments of Listerine.

Last week, I bought a special supplementary brush, for cleaning tops of teeth only. I'm considering a mirror on a stem, to inspect the backs. And I haven't washed my hair in days.

Mea Culpa Maxima

I'll make the shorter of my two confessions first. One night in 1967, at The Old Fell Bridge Hotel, near Haywards Heath, I opened the door of an empty lounge bar, looked in, vomited on to the carpet and quickly shut the door again. My second guilty secret is less disgusting but resounds louder in every particular to my eternal discredit. Here goes.

In 1969 I was working at *The Sunday Times Magazine* and living in Elgin Crescent, W.11., with someone I shall call Person A. One day in the office, my eye chanced to fall on a temporary secretary, hereinafter designed Person B. Swaggering up in one of the absurd white suits of the period, I invited her out to lunch. She accepted, in a clear, patrician voice.

Over lunch (champagne cocktails and moussaka) I struck my Jonathan Miller pose, questioning her minutely in a hawk-eyed, restless intellectual way about her background and family. What actually preoccupied me, I can now admit, was the rise and fall of the buttons down her blue and white matelot-style mini dress. I learned that she had been married but was now divorced and living at her parents' house in suburban south-east London.

Intensifying my hawk-eyed intellectual look, I leaned across the table. 'I'd like to see more of you,' I said. To which she replied, in that clear, patrician voice: 'Well, this weekend happens to be completely free.'

Living as I was with Person A, such an idea would normally have been unthinkable. But it chanced that Person A was due to go into hospital that very Thursday and remain there until the following Tuesday. The coast would thus be totally clear for me to entertain Person B on home territory for the whole of her fortuitously free weekend.

The slight difficulty was the journey she must make to my address from her parents' home in south-east London. I exchanged my Jonathan Miller pose for that of Aristotle Onassis. 'Just get a minicab,' I told her grandly. 'I'll pay it off when you arrive.' I didn't bother to take her telephone number.

On Friday evening I went to see Person A in hospital.

'I've got some wonderful news,' she said. 'I don't have to stay in here till next week after all. They've told me I can come home tomorrow.'

'Wonderful,' I said.

I walked calmly from the ward, breaking into a sprint as soon as I was through the perspex swing doors.

Clearly it was imperative to contact Person B and stop her arriving by minicab the next evening outside a flat now re-occupied by the convalescent Person A. But how was I to reach her now, on Friday night, all office work finished for the weekend? I hadn't her telephone number or address. I knew only that she was living with her parents out in south-east London.

Her surname, at least, was an unusual one. I'd just have to look in the phone book and try everyone of that name. Then, with a dull thud, I remembered something else. She'd told me over lunch that she was a divorcee. Her parents' name wouldn't be the same as hers. The phone book was no good at all.

So what did I do, you will be clamouring to know. I'll tell you. I abused my position and powers as a journalist.

I rang up the police in the suburb where Person B had told me her parents lived. I said I was a *Sunday Times* reporter on an important investigation, trying to trace a young married woman staying in that area with parents whose surname I didn't know. I persuaded the duty sergeant to go through the entire local Electoral Register to see if anyone with Person B's surname was listed in any household of another name.

The sergeant – believing himself engaged on a matter of public interest – was endlessly patient and painstaking. But no one with Person B's surname appeared on the electoral roll.

By Saturday morning the situation was desperate. In less than two hours the minicab would arrive in which I was to collect Person A from hospital. I still had no idea how to call off the minicab scheduled to deposit Person B outside my front door at around eight o'clock that night.

That I could meet Person B outside, quietly explain matters to her and pay her minicab to return her to south-east London, all without Person A's knowledge, was altogether too much to hope. Our flat was but a single large room with a bay window over the street where Person A would undoubtedly be seated, recovering from hospital. To move Person A from the window, if she was there, and simultaneously reach Person B before she could ring the front doorbell, would require almost superhuman luck, speed and co-ordination.

My only recourse seemed to be to waylay the minicab bringing Person B and turn it back before it could discharge its passenger under the, to say the least, speculative gaze of Person A. The problem was how to waylay it. True, I might manage to absent myself from tending to Person A's convalescence during the half-hour surrounding Person B's E.T.A. but Elgin Crescent is – as its name implies – crescent-shaped. I had no idea from which direction the minicab would come.

Alternatively, I might contrive matters so that when Person B arrived there would simply be no one at home. But could I in all conscience (let alone plausibly) suggest to Person A that what she needed, an hour or so after being discharged from hospital, was to go out for the evening?

Then inspiration came. It occurred to me that as a temporary secretary Person B must be known to *The Sunday Times'* personnel department.

I rang *The Sunday Times* switchboard and said that, as a matter of high editorial importance, I needed the home telephone number of the then Thomson Organization's personnel manager. I rang the personnel manager and told him I urgently needed to contact a temporary secretary who'd been working with me on a story and had taken home some crucial documents, not realizing I'd need them over the weekend.

The personnel manager told me that hiring temporary sec-retaries was the province of his deputy. With helpfulness that lanced through to my bone marrow, he gave me the phone number of the deputy's weekend cottage in Oxfordshire.

To the deputy personnel manager I told a still more dramatic tale of temporary secretary taking home documents frantically needed for a scoop story in the following day's paper. Could he suggest any means of discovering her phone number or address?

'The only way I could identify her would be from the files in my office,' the deputy personnel manager said. 'If it's important, I'll willingly drive up from Oxfordshire and look out her name for you.'

Here, at least, scruples took hold. I said I couldn't allow him to do any such thing.

'I can tell you she could only have been supplied to us by one of three temp agencies,' the deputy personnel manager said. 'I'll give you their numbers and you can ring them. Of course, they may not be operating on a Saturday . . .'

Eyes uplifted to Heaven and heart in region of elastic-sided boots, I dialled the first temp agency on the list. They did operate on Saturday. They *were* the agency which had supplied Person B! They said they couldn't, of course, give me her home telephone number. But they would try to reach her and ask her to call me back.

Her call came through 10 minutes before the minicab arrived to take me to collect Person A. I said we'd have to cancel our plan because *The Sunday Times* was sending me off on a foreign as-signment.

Incidentally, the night I threw up into that room at The Old Fell Bridge Hotel, I was en route to the Shetland Isles, where I did something else rather unpleasant. But that will have to wait for another time.

I'll Try To Get Back To You

Hello. I'm sorry I'm not available to take your call. Well actually I'm not a bit sorry. Please leave your name, number and a brief message on this machine. But don't count on my getting back to you.

If you're calling me professionally, the chances are you work in publishing, broadcasting or the pop music business. I'll have to decide if I can go through the weary rigmarole of finding out what you want.

There is first the wait for your organization's main switchboard to answer. If I'm trying to reach you at a national newspaper, the fruitless ringing can easily go on five minutes or more. At such times, I wonder how I'd feel if I were a reporter trying to ring in the exclusive story of Judgment Day.

When your switchboard finally does answer, it may well profess never to have heard of you, even though you've worked there in senior posts for the past decade.

More minutes will then elapse while your extension is traced. If your organization is particularly chic, some tinny Muzak will be played down the phone in the mysterious belief that it makes my wait more agreeable.

So, finally, do I get put through to your office. And the real carpet-biting telephone torments begin.

Very often when your secretary lifts the receiver, she will be talking to a friend in the office. She will therefore leave me unacknowledged, hanging in mid-air, while she finishes her mirthful account of what he said to her last night, up the disco.

I will state my name and ask to speak to you. 'One moment,' she will reply. 'Who's calling?'

You, at this point, if I know you, will be drinking tea and

joking with a colleague perched on the edge of your desk. Your secretary will gaze at you for a rapt moment before resuming her blank stare into the receiver at me. She will then tell me that you can't speak to me because you're 'in a meeting'.

I can't decide which I hate more about this phrase – its demonstrable untruth or its faint but unmistakable bouquet of illiteracy.

You may, of course, be a friend, calling me about friendly things. Even so, don't hold your breath waiting for me to return your call, the most beloved of my friends have telephone habits and mannerisms that make me want to rip out their wires.

You could be the friend who, when I say 'This is Philip Norman' (on the reasonable assumption that he knows more than one Philip) always replies 'Hel-*lo* Philip Norman' in a tone of gently mocking joviality.

You could be the friend who, on calling me at midday, always says, 'Did I wake you up?' as if I am some Frank Sinatra figure, sleeping off a a night of crap-shooting and blackjack in Las Vegas.

You could be one of several friends who – adroit and sensitive as they are in every other way – simply don't know how to get off the phone. I dread those conversations in which natural endings keep rumbling past like boxcars one longs to leap aboard. (The Bloomsbury Group's habit of ringing off without warning may have had some sense in it.)

You may be the friend who, from some painfully misplaced sense of whimsy, allows his three-year-old child to answer the telephone even in business hours.

'Hello. Is your Daddy there?'

'Ya-a-as!'

'Can I speak to him?'

'Na-a-aw!'

If it's you, don't expect me to ring back until – quoting the immortal P. G. Wodehouse – you've put a green baize cloth over that kid.

Possibly you're not so keen to get hold of me now. If you still are, I think there's just enough tape left on the machine. Speak – weighing each word – after the tone.

Beep!

Going Native in the Big A

Putting aside one's Englishness in New York is more than a matter of forbearing to cry 'Oh, I say – thanks *awfully*!' when the soda jerk slams down your grilled Reuben and fries. To become fully integrated, one must dispense with almost all the notions British people grow up with about what is done and not done in polite society. The following are just some of the starchy inhibitions – or you may call them trappings of civilization – that must be shed by anyone truly wishing to look and sound like a New Yorker.

Eating in public
This is not a city, like London, where one slinks along, taking covert bites from a Kit-Kat. New Yorkers – no doubt as a palliative against the daily ordeal of being New Yorkers – eat as ceaselessly and unabashedly in public as the Chinese. The breakfast hours in particular are an alfresco orgy of hot bagels, muffins, doughnuts and suppurating 'Danish', consumed on the run, in doorways or on packed subway trains. Receptionists eat while receiving you. Staff in exclusive shops eat while serving you. The most image-conscious young preppies do not mind being seen out of doors gorging shish-kebab, outsize pretzels or the great soggy spears of pizza that require the same concentration and dexterity as swallowing a sword. Food 'to go' goes anywhere, any time. Chili dogs with sauerkraut remain popular when the August heat liquefies the roads. In last winter's blizzards, the ice cream stall outside the Plaza hotel opened daily from 7 a.m.

Going through other people's rubbish
A thoroughly respectable pastime in a city whose wealthier residents commonly throw out almost new furniture, working order TV sets and appliances, even the occasional fur coat. Any skip in a good 'co-op' district attracts its steady stream of well-dressed scavengers. No stigma attaches to poking round in garbage-bins or sifting through the debris of the latest shop or apartment destroyed by fire. Next Christmas, I have decided, I will hold out against the Christmas tree extortionists on Madison. By six o'clock last Christmas night, such is the New York attention-span, people on East 85th Street had already begun throwing their trees out on the pavement.

Making an infernal noise in public
Forget your foolish British consideration for the peace and quiet of others. In New York you can, with impunity:

Bring misery to any park or residential area by playing rap music on a 1000- watt ghetto-blaster.

Own a motor car horn that plays snatches of 'La Cucuraca'.

Practise the electric guitar, with all your windows open, into the small hours.

Own burglar-alarms that malfunction day and night.

Walk down the middle of Bleecker Street in the Village on Sunday morning, singing at the top of your voice.

Threatening people with your attorney
Before I came to New York, I had never consulted a lawyer for any object more combative than a mortgage. In less than two years here, I have taken one American to court, and settled out of court with another. I have threatened a lawsuit for breach of copyright and plagiarism, and lain in wait for someone with a summons, just like in the movies. I have learned that what I once regarded as an extremity of inconvenience and embarrassment is as much an American national pastime as Lotto or the Stock Market. The bigger law firms advertise on television, hawking divorce and bankruptcy like soap powder, but mainly holding out promises of fabulous wealth to anyone with the

slightest excuse to sue a friend or neighbour. One of the largest firms, Jacoby & Myers, now has branches at department stores like Sears. One can imagine the conversation between shoppers as they approach. 'Okay honey – you go to Soft Furnishings, I'll check on the manslaughter rap, and we'll meet in the cafeteria . . .'

Wearing really silly hats

In Britain a man in a hat is usually derided either as a 'toff' or a homosexual. New York, however, considers all male headgear quite normal, especially in its terrible winters when radio bulletins repeatedly warn how much body-heat escapes through the cranium. A single subway car can contain a leather deerstalker, a Cossack fur, an Alan Quartermain bush hat, assorted Lenin caps and trilbies, and yet not arouse the most subversive punk fellow traveller to even a smile. The trendiest thing for young men downtown at present is the black homburg traditionally worn by Hassidic Jewish elders. Nothing that anyone can wear in New York ever seems to be regarded as excessive, eccentric or ridiculous, Browsing in a liquor store recently, I heard a man call through the door, 'Did I leave a bullfighter's cape behind when I was here just now?'

Loitering

Aside from Central Park, New York has virtually no open public space. Perfectly respectable people – as well as deeply sinister-looking ones – hang around on street corners, lurk in doorways or mooch aimlessly around the sterile ground floors of sky-scrapers through which there is public right of way. Magazine and bookshops seldom protest at their throngs of non-paying readers. The tiniest cigar store will have a counter for filling in Lotto forms and, often, a miniature space invader pit. With public seating almost unknown, it is socially acceptable to lounge across the bonnets of other people's parked cars, or sit on other people's front steps, depositing cigarette-ends, food wrappers and beercans. You will not be mistaken for a derelict. *They* are all too unmistakable. And they do not sit – they lie prone.

Talking about things British people don't mention
'Hi,' says the pretty girl on the TV ad. 'I'm Debbie. I have
bladder-control problems . . .' The open-faced candour which
New Yorkers so prize extends to discussion of their nasal
passages, stomachs, arteries, double bypass heart operations and
hypersensitive posteriors. Phlegm, mucus and haemorrhoids are
perfectly normal topics for the dinner table. A British friend of
mine on a luxury cruise to the Bahamas, hurriedly changed his
restaurant table after the opening conversation gambit of the
New York matron seated next to him. 'We almost didn't come
on this cruise. A week ago, my Harry came to me and said,
"Myra, there's something wrong. My stools have turned black
again . . ."'

Chewing gum with your mouth open
This is done by the smartest business types. A Brookes Brothers
suit, a St Laurent tie and a piece of spittly pink rubber snapping
against the front teeth, are the indivisible accoutrements of go-
getting. For choice, one should buy Stimarol, whose advertisements say 'At last! Chewing gum for the rich!' In business
circles especially, one should at all costs avoid that ancient
British schoolboy joke:
   Q. What's the difference between someone chewing gum and
a cow chewing the cud?
   A. The intelligent look on the cow's face.

Molly's Bloom

'Do you really mean it?' I said to Molly Keane. 'You don't remember your wonderful paragraph in Loving Without Tears about Edwardians understanding the "glamour and importance" of teatime?'

'No,' she answered with her guilty little girl grin. 'What did I say in it?'

'You talked about "the delicious contradiction between hunger and wafer food, scented tea and the greed they bring between them."'

'Oh – did I write that?'

'You *really* can't remember?'

'No, not a word.'

'What about the hunting bits in The Rising Tide? When you said that falling off a horse felt like a house falling on you.'

'No, got no idea about it.'

'Not even those marvellous characters in Full House? Miss Parker, the bearded governess. The woman whose face you said was "as fresh and taut as a new house"?'

'No,' Molly said, giggling.

'Not even that boy, Markie? Or the girl you know is nice because she throws away "almost a whole cigarette" to kiss someone?'

'No. Never heard of them before you mentioned them.'

The house – named 'Dysert' – stands on a high cliff overlooking Ardmore Bay in County Waterford. A few lower chimneys and their smoke float against the breathless sweep of sands and cold

sea. You descend steep steps from the road to a well-like rear
patio. The house is knobby seaside white, with a deep blue Irish
half-door. There is no sound but for plants stirring in their tubs,
and the long waves creaming over, almost a mile below.

I had knocked at the blue half-door several times without
success when Molly's younger daughter Sally came down the
steps after me with a baby wrapped in pink ski-wear. Sally let
me in and went to fetch Molly from the room underneath where
she was evidently still struggling with her 'lessons'. So the most
sumptuous novelist of manners since Elizabeth Bowen usually
refers to the occupation of writing.

Back they came together: Sally, a now fractious baby and
beside it, jiggling its foot, a slight, pretty woman with untidy grey
hair and a little turned-up smile like a shy girl's at a party. She is
one of those people whose clothes make you take to them. I
liked her olive green jersey dress with the brown checked shirt
poking out of its neck. I liked her orange wool stockings and
black pixie boots. Her figure is slim, her complexion lovely.
You simply would not believe she is 82.

We stayed in the kitchen while Sally gave the baby some
bread and Molly poured out whisky for Irish coffee with a
noticeably resolute hand. Her voice has no brogue in it, but is
downy with Irish endearments, impartially bestowed on daughter, baby, visitor and Hero, her spring-heeled crossbred chihua-
hua.

'Get down now, lovey. Do you want sugar, ducky? Is that
enough cream for you, love?'

'That's plenty for me, love,' Sally said.

'Sure, love?'

'Plenty, love.'

For a provider of such scrummy fictional dinners and teas, the
kitchen is not elaborate. Overhead hangs a wooden clothes-
horse, the kind you pull up and down. Above the Rice Krispies
and Chum Mixer are three fossilized servants' bells in graduated
sizes. Out in the scullery, a rusty old Frigidaire grinds like a
Dreadnought. The pantry also has linen airing in it. Only the
china stacked below hints at Molly Keane's immeasurably

grander Anglo-Irish past. Ancient steep-sided dinner plates sit on oval meat-dishes, recalling eras of cooks and butlers and gorgeous banquets eaten on half-fearful Twenties summer nights.

I told her how her writing made me hungry even for food I wouldn't eat – like Jasper's pigeon pie in Time After Time. Or the scene in Mad Puppetstown where the children toast just-killed snipe in front of the nursery fire.

'I'd forgotten that,' Molly said.

'What – even the bit about the blood mixing up with the butter on their toast?'

'Yes'. It had completely gone.

We talked in her small sitting-room, overlooking the harbour. It is a snug eyrie made from sky, flowers, soft slip-covers and occasional stately mementoes of that former life. A cabinet displays bone china cups, for teatimes possible only in the Anglo-Irish Raj. Georgian table-legs do their best from the alcove where they have had to be confined. A pair of deep blue Meissen urns hide in alcoves among the not many books. Sea wind thudded and rustled behind the fire of nuzzling grey logs. Its sound, Molly said, keeps her company when she's up here on her own.

She sat in a wing chair, laughing as Hero sprang in and out of her lap. Beside her lay a patched, spilling-out needlework bag. A picture of bright-eyed nanny sweetness and simplicity until one took in copies of *The New Yorker* spread on the table and books by all the latest names piled on a stool underneath.

Early in our talk, she mentioned her American hardback publishers and, with nannyish diffidence, asked me what I knew of them.

'They're a very famous house.'

'The trouble is, they know they're a very famous house,' Molly said. 'I just wish they'd fucking well get behind one's books.'

I had arrived (it is better to confess) long after the literary pack. Travelling as I was in 1981, I missed all the furore when Good Behaviour broke Molly Keane's 30-year silence as a novelist. When Time After Time followed it in 1983 – also deserving but, of course, not winning the Booker Prize – I managed to miss that, too. My initiation did not come until the television version of Time After Time, after which I read both it and Good Behaviour in one champagne gulp.

They are heavenly reading – Elizabeth Bowen elegance, spiked with the over-the-top mischief of an unreformed Beryl the Peril. They are the sort of books one buys almost wholesale to press on friends. Their wickeder moments become practically one's personal anecdotes . . . Aroon, the galumphing narrator of Good Behaviour, cheerfully choking 'Mummie' to death with rabbit mousse . . . Jasper, in Time After Time, supplementing his *haute cuisine* dishes with bits stolen from the dogs' bowls. And, everywhere, writing that makes this competitor, at least, feel happily sick with envy:

'. . . A steep distance below the house the river gave up an evening daze of fog. A lavatory clattered and shushed. Obedient to its plug and chain the contents went down the perpendicular drain to the open water. Faint pieces of paper floated among the starred weeds and iris leaves of flags . . . Once there had been an open, not a covert drain. Every morning housemaids lifted a grille and sluiced buckets into a sloped stone spout from which the doings of the night before flowed down their paved way to the river . . .'

It truly is no good quoting her good lines back to Molly Keane. For most novelists who write with pain, the finished paragraphs tend to hang around ever afterwards like unwanted furniture. Molly has always forgotten hers utterly. She finds it hard enough to remember what she did in Good Behaviour and Time After Time. The 11 books she published as 'M. J. Farrell', between the late Twenties and early Fifties, are an almost total blank. The more I reminded her of them, the vaguer her expression became.

The world of M. J. Farrell is that which we glimpse round Jasper and his sisters at its glorious, sleazy sunset in Time After Time. It is the world of the Anglo-Irish gentry into which Molly was born – the world of big estates, of Georgian houses named Rathglass, Aragon, Garonwood, Puppetstown; of horses and hunting, and motors and Majors, and 'Troubles' ever present but never quite troublesome enough to put off a tennis-party.

At her best, Farrell stands comparison with the best of Elizabeth Bowen's Anglo-Irish stories. There is the same fastidious eye and ear, the same stitchless unity of narrative that turns houses, rooms – even chair-covers – into living, revealing presences. But Farrell, unlike Bowen, does not stop in the drawing room. She takes us through the green baize servants' door, on wonderful stone-flagged journeys among ironing-rooms and knife-cleaning rooms, into vaulted kitchens, hot with the breath of new scones, where majestic, mad or drunken Irish cooks do their inimitable work.

Whereas Molly Keane is focused force and crystalline malice, M. J. Farrell is a mirror always half turned away. The writer's amnesia of Keane may partly derive from Farrell's early writer's shame. She dared not let them know she wrote novels in Anglo-Ireland in case it put off young men from asking her to dance.

She grew up in County Wexford, in a house named Ballyrankin, not much like her fictional Aragon or Puppetstown. For one thing, the cooking was awful. 'In those old Irish houses, it so often was. Especially for children. Oh . . . *filthy* diet! No wonder none of us grew up to be very tall. No eggs, except on Sundays. Filthy white bread and butter. Awful mugs of milk. Rabbit stew for lunch . . . or liver. I can't tell you how much I *hated* liver.'

Her father was a classic Anglo-Irish squire who hunted every day and – like Papa in Good Behaviour – conversed almost entirely in variants of 'Whoa, steady'. Her mother, by extreme contrast, was an Irish intellectual, given to writing history and poetry and long, learned reviews for *Blackwoods Magazine*.

'I never really got on with my mother. When I was born, you see, in 1904, she was already over 30. She had every single value and prejudice of the Victorian age . . . about religion, the Irish question. A code that couldn't be broken. We never understood each other, especially after I'd started to become a bit of a tearaway. Right at the end of her life, she said to someone, "I made a lot of mistakes with Molly". I still don't know if she meant she wished she'd understood me or hit me more.'

Mothers sprinkle poison pins of cruelty through M. J. Farrell, and receive that dreadful symbolic rabbit mousse comeuppance in Good Behaviour. They are not based on Molly's own mother so much as on her Aunts Bijou and Lulu, who lived permanently with the family.

'Aunt Bijou has been married . . . not for very long. I remember, much later when she'd got a bit gaga, she once said to me "Oh, my darling, I shall never forget my honeymoon. It was the most *horrible* time of my life."'

'Aunt Bijou was a jolly good watercolour painter. And Aunt Lu was very good-looking and perfectly beastly, and hated men and *loathed* my father. They both had this funny Victorian girls' thing about worshipping their brothers, so my brothers Charley, Godfrey and Walter could do no wrong. But Susan, my sister, and I were anathema to them. I remember when I was going off to school for the first time, I went in to say goodbye to Aunt Lu. She snapped her book shut – I can hear it now – and said, "Now remember, Molly, when you get to school . . . *don't tell any more lies!*"'

A girl's upbringing in that society was hardly less rigorous than a boy's. Girls, too, were expectd to ride and to hunt, never shirking hard jumps or crying when they were thrown. The worst thing Daddy or Mummie could call you was 'a little funk'.

'The Troubles', for a long time, barely picked at the edge of that 18th century hunting print. Though gunmen might lie in wait, young British Army officers still drove out in their open two-seaters to the meets or hunt balls. Farrell's Mad Puppetstown gives a glimpse of an old-fashioned, strangely chivalrous and considerate Irish Republican Army. Houses are not burnt if any light shows in them. English children are turned back from ambush areas and given a password to get them safely home. The IRA chiefs use romantic pseudonyms like 'Rory of the Hills'.

'They did come and burn our house in the end, of course. It happened when Susan and I and my brothers were all away at school. My father got hold of this old bayonet thing and tried to go for them with it. "Please don't do that," these men said, "or we'll just *have* to shoot you."'

In her teens she was semi-adopted by a couple named Perry, with whom she would spend months at a time at their house, Woodrooff, in County Tipperary. That was her introduction to the cuisine M. J. Farrell would write about. 'Dolly Perry was *the* most wonderful cook. And they kept a good Irish cook as well, named Murphy, who'd a very heavy growth of hair on her face. On her afternoon off, Murphy would go to her room, shave and then start playing her fiddle. The Perrys lent Murphy to a house in London once, and the very first time she went out on her own there, she got lost. So she sat down on the pavement, waited until a policeman came, then just said "Send for Lord Waterford."'

The writing began during a long spell in bed with suspected tuberculosis. The result was a blush-making romance called The Knight of Cheerful Countenance, which was accepted by Mills and Boon. She took the name Farrell from a bar she passed one day, riding home. 'I had to keep it a secret as long as I possibly could. Young men in that circle would have been afraid of you if they thought you read, let alone wrote. Anything out of the ordinary had to be turned into a joke. It was the armour people used to have.'

She carried on writing for the simple purpose of boosting her clothes-allowance. 'Clothes were an *endless* worry – and you ran into such debt all the time. Because you were always going to tailors, getting a coat and skirt made, or riding breeches. Of course, the tailors would let things run on for ever. There was this wonderful man named Mr Tyson at a sort of Jermyn Street men's outfitters where you'd go before the races to get a scarf with a bird's eye pattern ... you were always going to get *something*. Mr Tyson would say "Are you going to the Leopardstown this afternoon? Then perhaps you'd like to put £10 on your account", and he'd just hand you out £10.'

'Everything felt like a family then, you see. The Shelbourne Hotel in Dublin was like our club. I remember going in there after some race meeting and George, the hall porter, said to me, "Miss Skrine" – as I was then – "Miss Skrine, are you a friend of Major Watts?" "Yes," I said. "Well, hurry Miss Skrine," this

George, the hall porter, said. "The Major's just gone down to Switzers to buy hats for all his friends."'

Not that she was stuck in Irish provincial life. In 1934, M. J. Farrell published Devoted Ladies, a lesbian domestic drama very bold for its day. Her work was praised by Hugh Walpole, Herbert Read and Compton Mackenzie. Full House, published in 1935, went through five impressions in its first years. Her publisher, 'Billy' Collins, was a close friend. So was Elizabeth Bowen whose house Bowen's Court (fictionally, Danielstown) was not far from Molly's. 'Though, oddly enough, I first met Elizabeth in London, at a party I'd taken myself to. From her writing I expected her to be small and neat. But she looked like an Elizabethan adventuress.'

The love of her life was Bobby Keane, a gentleman farmer she met at a hunt ball. Because he was five years her junior, she felt uncomfortable about marrying him until they both got older and the difference seemed less. So for a long time they lived together – old parlance for sleeping together – at friends' houses or on trips abroad. 'Of course it was done a lot then. But never talked about, the way it would be now. Even my best friend Daphne never never knew.'

She married Bobby in London because he had a slight stammer and she didn't want to put him through the speechmaking at a big Irish affair. They lived in a house called Belleville, in the Blackwater Valley, with six indoor servants including a butler. Bobby enjoyed her books but preferred not to read them until after publication. There is a fond phrase in M. J. Farrell about a man with 'absolute sanity' shining from his eyes.

With the Perrys' son John she wrote a play, Spring Meeting, produced in 1938 by 'Binkie' Beaumont and directed by John Gielgud. It gave Margaret Rutherford her first major West End role, and was a runaway success. 'That was the greatest exhilaration I can ever remember from writing,' Molly says. 'After the reviews of Spring Meeting had come out, and Bobby and I met for lunch ... Huge excitement, and then starting to feel rather sick.'

Bobby Keane died in 1946, aged only 37. Thereafter, the

novels began to dwindle. 'I stopped writing because writing makes you think and I didn't want to think.' Elizabeth Bowen was a staunch friend in anguish she can still barely discuss. 'Elizabeth said to me, "You've got a play to do, I've got a book – come and stay at Bowen's Court, and you can write all day." But I couldn't write a word. I kept thinking of Elizabeth tapping away at the other end of the house.

'Besides, there were a lot of money problems. I'd got two girls to bring up. And no book I'd ever done with Billy Collins had earned more than about £400.' The coup de grace came in 1956, when her play Dazzling Prospects was put on in London at the same time as John Osborne's Look Back In Anger, and was slaughtered for its contemptible old-fashioned wit and style.

For a while she tried to run Belleville on her own, but the expense was too much – and, besides, the house proved as full of stored-up emotion as any in her fiction. So, after a long struggle, she sold it and moved to the cottage overlooking Ardmore, where she had brought her daughters to watch John Huston making his film version of Moby Dick.

The late Fifties and the Sixties were a perpetual struggle to make ends meet. Friends helped, especially with her daughters' education. On the strength of her past work, the Irish Government named her one of 'Ireland's Treasures', which brought – and still brings – a useful stipend.

Her decision to start writing again had no mysterious or cosmic element. 'I thought it would be nice to make a bit of money.' She finished Good Behaviour in 1978 and sent it to Billy Collins, who declined it because, he said, the characters were all so unpleasant. Molly put the manuscript in a drawer, where it stayed until her old theatre friend Peggy Ashcroft read it on a weekend visit and begged her to try it elsewhere. The ensuing story is a lesson to all authors ever shrivelled by a wise publisher's rejection letter.

Literary stardom has brought bits of money that M. J. Farrell never dreamed. Macdonald last year published The Molly Keane Nursery Cookbook, with 'receipts' garnered from old Irish kitchens and cooks of yore. 'Shall I *tell* you how much they paid me to write it?' She told me, as if repeating barely decent gossip. '. . . and before I'd even put pen to paper!'

She is mildly amused by the fuss they make in London now over 'an old woman from Ireland' – House of Lords dinners, Terry Wogan interviews. 'Now down in the village they call me Molly. For years it used to be Mrs Keane . . . or Mrs Bobby. I'm asked to open little libraries and things, which is a cursed nuisance. And I'm hugged and kissed a lot. That's because they've seen you on telly.'

M. J. Farrell, too, is receiving a new crop of praise. The Rising Tide, first published in 1937, is high on the American 'classic' bestseller-list. That and three more Farrells have been paperbacked by the Virago Press in their campaign for undervalued female writers. Molly wondered about Virago at first, but has been won over. 'I thought they'd just be a lot of old dykes. But they've got husbands, lovers, babies . . .' Virago for their part remark on the effort it is to get M. J. Farrell even to open one of her reissued books.

There has even been a whisper about reviving her most successful play, Spring Meeting. 'It *was* a funny play. It was all about my Aunt Bijou. But do they want that kind of funniness now? I don't think I could go through all the rehearsals again . . . not the way John G [Gielgud] ran them. "*Not* a very funny line, darling . . . run along and write a funnier one."'

Beside her wing chair, with the needlework bag and Hero's pink squeaky dog toy, is a biography of E. B. White, the *New Yorker*'s most tormented wordsmith. '*Isn't* he divine! He's my total idol. And the suffering, the agony and thinking it was no good that went on all the time he was writing. Then he writes those children's books that make millions.' She laughed and said what sounded like – but surely could not have been – 'I should be so lucky!'

She is at work on a new Molly Keane novel, provisionally entitled Queen Lear. She works, unhappily, for three hours each morning, then has a couple of baked potatoes for lunch. 'Cooking just for myself bores me. At seven o'clock, it's din-dins for

Hero and a drinky for Gran-Gran. Quite a big drinky, actually. After that I might feel up to cooking myself a cutlet.

'What I'd really like to do is make a nice lot of money and go back to how I was in the old days *between* novels – having people to dinner, playing poker, thinking about the garden. I was always happiest just cooking and gardening. With all this writing business, the garden has got *terribly* neglected.'

She has been pressed to write her autobiography, but is adamant she never will. 'There are too many people still around who'd be hurt by it. And a lot of it, I think, readers now simply wouldn't believe. Like the Victorian code my mother lived her life by. Moral precepts about everything . . . if you got an anonymous letter, you must *never* read it. She got sent one about me once, and she didn't read it. But she didn't show it to me either. It went straight into her file, for ever.

'There's a Battersea teapot over there that used to be my mother's and that, for some reason, I always loved when I was young. When she came to make her will with my brother Godfrey – who was a solicitor – she said: "Now, there's that teapot Molly always liked. That's to go to Susan."

'Oh, and the way people didn't communicate and kept silent – especially men like my father. He's a complete mystery to me, even now. I remember the worst thing I ever did as a gel; it was to disobey both my parents and go off hunting somewhere they'd said I shouldn't. I just left a note saying where I'd gone, and went.

'Years later when my father died, I found he'd kept that note among his papers. I still don't know if that meant he was on my side all the time.'

Telecom Britain

I have here a newspaper filler of the minuscule size once associated with kittens trapped up trees. It says that plans are on course for privatizing the London Underground. Don't let me hear anyone from now on accuse the Russians of being secretive over their national disasters.

Oh God, not the London Underground *too*! How much more of our infrastructure is to be turned over to State-licensed spivs? Isn't it bad enough to have to live in Telecom Britain? Haven't we learned our lesson from that realm of darkening technical chaos, maniac advertising, and avarice so pettifogging as to have sub-franchised even the Speaking Clock?

In a London laid waste by bureaux de change, Next boutiques and blue denim-clad refugee columns from Scandinavia, the Tube is one of the last things to love. Alone among public transport systems (save, perhaps, Moscow's), it was made with the conscious intent of giving aesthetic stimulus to its passengers. Even at rush-hour on the Bakerloo, the eye can find something pleasing. The logo must be the most satisfyingly explicit ever drawn. The map is a thing of beauty as well as a marvel of clarity. By even less easily imaginable tradition, Underground signs (in that lovely exclusive typeface) are literate. Indeed, I sometimes think they may be the last refuge of clear, concise English in the land.

Try the New York subway sometime, and you'll see what a treasure London has. Try finding your way around that dementedly illogical system of colours, numbers, letters and almost psychotic misnomers (for instance, the slow-grinding inner Manhattan train ludicrously dubbed Pelham Bay Express). Try sitting on those naked metal benches in carriages bejungled by graffiti, awash with urine, overrun with winos, shootists, beggars and crazies. By contrast, my Central Line journey from Lancaster Gate feels like sitting in the Athenaeum.

Taking British Telecom as our guide, the stages of privatisation can be easily imagined.

A 'watchdog' body will be set up, sworn to maintain the spirit and values of the London Underground. Then the fares will triple. Men wearing Next blousons will be brought in to give the design a 'facelift'. Six billion pounds will be committed to advertisements telling us there are underground trains, via the medium of talking animals. The logo, the map and the clear English will go. Signs will be put up everywhere saying 'Thank you', that well-known American preamble to getting kicked in the teeth.

Later on some whizzkid may get the idea of putting individual lines up for private sponsorship. We shall change (if we can find them) from the John Player Northern to the Durex Piccadilly. Escalators and lifts will be franchised to private operators. Station announcements will include advertising. 'The next train is brought to you by NatWest . . .' And *won't* it be good for all of us.

I specially resent what privatisation has done to the cross-Solent ferries, which I've known since childhood. I can remember crossing from Ryde to Portsmouth on ships with holystoned decks, varnished seats and green leather-upholstered refreshment saloons. At midsummer, when the service became virtually non-stop, Victorian steamers used to be brought out of retirement, strumping blue-black foam through their gold-emblazoned paddle wheels.

The privatized Sealink service, here at least, is disgusting. They seem unwilling to put to sea at all unless loaded to the gunwales. The ferries can vary from a small freighter to a wobbly motorized catamaran. My mother crossed in one of the latter last weekend, after an hour's wait in conditions she says were 'like a concentration camp'.

Sealink crewmen now wear dark blue crewneck sweaters with epaulettes and leather shoulders. Have you noticed these sweaters? Meant to evoke Jack Hawkins as Captain Ericson in 'The Cruel Sea,' they are coming to signify all kinds of social oppression, from security men to anti-hippy police. There is space on the breast for a badge and motto. How about Sod the Public?

The originators of Sod the Public, of course, were supermarkets, which to my amazement still generally refuse to give customers a proper bag to carry away their purchases. As well as greedy, it is stupid, since one responds by buying only what will fit into the undersized white paper sheaths they provide gratis. Even in New York, the greediest, most anti-people city in the world, any purchase automatically brings a stout brown paper bag *inside* a carrier. The result is huge impulse buys in bottled seltzer water or outsize tubs of Haagen-Dazs Swiss almond ice-cream.

I was leaving my local Budgen (empty-handed) last week when a man at a promotion desk called out 'Sir. Have you ever thought of buying *Encyclopaedia Britannica*?'

I suddenly realized I'd been thinking about it for something like 20 years.

'Yes,' I said. 'I'd like a set. How much are they?'

The *Encyclopaedia Britannica* man looked at me as if I'd shouted a four-letter word.

'I'm not allowed to discuss price here,' he murmured out of the corner of his mouth. 'But if you'll let me call on you and explain the payment options . . .'

'You don't have to sell it to me,' I said. 'I *know* I want a set. If you've got them round the corner in a truck now, I'll have them.'

He gazed at me stupefied. Clearly, nothing in his whole indoctrination course had prepared him for a situation like this.

'Couldn't I just ring you up and explain the payment options?' he pleaded.

'I don't want payment options,' I said. 'I'll take them now, or no deal.'

'Can't I even give you my card?' his voice floated after me, piteously.

That is how I went into Budgen for a lemon and almost came out with a set of *Encyclopaedia Britannica*. Anyway, I don't suppose the damned shop would have given me a bag to carry them away in.

The Game of the Rose

British politics will probably never see another television communicator like Harold Macmillan. Mostly, it's true, he resembled a moth-eaten sealion, dozing on a rock. But when goaded to action, he was stupendous.

In the 1959 election, Labour seemed set for victory with the first campaign ever to create a TV image. Its front man was young Anthony Wedgwood Benn, keen-faced and Italian-suited, bombarding Tory old-fashionedness set about by grainy photographic blow-ups, for all the world like some trendy presenter of Monitor or Tonight.

The government's TV pitch, by contrast, couldn't have been worse. Macmillan was shown with his ministers seated in clubmen's armchairs, agreeing that everything was going on *jolly well*. The advent of button-down Socialism seemed assured.

Then, when it seemed too late, Macmillan went on television alone. His only prop was a globe, which he turned under his hand as he spoke. The tremulous voice oozed Earth-embracing wisdom, tinged with generous sorrow. 'When I look at other nations, what do I see? Much pain. Much uncertainty . . .' Could Wedgewood Benn turn the world under his thumb? Of course not. At the polls, the Tory majority doubled.

Harold Wilson, oddly enough, began as a poor communicator. Lady Falkender has related how, in early TV appearances, his right forearm kept jumping up like an embryo Black Power salute. The solution was to give the inveterate cigar-smoker a pipe to gesture with.

But once he got going, he could play an electorate along like the finest stand up comic. 'I saw the Earl of Home on television the other day (Titter) I *did*, you know! (Louder titter) I'm allowed to watch television, same as you are. (Guffaw). I've got my favourite programmes, too – and this wasn't one of 'em.' (Collapse of audience and Earl of Home)

Edward Heath's authentic tragedy was his failure to communicate in any medium. I once spent a day with him and found him far from his stiff-necked public persona – easy, funny, rather endearingly Bunterish. His phrase 'the unacceptable face of capitalism' continues to reverberate through our times. And in retrospect he seems a great humanitarian.

It was despair at Heath's unmarketability that sent the Conservatives to Saatchi and Saatchi and their subsequent manufacturing triumph. Since then, a complete change has occurred in the way politicians speak and project themselves to us.

Under Mrs Thatcher, politics has all but lost its traditional primary means of communication. Words, to express policies or ideals, are at an all time nadir of banality and impotence.

For this Mrs Thatcher must take most blame. Generations far into the future will feel their sphincters shrivel with despair at her leader epigrams like 'The Lady's not for turning.' But it isn't exclusively down to her. Across the gangway is an Opposition leader who thinks he can reincarnate Lloyd George by running through Roget's Thesaurus. 'Is the Right Honourable Lady aware that what she says is untrue, false, lying, fraudulent, misrepresenting . . .' In the nation's great duelling-place all we have is nanny slapping a grizzler round the legs.

Whatever problems the Tories may have, media image is not among them. All Mrs Thatcher's ministers look strangely alike, younger or scrawnier clones from Sir Geoffrey Howe. Aside from the fact that Hurd bleats, Baker mumbles and Fowler reminds us of Aids, they shelter securely within the same visual monotone. Much is explained by Sir Geoffrey's appointment as media team 'anchor' man, since that is precisely what falls on one's head each time he opens his mouth. (He it was, you remember, who described the 1981 recession as 'growth going the other way'.)

It seems a pity that the spotlight is to be denied Edwina Currie. Like her or not, she is the second most compelling woman in politics. The Tory team's only truly distinctive performer will thus be Cecil Parkinson, who has an oddly myopic tearful delivery, like someone telling you about their operation or Frankie Vaughan describing the Boys Club movement.

It must benefit the Tories greatly that, barring Norman Tebbit (as one must) all their chosen media stars are blessed with luxuriant heads of hair. Baldness is an essential Labour problem, though great wisdom lay in making Neil Kinnock become what Clive James calls 'an own-up baldy'. Those former Scargillesque ginger cobwebs could have cost votes by the hundred-thousand.

The hirsute Labour wing, alas, may be just as much a liability. Denis Healey's eyebrows grow more derangedly unpicked the further he advances into second childhood. Hattersley is already a proven crowd-repeller with his 'News Quiz' appearances, his maunderings about football and cigarette-cards and his fondness for running into public meetings, arms outstretched like a cream bun-fed Bruce Springsteen.

Labour's image-makers would do far better to concentrate on the second rank of unquestionably good communicators who will be their real strength at Election time. Some small external touches would make all the difference. Bryan Gould should be told to comb his hair, John Smith to wear less painfully tight suits, Jack Cunningham – the most impressive of all – to lose that South Shields night club doorman's glare and give us the odd 'hinny' and 'wha-hey'.

As for the Alliance's image problem, it is well known and intractable. They are – O sign of our age! – 'too normal'. Nothing, it seems, can stop their unraised voices and balanced views from disturbing and unsteadying voters throughout the land. Owen and Steel always come over well: that's their whole problem. We see them as Parliament's Gatsby and Daisy, vainly trying to recapture a roseate past of consensus, compromise and the mixed economy.

If the Alliance truly can't grow fangs or learn mixed metaphors, here are a couple of minor suggestions. Invent some sort of hand set to stop David Alton's sentences collapsing into puerility. And send that nice young Simon Hughes's shirts to a laundry that's kinder to collars.

May I also, in case of rain, propose an all-party ban on anoraks? They are equally repellent worn over Tory Bing Bang pinstripes or Labour flares. Let me tell you, I can remember a time when politicians wore smart new rubberized raincoats with collars of Black Watch plaid. God, am I getting *old*!

What Makes Sammy Rhyme

When one interviews Sammy Cahn, a little time must first be spent in getting past The Patter. This patter is beguiling enough. It has satisfied Michael Parkinson and a succession of audiences at one-man shows. It dances down the decades of Sammy's life as a hit lyricist as easily as moon rhymes with toon. But behind it there is a still more delectable refrain. Like the little ol' ram, in one of his more famous couplets, you just have to keep buttin' that dam.

'Where were you born, Sammy?'

'I was born, nineteen hundred thirteen, on the lowest part of the Lower East Side of New York. Unhappily, I never had a formal education . . . It's like I say in my one-man shows, the key to existence for me is paradox. If I had to sum up all of my life, it would be in that single word, paradox.'

'Mm hm. What street on the Lower East Side?'

The lyricist is like a slim wood shaving planed from the side of the Marx Brothers. Being married to a young wife, he is dressed in a Gucci safari suit, the cuffs turned correctly back, and twinkly oxblood pumps. Gucci cannot help the little bald head, the darting eyes or the thin grey moustache, beached on his upper lip since the last days of vaudeville.

Our time endlessly dissects and wonders at what other eras took for granted. In the Twenties, the Thirties, Forties and Fifties, there were no 'lyricists'. There were just men who put words to music for Hollywood movies and Broadway shows. Albeit known by name, they were not famous or any way glamorous. They worked as much to order as hamburger chefs, responding to the panic of publishers, pluggers and producers at wirebag pianos in Tin Pan Alley offices, frequently expostulating, cursing and chewing on wet White Owl cigars.

Now we know that Lorenz Hart wrote exquisite haikus of cynical seduction, that Cole Porter first set the orgasm to melody, that Ira Gershwin was hardly less a genius than George. And there's this great sackful of songs wherein we can now see past Sinatra or the Andrews Sisters, to savour the ironic shrug of Grouchoish shoulders and the twist of a small moustache.

For those who grew up in postwar years, Sammy Cahn lyrics are so bound into personal memory it's hard to believe someone actually sat down and wrote them. 'Give Me Five Minutes More' was sung to me as a baby at our St Neots hotel. 'Love and Marriage' I still hear drifting over the roofs and past the meatsafe at my grandmother's seaside flat. 'Come Fly With Me' used to waft Sinatra's Stratocruiser chic over the toilsome din of my father's pierhead cafeteria. Then there's that familiarly mysterious one, beloved of cabaret entertainers, whose words sound like 'Buy beer, Mr Shane'.

Sammy can – and does – sing virtually every lyric he ever wrote, from the late Twenties to earlier today in his suite at The Dorchester. His voice is light and young, with a tiny splash of Sinatra. Frequently he jumps up to sing, knocking over the same occasional table.

'My whole career, I've performed every song as I wrote it. To me a word is only ever as good as the note that's curled underneath it. A song has got to have what I call singability. Now, Shakespeare would have been a lousy lyricist. S'true. Listen what I'm saying. Shakespeare once wrote a line 'Love laughs at locksmiths'. And you cannot sing 'locksmiths'.

'Don't ask me where all those lyrics came from. I hear the music, and it just speaks to me. I get the title, and the song's written. 'Love is lovelier, the second time around . . .' Written! Or 'I like when it rains'. Once through the typewriter and it's done! Julie Styne – who wrote the music to Let It Snow, It's Magic and all those – used to say 'Sammy's trouble is, he writes like people talk. He does it in 15 minutes and it takes us hours to make it sound good.'

'For me the greatest lyric-writer isn't Ira Gershwin, it isn't Cole Porter, it isn't even Larry Hart. It's Gilbert, out of your Gilbert and Sullivan. I love the one where the judge fella sings "When you're lying awake with a dismal headache . . .' And "I am the captain of the Pinafore . . ." That guy's just *alone*."

We are through The Patter now, and into a whole fresh set of verses. About Broadway in the Twenties – Loew's Delancey vaudeville house, Roseland and the Cotton Club – travelling to Hollywood in the club car of the Superchief – Jolson, Satchmo and Sinatra, and what Harry Cohn said on the Columbia lot. It's like settling down to an afternoon movie in cosy Fifties Technicolor.

'Number 10 Cannon Street, I was born, in an apartment over the American Pie baking company. My parents had come from Galicia in Poland. My father owned a restaurant two blocks away on Madison Street. Just a little place with a coffee urn, some wrought iron tables, a glass counter with some hors d'oeuvres. Next door was a saloon, where they'd send me to bring in a bucket of beer. When I was small, I had a very bad lisp. In the saloon they'd stand me up on the bar and make me sing 'I mith my Swith, my Swith mith mitheth me . . .'

'My father was the most decent man God ever created. The whole of his life, I never knew him do a bad or dishonourable thing. I'd go to Synagogue with him on the high holidays, and there's this section of the service called "Do not punish me". You say that, and beat your chest, and there's five pages of things you can be punished for. We're standing there one time, beating our chests, and my father turns to me and says "I don't know why I'm beating myself. I haven't done *anything*!'

'I grew up in the dying days of vaudeville. If I'd have been born in 1900 'stead of 1913, I'd have become George Burns. I used to go to Loew's Delancey vaudeville house, where they had a seven-piece orchestra led by a man named Rudy Zwerlin. I used to love to sit in the first row behind Rudy Zwerlin and read the cues for the performers written on his music-score. For a comic, it'd be a funny cue. Like "When I lean down to shake your hand, wait till I take my ring off first."

'My mother said I should learn the violin. I used to play in a little six-piece band in our neighbourhood, called The Pals of Harmony. For some reason, the publishers' stock arrangements only put the words on the violin part. I'd sit there playing and reading "Mary Lou, Mary Lou, cross my heart I love you . . ." and I'd think "*I* could do that."'

His first hit was 'Shake Your Head From Side To Side,' written when he was so young, his father had to sign the publishing agreement. 'My mother despaired. She had gotten me a job as candle-boy at the United Dressed Beef Corporation, down by the East River where the UN now stands. I had to go into the Frigidaires with the beef-grader and hold the candle for him. One morning, I just decided I had to run away. Where else does a kid from the Lower East Side run away to but Broadway?'

With his first musical arranger Saul Chaplin he wrote a string of late-Twenties knee-bangers – 'Rhythm Is Our Business', 'Wrap Your Cares In Rhythm And Dance', 'Rhythm In My Nursery Rhymes'. Tin Pan Alley still jangles and shouts unforgettably in his head. 'When you say that, I always see this one big place, at Seventh Avenue and 49th Street, called the Da Silva, Brown and Henderson Building. Eight floors, 10 publishers on each floor . . . a hot day, every window open, and about 50 pianos going . . .'

A hit song in those days was calculated, not in record sales but in sheet-music. He could stand in music stores along Broadway and watch the rolled-up copies being frantically bought. 'Give Me Five Minutes More' sold 600,000 copies. His all-time hit 'Bei Mir Bist Du Schon' was, implausibly, a traditional Yiddish air he heard performed as a swing number, of all places, up in Harlem.

His great career, though, was in Hollywood, writing what producers called 'the money song' to guarantee success for lush love epics like 'Three Coins In The Fountain'. (Another term was 'the rocking-chair song' because, with luck, it would allow the publisher to do nothing more for the rest of his life.)

In Hollywood, to his bewilderment, he became bosom friends with Harry Cohn, boss of Columbia Pictures – a man so hated that at his funeral several mourners said they had come only to make sure the bastard was really dead.

'There's a lotta stories about Harry. Someone else said he wouldn't go to the funeral unless they were burning Harry alive. One time, Harry calls in a young musical director and says "How's the Chopping picture?" The young MD says "It's Chopin." "Keep talkin', kid," Harry says. "You'll be outa here by the end of the week."

'One night at Harry Cohn's birthday party, Al Jolson comes up to me. He's wearing a white suit, white turtleneck sweater – he's the biggest thing ever known in show business. He says to me "Whaddaya think of this Sinatra kid?" I say "I think he's pretty good." So Jolson takes out this wad of legal papers, and the first thing I read on it is a notation for 10,000 shares in the Bell Phone Company. Jolson shoves it under my nose and says "D'ya think Sinatra will ever have *this*?"'

With composer Jimmy Van Heusen he became Sinatra's court composer, the psyche behind the black straw hat, the loosened tie, the glass of Jack Daniels ironically raised to squandered love at dawn. Gilbert might have applauded several lines from 'Come Fly With Me'. '. . . in llama land there's a one-man band that'll toot his flute for you . . .'

'Sinatra was always very easy to write for. If you'd got a song to pitch to him, he'd always say "come over for breakfast" – so you'd know to go at six o'clock at night. He'd just sit there listening, kneading his lower lip with his finger. At the finish he'd just nod and say 'That's OK'. He'd moved into the lyric like it was his house.'

Sammy and Jimmy socialized with Sinatra, too, though the experience was sometimes nerve-racking. 'Sinatra has this theory that in every men's room in the world there's someone wanting to shake hands with him. It can make you crazy, a little bit. One night we're all at Romanoff's in Beverly Hills. This guy comes and sits next to Sinatra and starts staring into his ear. Sinatra turns and says 'Can I do something for you?' . . . and the guy goes into shock because Sinatra's just spoken to him. They have to come and take him away!

'Another night, we're all sitting in a restaurant booth, drinking soup – and there's a guy over at the bar, staring at Sinatra. In the end, Sinatra can't stand it any more, he jumps up, rushes over, grabs the guy by the lapels and screams at him "What the *fuck* are you staring at?"

'The guy says "I love you. I'm your number one fan in the world." So Sinatra lets go his lapels, drops him back on the bar-stool and says "Give him a drink."'

Hollywood brought honours given to no other lyric-writer. He has received four separate Academy Awards for movie songs, including Three Coins In The Fountain and Thoroughly Modern Millie. He remains proudest of the historical details in Millie, and having had the bare-faced cheek to rhyme 'adorable' with 'Sodom and Gomorrhable'.

'And is there a rhyme for "paradox"?'

'Oh sure,' he said without a pause. 'Parasocks.'

These days he spends less time on new lyrics than on rewriting old ones to special order. 'The de Beers diamond people asked me to go down to South Africa and do a whole bunch of my lyrics in a way applicable to them. So I wrote "three rings on each finger" to the melody of Three Coins In The Fountain. Another one was for the Pacific Phone Company. "Time after time, I take the normal dime . . ." Or how about "Birds do it, bees do it, history proves that some MPs do it"? Just this morning, I wrote a special lyric for some friends in California named Jack and Rhoda. "Jack and Rhoda, Jack and Rhoda . . . go together just like Scotch and soda."

'See, everything I ever wrote I could have written any number of different ways. If ever I can't go to sleep at night, I just run through all my lyrics, putting in new lines. 'Whadda they do in Albuquerque, when skies are murky . . . Whadda they do in Tallahassee, when streets are glassy . . .'''

He had been talking, and singing, for more than three hours. Only the intervention of his young wife, Tina, prevented him from continuing three further hours. He looked at her with fond deference. 'Tina sometimes asks me, "Who came first, Sinatra or you?" I always tell her "the song!" '

Before I left, he insisted on taking me into their bedroom. Next to the left-hand bed was a wheeled table with a black IBM typewriter on it. 'See?' he said triumphantly. 'Straight outa bed and into work. I never forget what my mother used to tell me. "Always keep moving because if you ever stand still, they'll throw earth over you."'

Telly Goons

Most of television's conventions we accept with the blind acquiescence of babies sucking on blankets. Programmes that purvey information must be presented by two people constantly alternated, so as not to tax our retarded attention-span. Entertainment programmes must come with built-in, orgiastic applause. Weather forecasts must be delivered by human hamsters wearing jackets of Third World check. The final item of each news bulletin – even on Domesday itself – must be such as will allow the newscaster's face to dissolve into a quizzical smirk.

One dissident question, however, continues to kick feebly but persistently against the walls of the medium's complacency. Why are interviewers on television – all save an isolated and undervalued few – so problematically bad? Specifically, on shows where people are questioned in turn by people earning higher salaries than the Prime Minister, how has it become a convention that we learn and understand nothing whatever?

It can be argued, I know, that TV chat shows aren't about interviewing at all. The music, the graphics, the empty chairs and illuminated staircase are what principally excite the audience. As Kenneth Tynan said of America's 'Johnny Carson Show', it is television's nearest equivalent to foreplay. Carson's nightly coast-to-coast performance is the ultimate example of how people can be aroused to a near-orgasm of expectation, utterly unrelated to anything they will subsequently see or hear. All they see, as for two decades past, is a man with a curious little-boyish skull, sitting at a desk and asking questions with a flippant apathy that makes Terry Wogan, by contrast, seem like Judge

Jeffreys. Yet millions – billions – have tuned to him, and been sated.

Other American chat shows have proved it possible to talk sensibly to people, yet sacrifice nothing in showbiz glitz. Merv Griffin does it by thrusting his face – a very earnest, though thickly-pancaked face – only about two inches away from each guest's. Dick Cavett, a sort of preppy Hamlet, was excellent in his day. There was also, for a delectable season, a host with a highly-publicised false leg who sat in an arbour smoking a cigar, calling his guests up one by one to a lectern, occasionally bawling at them stimulating things like 'Aren't you ashamed to call yourself an American?'

Whatever their aberrations, American chat show presenters are at least always firmly in charge. In Britain we expect the lighted dais, the sweeping stair and waiting couch to constitute a torture-chamber. From Eamonn Andrews through Simon Dee to Harty and Wogan, the essential spectacle has been that of a man on the rack.

There is no mystery about the reason why. Andrews and Dee were palpably unequal to the job in its simplest form. Harty was pseudo-intellectual and inarticulate. Wogan is an almost visible mass of self-inflicted love-bites. While most guests accept the presenter's incapacity as a *sine qua non* and exploit it for their own purposes, there will always be someone – like HRH the Duke of Edinburgh – who decides it has gone far enough. The resulting humiliation for all concerned with the programme is referred to, inexplicably, as 'good' television.

Interviewing, really, is the most straightforward of journalistic skills. Television's demands and confinements make no difference to its basic requisites. Take an informed interest in someone, on camera as off, and they will usually respond well. Ask a question someone wants to answer, and they'll answer it. Do not talk about yourself or show off to the gallery. Follow a train of thought, and you will nearly always stumble on something fruitful. Good interviews are good for everyone.

The point is proved for all time by recordings of John Freeman's 'Face to Face' programmes – not an intellectual byway, as is sometimes claimed, but prime time entertainment telly, avidly watched by the whole nation. It remains spellbinding to

see even so crustacean a cynic as Evelyn Waugh, even so
nervous and nebulous a spirit as Tony Hancock, coaxed to
self-revelation, under that focused light amid private darkness,
by that muted, sympathetic but remorseless probing. A lesson
for his whole milieu should have lain in the fact that, throughout
these brilliantly human, brilliantly entertaining encounters, John
Freeman himself stayed almost invisible.

Where has John Freeman gone? And the other real interviewers of yesteryear to prick the stupendous bores, the grimy
con-men and con-women of today? Robin Day has become a
deranged-looking old gent, not so much incisive as irascible and
rude. Parkinson presents 'Give us a Clue'. Levin does only travel-
ogues that show his knees. Frost – once the great innovator – is
out to grass with the pink pullover brigade at TV-AM.

The trouble with the new generation of TV interviewers isn't
just that most are lazy and conceited. A great number also seem
scared to death of going before the cameras. It seldom crosses
their minds that the person decanted into the desk or couch next
to them might be nervous or uncertain about studio procedures.
All that concerns them is getting through the next three minutes
somehow. As an interviewee, you can say more or less what you
like as long as you keep making the interviewer look good, and
never stop smiling. At the conclusion, invariably, you will be
left to see yourself off the studio-floor while your interviewer
seeks reassurance from his producer that he really was all right.

The vacuum, needless to say, is ruthlessly exploited by all
peddlers of books, films, records and political doctrines. 'Interview',
in our mental TV contradictionary, means 'Plug'. 'Wogan', in
particular, reminds me of one of those old TV 'advertising
magazines' where products used to come on in the guise of people,
and the spontaneity weighed like lead. 'Hello Neil. Is that a Party
Manifesto you've got there?' 'What, this? Oh! Yes, Terry. It's really
good. Shall I show you how it works?' 'Ooh, yes please . . .'

The TV companies themselves seem unconcerned – or, if
concerned, unwilling to give the problem any concerted adult
thought. In both the BBC and commercial companies, star
interviewing jobs have traditionally been the next step up the ladder

after – for God's sake – news-reading. Angela Rippon, Anna Ford, Selina Scott have all been tried, seen to be less than spectacular and signed up for another series. After all these years, the selection procedure remains ludicrously hit-and-miss. Because an ex-MP, Brian Walden, had a good run on *Weekend World*, other programmes have begun frantically signing up ex-MPs as presenter-interviewers. It is exactly like the pop music business after Craig Douglas's first big record, when talent scouts were sent to scour Britain for another singing milkman.

Why should they bother, anway? Having foisted all those earlier travesties on us, they know there is virtually nothing which the power of habit will not, eventually, let take root. The same rule operates at all levels of the pitch. For 10 years, the only prominent interviewer in the field of performing arts has been Melvyn Bragg. No one questions how a writer of dull books and sloppy journalism has unflinchingly promoted himself to converse on equal terms with the pacemakers of our culture. The gorge scarcely rises any more as Melvyn, in his Seventies clothes, twists round his chair with sycophantic ecstasy, uttering the glotteral grunts that are meant to signify 'Yes, yes. I am an artist, too. I understand.'

A few bouquets need to be handed out. Peter Sissons, the Channel 4 news presenter/interviewer, is a crack shot. Seeing him recently bring down Geoffrey Dickens MP like a big, ugly barrage balloon, I suddenly felt there might be hope. Clive James is wonderful, if only he would forget his one-liners. Ditto Peter Jay, if he would forget his Destiny. What makes me angriest is that the craft is alive and well among people receiving low wages and zero credit. Hundreds of good interviewers contribute anonymously both to special interest documentaries and high profile programmes like 'The South Bank Show' (whose smallest size in notepaper does not lose the opportunity to proclaim it is 'Edited and Presented by Melvyn Bragg').

Lionel Blair could be good. No, I'm serious. On 'Name That Tune' he gets further with his contestants than Terry would in a month of 'Wogans'. He proves, not how much you need for the job, but how little. You just need to be a little bit interested in other people. And – if you can't be brilliant – just a little bit nice.

Death under an English Heaven

As a small boy, I often spent holidays in Fairview Road, Hungerford, a few doors from the house where Michael Ryan went berserk. Of all the quiet, uneventful places in my Fifties childhood, Hungerford was the quietest.

My grandmother and I would get off the coach from London at the Bear Hotel and carry our cases, stopping frequently for rests, up the broad main street with the redbrick clocktower, where this week dead bodies lay and police marksmen cowered. Invariably, the town clock would be tolling its slow, flat note, assuring us that, whatever might be happening elsewhere in the world, nothing ever happened here.

We used to stay with a widowed cousin of my grandmother named Aunt May. She was a shy, faltering old lady in a black straw hat, with faded blue eyes and a Berkshire accent as gentle, and hard to understand, as a string of blown soap-bubbles. Her house was like so many there, a redbrick villa that seemed permanently asleep in afternoon sun, net curtains drawn across its parlour window, front door used only on occasions of high ceremonial.

We would sit with Aunt May in her back kitchen, looking down her old-fashioned cockleshell garden to Eddington Bridge over the River Kennet. The only sound would be the tick of a long case clock with a swan on its face, nodding in time, and the muted fizzle of something in a saucepan on the old iron range. In late summer, smoke from burning stubble would drift over the tousled heads of roses in Aunt May's garden. Often, the stillness and silence of everything would oppress me, and I'd pretend the stubble smoke was racing car exhaust, and that Aunt May's villa was actually a spacecraft, rocketing us at huge velocity through the deep-blue four o'clock sky.

There she stayed, year in, year out, tending her cacti, sending me five-shilling postal orders, listening to the tick of the clock with the swan face. The only shadow on her existence – one cannot even call it a fear – was the presence of the old Victorian asylum across the cattle grid on the Common.

To my late father, in his disastrous days as a seaside impresario, Hungerford was Nirvana. Often, amid the glum carnival nights he organized on Ryde pier, he would speak of his dream – to sell up his pleasure dome; forget about tea dances and slot machines; move to Hungerford and do nothing for the rest of his days but fish for trout and grayling on the Kennet.

Unlike his other dreams, this one came true. In 1961 he bought a block of three cottages in Hungerford High Street – just a few yards away from where the local taxi driver was slaughtered this week. That bloodstained place, so avidly revisited by television cameras, is where my father spent the last six years of his life, and found the nearest to contentment and stability he could ever know.

Entailed with the cottages was status as a Freeman of Hungerford under the charter given to the town by John of Gaunt. As well as fishing and grazing rights, this brought obligation to hold office in the ancient annual ceremony of 'Tutty' (Tithing) Day. My father served as 'ale-taster', 'Constable', and, finally, 'Tutty Man', parading through town in morning dress, kissing maidens and throwing pennies and oranges to children (perhaps Michael Ryan among them).

I often visited him there, though I myself had no interest in fishing, and Hungerford was too quiet to keep me long. I remember those utterly motionless summer afternoons in the high street, when the only person abroad would be Doug, landlord of the John of Gaunt pub, going to post a letter. One afternoon, I climbed the hill to the old town picture house to see Tony Curtis and Kirk Douglas in 'The Vikings'. I was the only member of the audience.

Both my father and grandmother died in Hungerford: drawn out, painful deaths that could have been worse but for the sweetness of people in the town. During my father's last days, the Queen was visiting the Shah of Iran and I wanted him to see it on colour television. Within minutes, a man from the electrical shop arrived to fit the aerial. In minutes, another brought the shop's only available colour set.

A piece of Hungerford faces me as I write – the long case clock with the nodding swan from Aunt May's kitchen in Fairview Road. Looking from it to the television screen, I still don't believe what I'm being told.

On the back road from Hungerford to Lambourn, half buried in hedgerow, is a monument that few passers-by notice. It commemorates two policemen, murdered there by a gang of robbers in the 1870s. Until Michael Ryan took up his arsenal on Wednesday, that was Hungerford's sole experience of public slaughter. I hate to think how our age has reached in, among the sunshine and peace and net parlour curtains, to create yet another charnel house.

Loony Tunes

There is a young man in P. G. Wodehouse who can always
contentedly beguile the hours spent waiting for his beloved by
calculating how best to hit a golf ball from St Martin-in-the-
Fields to the dead centre of The Strand. I am fortunate in
possessing the same inner tranquillity. Whenever I am forced to
wait about, two perennial questions return to exercise me.
Which is the best pop song ever recorded? And which is the
worst pop lyric?

The first category I have narrowed down to 'When' by the
Kalin Twins, 'Good Golly Miss Molly' by Little Richard,
'Tangled Up In Blue' by Bob Dylan and 'Perfidia' (an instru-
mental) by The Ventures. I think 'Perfidia' must win, for the
weight of personal memory involved. As my fingers shape its
unheard chords, I see the same ménage-à-trois in Ryde in 1960:
the girl I adored, named Pat, and the girl I used to hide from,
named Joan the Bone.

The worst pop lyric also used to be a walkover. Discounting
pure gibberish (which often made the *best* pop lyrics), one was
looking for a special blend of pretentiousness, laziness and
kindergarten literacy. Until the mid-70s I would unhesitatingly
have awarded the prize to Peter Sarstedt's Where Do You Go
To, My Lovely? which scooped the board, as much as anything,
for sheer horrendous length. There are what seem like dozens of
verses, each one dropping a snobby name, then following it up
with a moment of almost concussing bathos. 'I've seen all your
qualifications/You got from thee Sorbonne/And the painting
you stole from Picasso/Your loveliness goes on and on.'

In the light of more recent offerings, however, Where Do You Go To, My Lovely? has begun to sound positively Proustian. Recently at dinner, I even found myself joining in a nostalgic chorus of its most famous cruncher, remember? 'Your name is heard in High Places/You know thee Aga Khan/He sent you a racehorse for Christmas/And you keep it just for fun . . . for a laugh, ahaha.'

There can be no question about the most sphincter-shrivellingly awful line put into a song in any era. It is the line sung by Tim Rice's Eva Peron before the mob, confessing that she is 'dressed up to the nines . . . at sixes and sevens with you'.

The stupendously complacent badness – one turgid anachronism excitedly sparking off another – is unique in the annals of leaden lyricists. Though millions have apparently heard the song without objection, I know there are some who share my burning desire, someday, to ram a copy of it up the lyricist's nose.

The effect of 'Cats', 'Time', 'Mutiny', 'Chess' – all these ghastly one-word meringue musicals – has been to send me back to W. S. Gilbert, a lyricist whom Rice and Co. should be force-fed ten times daily. There is proof, if it were needed, that brilliant words can be universally popular. I thought I knew every treasure in Gilbert, but then suddenly unearthed a new one in 'Ruddigore', where Despard Murgatroyd makes a perfect rhyme by lapsing into Dickensian Cockney. 'My story would have made a very interesting idyll/And I'd have lived and died a very decent indiwiddle.'

Not that a lyric must do handsprings to qualify as art. Gilbert's only equal, to me, was Lorenz Hart, who was clever and witty, yes, but also on occasion as sweetly simple as a cigar-chewing Wordsworth. What could be better than 'When the steeple bell/Says "Goodnight, sleep well"/We'll thank our small hotel . . .'?

Pop has produced its share of good wordsmiths – Lieber and Stoller, Smokey Robinson, Hal David, Joni Mitchell, Harry Chapin, Ian Dury. A special category award always goes to

Jackie de Shannon for 'I close my eyes for a second and pretend it's me you want/Meanwhile I try to act so nonchalant.'

The undisputed masters, Chuck Berry and Bob Dylan, are able to bend scansion and stretch syllables to their command as audaciously as Gilbert and Hart. Stevie Wonder rarely pulls off even the semblance of a rhyme, but gets away with it on sheer feeling. From Hoagy Carmichael onward, the best pop composers have been performers with mastery of at least one instrument. A guitarist like Mark Knopfler or Chris Rea can frame the most commonplace phrase in a sumptuous chord, and make it resonate for ever.

Then, of course, there are the other 99%. Pop music has become the commonest element after oxygen, the universal con automatically invoked to sell all consumer goods, however ludicrously far removed from youth. I notice it now sells, among other things, Kit-E-Kat, East End car auctions, Sanatogen and (with even less irony) the US military draft. The declaration of the Third World War will doubtless be put out as a soul brother rap.

Yet for all its utter commonness, pop still allows its newest, dimmest would-be stars the affectations of an art form. They still announce they are 'going into the studio', as if the studio were some bleak intellectual proving-ground rather than a basement full of fag-ends and engineers who do it all for you. Studio technology has, if anything, increased the posturing. Hunks of machine-made disco sound are now issued serially as the 'London mix' or the 'special mix', as if compounded on the palettes of so many Leonardos.

Whatever the bizarre new sound or look, the same exhausted old rhymes come rumbling back like pantechnicons: 'walk' and 'talk', 'California' and 'warn yer', 'make it' and 'fake it', 'you' and 'the things you do'. (What are these 'things'? If relevant, specify.) Was it possible that as late as 1983 the allegedly cerebral Police could *still* begin a song 'Every step you take/-Every move you make'? Sting, in fact, gets a Tim Rice raspberry for many things, not least his highly self-satisfied rhyming of 'failure' with 'jail yer'.

Leaving aside Kylie and Jason and Tears For Fears, what is the most embarrassing moment to be heard on any pop record? I would have said it was Bryan Ferry whistling Ronnie Ronalde-style on 'Jealous Guy'. But then I happened to hear the live cabaret album where Jack Jones sings 'Everything is Beautiful' with one line totally back-to-front. The result is a plea for universal brotherhood more interesting than the composer ever intended. 'We shouldn't care about the colour of his hair . . . or the length of his skin.'

Getting Up My Nose

It amazes me now to remember for how many years – how many decades – I was completely indifferent to cigarette smoke. As a reporter in the North-East I would quite happily go into clubs or miners' lodges that were literally sky blue with it. As a pop music critic I used to sit in Hammersmith Odeon night after night letting the hazed continents of it drift around me without so much as clearing my throat.

I once worked on a television script with a woman who had only to suck on a cigarette to melt it instantly down to the cork tip. We scripted and she smoked for three straight days. A whole week with every window wide open still would not banish the smell. About a month afterwards, I opened the case of my typewriter, which had been closed since our joint labours, and out, like a genie, popped this mischievous little coil of cigarette smoke.

With such a record of acquiescence behind me, is it any wonder that my attitude to smokers today is like Dr Van Helsing's to anyone who stays in until after sunset and doesn't care for garlic.

Like the man in the Edgar Allan Poe story I suffer from 'a morbid exaggeration of the senses' that has tuned my nostrils of VHF and sharpened my ears to detect the flare of a match at 50 paces. In restaurants I cannot relax unless separated from smokers and potential smokers by a swathe of empty tables. When people arrive to sit near me I watch them like a tail-gunner scanning the skies for Messerschmidts. I am waiting for that heart-sinking preliminary gesture when squishy cigarette packet and pseudo-French petrol lighter are brought out together in a wedge and laid tenderly – almost proudly – on the cloth.

What especially mystifies me about smokers in restaurants is why, having lit a cigarette, they do not then proceed to smoke it but instead hold it flourished aloft, elbow raised from the cloth, forefingers parted as for a Churchill V-sign. Evidently the pose is meant to communicate sophistication. In that case, why not leave out the cigarette and make the fingers alone a recognition signal among sophisticated people, along with Volvos, hair-streaks and outfits from Next?

Not even on American airlines am I so candid in my responses as when I smell my air-supply being singed and espy one of these pestilential V-signers. Seldom do I even bother with the politer option of coughing, retching and flailing my arms about. Usually I go straight into rehearsing aloud my plan for legislation obliging all smokers to wear divers' helmets with pipes leading from the nostrils directly back into the mouth. I remember a rather wonderful dinner in a smoke-filled French restaurant when a companion and I developed an idea for a retaliatory incense called Skunko, to be marketed under the slogan Makes Smokers Vomit.

That I do not myself smoke is, I admit, just the mercy of Providence. For I grew up in that great unquestioning age when yellow-brown fingers denoted manliness, and smoke mingled as a matter of course with cinema projector-beams. I was as suscept-ible as anyone to the eroticism of cigarette ads. 'We didn't speak . . . we sat and smoked our Player's . . .' 'Today's cigarette is a Bristol . . .' 'Don't you like the crisp way the Cellophane slips off in your hand . . .?'

For schoolboys in my time there was no other way to achieve depravity. I remember one classmate who cherished the nicotine burn on his upper lip as tenderly as any guardee moustache. School trips abroad always began with a stampede on the cross-Channel ferry to buy 250-cartons of Senior Service. Another boy, named Peck, used to smoke himself almost inaudible even before we disembarked. His croak of 'Wanna fag?' on the Calais dockside echoes down the years.

I never smoked cigarettes but under Godfrey Smith's tutelage at *The Sunday Times* I did acquire a taste for Havana cigars. I confess I used to enjoy the rolling, sniffing, snipping and general 19th-century posturing. I still have an immense stack of beautiful, aromatic boxes labelled Bolivar, Henry Clay, Romeo y Julieta. Among my more bizarre journalistic souvenirs is a cedarwood humidor given to me by President – now deceased ex-president – Ferdinand Marcos. It was meant to have contained 50 cigars. I do not remember whether the count was accurate.

I abandoned cigars when I stopped going daily into a newspaper office and there was no one, other than the cat, to see me posturing. I also took up running, which introduced me to the palpable miracle of my own lungs. I have been extremely fond of my lungs ever since.

Anti-smokers do not have it all their own way, as is so often alleged. In all restaurants bar an enlightened handful, one is beset on all sides by sophisticates holding their fingers in the air. No Smoking areas are of little use in open spaces when those elegantly raised forearms succeed in spreading the unpleasantness so wide. Cigarette ads are still erotic, albeit in a subliminal way. Though people my age seem to be smoking less, teenagers seem to be doing it more, girls in particular, thanks to the new Madonna guttersnipe look. During a recent visit to Liverpool I met an 18-year-old with a nicotine burn on her upper lip just like that depraved schoolboy I used to know.

Nor does even my 'social pressure' seem to have much effect. Objectors in Britain are still thought cranky. By contrast, a friend who lives in New York tells me she saw the start of a near riot at Madison Square Garden when someone in the audience brought out a cigarette.

I get almost as enraged by the insincerely apologetic grins some people now give when asking the purely theoretical question 'Do you mind if I smoke?' The best reply is still the one attributed to Bernard Shaw, while travelling on the Great Western Railway.

'I hope you won't mind if I smoke,' a woman in his compartment said brightly.

'No,' G.B.S. replied. 'And I hope you won't mind if I'm sick.'

'I'll have you know,' the woman said hotly, 'that I'm one of the directors' wives.'

'Madam – if you were the director's *only* wife, I should *still* be sick.'

Brighton's Glorious Ghost

The closest you can get to Brighton's West Pier these days is to walk along the Palace Pier, half a mile eastward. The Palace Pier is a famous enough feature of Brighton with its clock tower and aquarium: it has slanted planks, sun-faded wood and lacy iron-work enough to satisfy the ordinarily nostalgic heart. It has prospered by turning itself half into an Eastern *souk*. As well as ice cream and candy floss there are vendors of glassware, table-cloths, T-shirts and costume jewellery. There is even a Palace Pier deejay, rabbiting against the waves. Few who stroll along here do so for the view. Fewer still even notice that view of a second, silent pier, outlined as in pale sepia among the sea mists far to starboard.

Beside the Ghost Train is a booth advertising 'Speedboat trips', attended by a solemn small boy. On receipt of £1, the boy directs you down an iron companionway through the legs and cross-girders to a rocking, unluxurious launch. This, presently, curves under the Palace Pier walkway, out before the dull gold beach, the fine Nash terraces and hideous tower blocks. The driver is an oil-smeared youth who leans sardonically inward just before each wave smacks over his passengers. To him the West Pier is just a turning-point. As the launch skids round you glimpse what looks like a forsaken Oriental city of minarets and domes, marooned on a weed-draped forest of cast iron. Then you are racing back, dodging the spray, wishing your driver would not take *both* hands off the wheel.

For 11 years, that melancholy sepia shape has been the enigma of Brighton. How could a town otherwise so preoccupied with its image have tolerated the abandonment and decay of what is, undisputedly, the most gorgeous seaside pier ever built? A pier, moreover, which has enriched Brighton's celebrity in literature as well as fact. Hales, the poor fugitive of 'Brighton Rock' sits and envies the waves their unconcerned curling around the West Pier's legs. Patrick Hamilton gave its name to the funniest of his novels about the the predatory Ernest Ralph Gorse. Every celebrant of Brighton in pomp and seediness, from Max Miller to John Osborne, has had the West Pier somewhere in mind, marching from shore in its broadening tiers of concert hall and theatre, aglitter with bands, flags, brilliantine and glorious cheap sugar.

Yet since 1975 it has merely stood there and rotted, its entrance a dismal blank of hardboard and barbed wire. Neglect, ironically, makes it look still more sumptuously dramatic, a barely believable ghost looming out through the long-backed waves. I remember staying at the nearby Metropole hotel a few years ago and suddenly catching sight of it outside my window, almost vertical in the milky dusk, its terraced labyrinths seeming to collapse and dissolve into each other like some great sea-sodden wedding cake.

There are two cheerful developments along Brighton seafront this summer. The Grand Hotel, gutted by a terrorist bomb in 1983, is undergoing careful reconstruction. And the West Pier is not to be let fall apart in the sea any more. After a decade in offshore limbo, it has been acquired by a trust whose supporters include Lord Olivier, Nikolaus Pevsner, Graham Greene and Spike Milligan. Work is underway on the £1 million first phase of a scheme to restore it to its old improbable glory.

The cost will, of course, be phenomenal. The £1 million initial phase merely covers the shoreward end, plus the most urgent structural repairs. Restoring the whole deck will take upwards of £4 million, with perhaps as much again for the concert hall, theatre, rotunda and outlying pagoda shelters.

Set against this, however, is the belated official recognition that the West Pier is a public treasure, pulled back from a watery grave just in time. In 1982, it became the only seaside pier to receive Grade A listing as a building of outstanding architectural interest. Of the half million pounds already raised by the West Pier Trust, £400,000 is guaranteed by the government's Historic Buildings and Monuments Commission, jointly with a local authority which, throughout the 70s, seemed indifferent to the West Pier's fate. A further grant has come from the EEC. Many foreign conference delegates, over the years, have looked out of their hotel windows and marvelled at the terrible waste.

The West Pier Trust has lately acquired an office and a full-time chief executive, Donald Phillips. Mr Phillips is a retired Lieutenant-Colonel, Royal Engineers, whose expertise in deep-sea diving has proved invaluable in checking the disintegration of the pier's superstructure. During last winter's gales, unknown to anyone on shore, one of the two giant pagodas at the seaward end fell directly through the deck. Donald Phillips persuaded his old RE friends that probing for it in the shallows underneath would make a useful training exercise. The divers rescued bits of the lost pagoda, and added to existing reports on the state of cross-girders below the waterline.

Though £500,000 still has to be found for the first phase, Mr Phillips is confident it will appear. 'There's a tremendous feeling now for the West Pier all over Brighton. And, more important, nationally. We've proved we're not just a bunch of enthusiasts or fanatics. The government, even the EEC, agrees with us that it's a thing of national historic interest.'

Brighton, above all resorts, should cherish piers. It was here, after all, that the odd notion of them as pleasure objects began. Long after the Prince Regent had arrived and commenced to flounder in the sea with his attendant 'Old Smoker', the town remained primarily a port, sending forth coal and consumer goods brought from inland by road. These were loaded into Dieppe-bound ships from a utility chain suspension pier built in 1823. Gradually it began to be noticed that ladies and gentlemen were walking out along the Chain Pier simply to breathe in the ozone. Shops and refreshment booths sprang up inside the hollow Egyptian towers that supported the chains.

The West Pier – i.e. west of the Chain Pier – was built in 1866. By then, railways had routed the coal elsewhere and

introduced the working class to Prinny's hideaway. The motive
was pure seaborne fantasy. The architect was Eugenius Birch,
builder of 14 classic English piers including Margate's, Eastbourne's, Hastings' and Deal's. The 300 screw-piles that Birch
drove into the seabed chalk at first upheld just a plain promenade
adorned by six outsize pagoda shelters. The 800-seat pierhead
theatre was added in 1892 and the concert hall, midway, in 1916.

The Palace Pier arrived in 1891, immediately west of the
Chain Pier (which, four years later, was destroyed by a storm.)
Traditionally, the Palace Pier was for children while the West
Pier concentrated on plays, revues, symphony concerts and
outdoor spectacles like the high divers who invariably styled
themselves 'professor'. The West Pier was famous for a female
diver, Gladys Pawsey, whose speciality was riding off the high
board on a bicycle. Any Sunday through the eras of bathing
machines, beach minstrels, goat carts and 'hokey-pokey', 10,000
people would throng its promenades and booths, lingering to
hear the twilight sound of waves mixed with violins, and marvel
at the free show of prodigiously wasted electric light.

That era continued, fundamentally unchanged, until 1939 and
the turning of the South Coast's beaches into armed redoubts.
As with many a neighbouring pier, after the air-spotters had
gone, the barbed wire had been untangled and the mines lifted
from the waters round it, something about the West Pier was
never to be quite the same. Package tours abroad put an end to
the old, secure English seaside Raj. Falling receipts at the
turnstile combined with ever more horrendous upkeep costs
below the deck. Profits, once spun as easily as candy floss,
turned into an irreversible drizzle of debt.

In 1974, AVP Industries, the hotel group which had absorbed
the old West Pier Company, proposed a 'rationalization' plan
involving demolition of the pier's whole seaward end, including
the theatre. Seventies rationale seemed to be functioning perfectly. It was, besides, an era when Victorian piers seemed
possessed of an almost warlike attitude to their towns –
Margate's refusing to be dynamited and lingering as a defiant
offshore island; Ryde's (where I grew up) getting in the way of a

cross-Solent ferry and collapsing under a taxi; Southend's and Ventnor's disobligingly turning themselves to unattrative burnt-out skeletons.

Brighton wanted least truck of all with pernickety iron structures, absorbed as it then was with the money-gorging grey concrete phenomenon of its new marina. A town council committee recommended that AVP's application to demolish the West Pier's seaward end should not be opposed.

This was too much for the pier's hitherto unmilitant devotees. A local art gallery owner named John Lloyd organized a 'We want the West Pier' petition and, in barely a weekend, collected 5000 signatures. Lloyd and 600 of the signatories, including actress Judy Cornwell, marched on Brighton Town Hall while the Council was in session. Swayed by this evidence of popular feeling, the Council voted to block AVP's demolition scheme.

From John Lloyd's petition grew the idea of a trust to own and operate the West Pier as a thing of beauty. At first, the chances seemed remote. Structural repairs, even then, were estimated at close to £1 million. Brighton Council would make no financial commitment, beyond a contingency fund to demolish the whole pier if necessary. In 1975, it was condemned as unsafe and closed to the public. Two years later, the West Pier Company went into liquidation; the structure was disclaimed by the Official Receiver and passed into the hands of that remote entity, the Crown Estates Commissioners. Summer after summer, its flaking corpse returned to spoil Brighton's new 'international' image, distracting the visitor's eye from modern seafront marvels like the new ordure-coloured Conference Centre. Especially in 1983, as fire tenders and police cars screamed up towards the Grand Hotel, the fate of the West Pier seemed the last thing on anyone's mind.

Meanwhile, John Lloyd and his nascent trust were working away. Another of their early coups was to consult Donors International, the fundraisers behind successful conservation projects like the Mary Rose and the Iron Bridge Gorge Museum. Donors International advised them – and continue to – free of charge. In 1980, by special Act of Parliament, the West Pier

Trust was recognized as the pier's sole operator. In 1984, convinced of the trust's financial viability, the Crown Estates Commissioner agreed to sell the pier and its problems for a nominal £100. Last year came the real breakthrough, an offer of £200,000 from the Government, on condition an equivalent sum were guaranteed by Brighton Council. The Council – having undergone a manifest sea change since 1974 – agreed.

Anyone trying to demolish the West Pier, as threatened, would have found it no pushover. Each of Eugenius Birch's 300 screw piles would have had to be extracted from the seabed like wisdom teeth. Margate's far less complex pier vanquished the demolition men after a cannonade that broke windows in several hotels along the front. For all its outward decay, the West Pier remains a doughty testament to Victorian engineering. Its cast iron legs have held up amazingly against the endless swirl and collision of tides among them, the smash of shingle and throttling crust of barnacles. By contrast, the steel outer jetty, added for pleasure steamer traffic in 1901, has been battered to a ring of twisted stumps.

The first restoration phase – apart from succouring the pier's structure – will be designed to bring life back onto its shoreward end as cheerfully and simply as possible with stalls, open-air shows and games. The trust is determined to keep the accent on children, and on traditional, innocent pier pursuits like brass bands, shows, plays, perhaps illuminations like those which used to dazzle the Victorians. Whatever development may follow in pubs and restaurants, the essential users will be people with no motive other than a short walk out to sea.

Donald Phillips inserted a key into a padlock the size of a large tin of baked beans, and we passed through the security fence, down one of the twin ramps beside the shoreward plateau where a funfair always used to be. The West Pier's rails are of a unique mosaic pattern, like a Persian carpet in creamy iron. Every few feet is a serpent-entwined stem of the lamps whose orange orbs used to light the promenade across the evening sea. The iron benches round the promontories are tilted steeply back, to allow the Victorians to take the whole sun on their faces.

The concert hall has a shallow dome, traversed by a fairground-like wooden banister and ringed by heraldic shields. Its final use, before the pier closed, was for Bingo. The floor is a rubble of grime, glass and broken catchpenny signs. One can imagine its inaugural concert in 1916: the patriotic songs, the khaki, the blue suits and red ties of the convalescents, brought from their hospitals at Eastbourne and Hove.

We made our way down through a succession of gimcrack barriers with barbed wire as furiously entangled as if Hitler were still expected. Vandalism is a perpetual problem. The trust's brainwave has been to let all-night fishermen continue using the pier in return for acting as unofficial caretakers. Every so often amid the broken kiosks and shops, one stumbles on a corner made draught-proof and orderly, with gas-ring and coffee-mugs and the bait-carrying Oxo tins that mark the presence of the West Pier guard.

Inside the wind-peeled weather screen, canvas chairs decompose where they have been left. Before us rose the theatre with its Russian domes, its verandahs and balconies half adrift, like some ghost town in the Wild West. The 800-seat auditorium was long ago partitioned off to make extra cafes and bars. Upstairs in the old main restaurant, pigeons murmured among the rafters. Fossilized black stoves and fryers still sent forth a spectral reek of fish and chip fat.

Seaward of the theatre, Mr Phillips pointed out the symmetrical hole in the deck where, last winter, the kiosk plunged through. By now, the diagonal boards around us showed larger and larger rents of violent sea green. The rotunda was too dangerous even to approach.

As we came out onto the seafront again, we bumped into a pixie-eared man in a woollen hat, a tweed sports jacket and pastel-coloured flared trousers. He was Les Piper, one of the fishermen who guard the West Pier at night and weekends, bedded along the mosaic rail with their invisible rods, their tiny lights and Oxo tins.

Les Piper used to come fishing on the West Pier when an all-day ticket cost three old pennies. You need not be very old to recollect those old pennies, the newer ones copper-coloured, the *truly* old ones almost black and bearing the worn, watery image of young Queen Victoria. The pennies that were indivisible from piers, pressed into brassbound slots below that stern Victorian reminder 'For Amusement Only'.

He pointed out beyond the pierhead to the ring of steel stumps that was a landing-stage for steamers to France and the Isle of Wight. 'Right down at one end,' he said, 'they used to have this ruddy great brass bell.' A bell for shipping was that? 'No,' Les Piper said. 'For telling us fishermen when it was time to get off.'

Some of the fishermen think the West Pier may be haunted. Late at night, noises have been heard from the direction of the theatre. But no one is worried. The sound seems only to be of laughter.

Only When I Pray

The most eventful evening I ever spent in Los Angeles began at 6-30 with an appearance on Merv Griffin's TV show, and could have reached its natural end by nine when I and a pleasant female friend sat eating our Caesar salads at the Brown Derby restaurant. Instead, my friend dropped me on Santa Monica Boulevard and watched with deep scepticism as I set off through the twilight, looking for The Chateau Church Under the Ministry of the Gospel of Truth.

The church proved to be a small wooden house with a homely-looking front porch, belied by an elaborate entry-phone system. I rang, identified myself and was admitted to narrow stairs ascending to the reception area, where several worshippers already waited. All were male, and wore expressions of studied unconcern as they chatted to the half-nude black receptionist or leafed through back copies of the church's main literature, a magazine called *Beautiful Bondage Positions*.

The Chateau Church *was* a bona fide religious establishment. But – this being California – it also was a private club for sado-masochists, retailing bondage, torture and ritual humiliation at the rate of one dollar per minute. On the principle that these are not perversions but forms of therapy valuable to the American urban male, it held a genuine charter from a mission church known for sponsoring social work in 'unconventional areas'. Its proprietor, a worthy heir to De Sade on one hand, was on the other an ordained minister, empowered to perform baptisms, wedding and funerals.

My appointment was with 'Mistress Veronica', one of the

Chateau Church's six resident 'dominatrixes'. She joined me after a few moments, clad in a brief tiger skin leotard, leather gloves and high-heeled boots, and carrying a cat o' nine tails, a small metal vice, a riding crop, a collar and lead, an eyeless hood, police-issue handcuffs and a full-length buggy whip. Her face, framed by untidy black hair, wore a paradoxically good-humoured expression. That my interest in her was purely journalistic did not offend Mistress Veronica. 'I've written a few things myself,' she said modestly.

'The Chateau', as it is usually known, was founded by a former computer-programmer for the US Army named James Hillier. It was at once a spanking success, enabling Mr Hillier to open a second branch – with the same bona fide ecclesiastical status – in San Francisco. On the telephone from there, he told me of the great advantages in operating as a church – maximum tax breaks and minimum police interference. But there were obligations also. The flagellation of prominent Californians generates some income for charity work on the state, and helps to support a children's orphanage in Mexico.

Mistress Veronica, by day a shorthand reporter at the San Francisco law courts, was especially well-placed to spread the Chateau's Gospel. Eminent lawyers, and a good leavening of judges, figured high on the roster of men who found a good thrashing – or variations from wrestling to tickling – the ideal respite from a hard day's mental activity. 'It's guys under pressure,' Mistress Veronica said. 'Most people resist pain, but actually it can be a relief. S amd M is kinda like jogging, really.'

She beckoned me into the adjoining room where her next client – or 'slave' for the nonce – awaited her. In the middle of the room stood two ceiling-high carved whipping posts. In the left-hand corner stood a timber cross, festooned with leather thongs. In the right-hand corner, a heap of clothes rested on two spotlessly clean gym shoes. In the foreground – so much so that we did not see him until we looked vertically at our own feet – a naked man knelt with his forehead pressed Muslim-style to the threadbare carpet. Stepping over him, Mistress Veronica lifted a wall intercom and spoke into it. 'We're ready to begin.'

'Thank you,' said a voice from a floor below.

'You're welcome,' Mistress Veronica said.

Seated in a black wickerwork chair, I watched as Mistress Veronica, with much initial fumbling and several involuntary giggles, affixed her 'slave' to the cross by the numerous leather loops provided. She then set a metal clamp on each side of his nipples and slipped the eyeless leather mask over his head. 'Oops!' she cried as one of the metal clamps fell off. The most intricate work centred on the man's genitals, which she first tied up by a strap to his neck-collar, then bound in a web of thongs and finally fitted with a shroud rather like the lace-up toecap of a roller-skate. As a final obliterating touch, she clamped the small vice to his penis.

'How does that feel, slave?' she inquired.

'Wonderful, Mistress Veronica,' the man's muffled voice replied.

'You can still breathe, right?'

'Yes, Mistress Veronica.'

'One thing we do emphasize here is safety,' Mistress Veronica said, cranking a lever so that the cross, with its spreadeagled, hooded and trussed man, rotated to an angle of 45 degrees. 'We ask all our clients beforehand if they have any health problems, like heart disease, or even small things. Say a client has pulled a tendon in sports, it's going to be really painful for him to stay on his knees as my slave . . .' She ceased cranking and returned to the front of the cross. 'How does it feel to be upside-down, slave?' she inquired.

'Wonderful, Mistress Veronica,' the muffled voice replied.

Like all Chateau employees, Mistress Veronica had undergone 'training' – chiefly by acting the submissive role to customers with a taste for domination. 'Mr Hillier says that's the only way to learn about true domination. As a submissive, you aren't necessarily whipped or caned. Some guys just want to wrestle with you – that's fifty dollars for about half an hour. I was tickled for forty minutes one time. I also specialize in trans-vestism. There's a big Texan guy who comes to me once a month. I usually dress him up as a drum majorette.'

At 22 years old, Mistress Veronica doubted whether she would ever make a conventional marriage. Why should she bother when her 'personal slaves' – men, and some women – competed for the favour of attending her at home, between them doing all her housework, shopping and auto-maintenance. Favoured Chateau customers were sometimes given a bonus of such domestic domination. 'When I go out to the kitchen for coffee, I may make the slave follow me on hands and knees. A lot of my clients really appreciate doing that.'

The local Police, though generally quiescent, made occasional checks to see that actual sexual intercourse played no part in the Chateau's itinerary. 'There's no way I'm going to allow that,' Mistress Veronica said. 'That would make me nothing but a prostitute. I also studied martial arts for two years. The cops sent one of their guys in last month to check on me. I could tell right off who he was and what he was trying to do. I got him strapped to the cross, then I made him begin barking like a dog. This poor guy starts yelling "I don't get *paid* enough to do this!"'

For 40 minutes, she struck the man on the cross with her riding crop, her cat o' nine tails and – her personal trademark – the buggy whip. 'It's an antique,' she said over her shoulder. The man on the cross made no sound, and clenched and unclenched his hands rhythmically.

After he had padded off, refreshed as if by squash, on his clean white gym shoes, Mistress Veronica gave me a conducted tour of the Chateau's other specially-equipped torture-rooms. 'This one is called The Inquisition. We have a real rack. This in here is The Victorian. And this is the Frank Campbell Room . . .' I searched through my limited knowledge for the name of Frank Campbell among history's notorious sado-masochists. It turned out he was a local man, so regular and well-liked a customer at the Chateau that they had named a room in his honour.

'I do the job because I get paid, sure, but also because I enjoy it,' Mistress Veronica said. 'When I'm with a slave, I can become whatever and whoever I want. And I get some good relationships going in there. Last week, I was with a slave for an hour and a half – I'd humiliate him a little, then we'd talk. We just kept on going, talking and trying out new ideas. At the end of the session, he asked me to marry me.'

Great on Paper

From my vantage-point as a trainee reporter on the *Hunts Post* (county newspaper for Huntingdonshire) Fleet Street used to look a forbidding place. What I knew of it from movies and books convinced me I would not prosper there – would, indeed, last only minutes amid the whirl of roaring presses, dirty trench-coats and ranting news editors, the hiring and firing at the drop of a dented trilby hat.

Picture my astonishment then on reaching *The Sunday Times* and seeing how different was the reality. Instead of drudges in trench-coats I found pink-shirted young men named Godfrey or Nick. Instead of mad haste I found four-hour lunches at Chez Victor. Instead of ruthless sackings I found job security such as had previously been enjoyed only by medieval calligrapher-monks.

This was, of course, the era when London was swinging and advertisement revenues, especially from colour supplements, were at an all-time high. The editor of so fabulous a gusher as *The Sunday Times Magazine* could do virtually what he pleased as long as the moolah from After Eight mints and Kosset carpets kept rolling in.

My years on the Magazine I can liken only to life in Ancient Rome under one of the sportier Emperors. Our huge glamour and profitability made us accountable to almost no one. Blunders, lapses of taste, even libel writs vanished as by magic from the foreground of coloured shirts, guffaws and champagne. To apologize was unthinkable, let alone to resign, let alone be asked to vacate one's seat at the feast.

On balance I don't mourn those so-called great days. No journalist can be other than glad at the final busting of the print unions' protection racket. It's good that young people other than Balliol double Blues nowadays get a chance on national papers, and that the way to keep a writing job is, once more, to work one's butt off.

The new era in journalism actually isn't new at all – merely a return to how things were before that opium-eating Sixties interlude. It's practically a re-birth of Gissing's *New Grub Street*, with journalists again regarded as grubby pariahs, owners meddling the way Victorian owners did, and scarcely a week passing without the appearance of another brand-new title on the stands.

When Robert Maxwell launched his *London Daily News*, five months ago, I was happy to accept the offer of a fortnightly column. I did so mainly because its editor, Magnus Linklater, was a personal friend as well as the finest executive journalist I know. I also supported the idea of a paper that would represent and reflect London the way it had not been for more than a decade. Like many, I cherish a low-burning hatred for the connivance that killed off the old *Evening News* and gave the *Standard* its monopoly licence to be smug, bland and indifferent as an airport departures-board.

Writing my *London Daily News* column was, I confess, not hugely enjoyable. The staff, frantic with producing round-the-clock editions, had no time for the niceties one receives from weeklies and Sundays. The way I knew they'd received my copy was seeing it in the paper.

There also were endless problems over payment – an area in which all these new high-tech titles seem remedially under-equipped. Even the lofty *Independent* takes six weeks-plus to pay its contributors. *Today*, under its original management, took at least ten. In cheaper circles the practice is now rife of 'lifting' copyright material from other sources, hoping the authors just won't notice. The parody *Evening News* (relaunched by the *Standard* company merely to scupper the *Daily News*) resorted to outright piracy recently, lifting an entire V. S. Pritchett short story, with the subsequent absurd excuse that they thought it was 'out of copyright'.

No one ever denied that the *London Daily News* instantly became, and remained, a first-rate paper. Yet from the start one knew in one's bones that it just wasn't being read. At my local Indian newsagent's I would see piles of it remain virgin while the *Standard* rapidly disappeared. '*Very* bad seller,' the newsagent would say, shaking his head. 'Only 11 copies today.'

Myself, I wonder if the very soundness and explicitness of its aim mightn't finally have told against it. The modern British public prefers woolly inanity, as can be seen from the way two highly successful newspapers market themselves. *The Telegraph* declares itself, almost gibberingly, to be 'not boring'. The *Mail On Sunday*'s slogan is 'A newspaper not a snoozepaper'. There's clearly not much percentage in logic or literacy.

Magnus Linklater attributes the failure of the *London Daily News* to what he calls 'The Roland Rat Factor'. There was a missing ingredient they could never pinpoint. They seemed to be offering the public everything that was intelligent and relevant. Maybe what the public wanted was something totally stupid and irrelevant.

Robert Maxwell's next act, after folding the *London Daily News*, was to announce he would be starting three more papers soon. Naturally one must welcome them. But I wish these new titles didn't appear and disappear quite so much like spivs selling nylons from suitcases in Oxford Street. Anyone who's tried to get money out of them will know especially well what I mean.

Outlook Bilious

The nadir of British male fashion, one can safely say, is BBC-TV's nightly weather forecast. The men who discuss cold fronts and satellite pictures, with all the charisma of voles staring at car headlights, rarely appear in anything designed after 1969. Michael Fish was until recently the Brummel of the bunch with his claret-coloured, waisted velvet jacket. But Michael Fish has been thrown into total eclipse by Bill Giles's sweater.

Bill Giles's sweater was evidently given to him – by some very guileless or very malevolent person – for Christmas. It is bright emerald, blobbed all over with fierce primary black and white. Is the prevailing men's leisure look, meant to evoke ski lodges and Scandinavian stoves but, alas, more strongly suggesting a copiously regurgitated meal of spring greens, blackberries and white sauce.

Beastly though it be, there are men on TV with sweaters even beastlier. Richard Stilgoe owns a particularly foul specimen, of powder blue vertically cabled with misty turquoise. Chris Kelly goes for the patchwork look, weaving raw liver vermilion into hideous contrast with dried-blood red and Bisto brown. Balding sports commentators generally favour baby pink lambswool, sometimes with little lambs gambolling across the front. Noel Edmonds chooses hunky, zig-zagged grey Shetland to point up his custard-yellow programme sets and the highlights in his hair and beard.

An average evening's viewing, in fact, establishes the basic British fashion picture at present. Women – even those one doesn't specially care for, like Sue Lawley or Janet Street-Porter

– have never looked better and classier. Men, on the other hand, have seldom looked so thoroughly disgusting.

It's rather unfair if you think about it. For years, British men were reproached for being unflamboyant in their dress, sticking to their eternal pinstripes and clerical greys. All that changed with a vengeance, almost at the precise moment women discovered the virtues of pinstripe and clerical grey. She, as a result, looks sleek, neat and purposeful. He is a shifty shambles of bilious 'leisure' hues, not a peacock so much as a poor old pigeon over which someone has poured a multicoloured milk shake.

The colours worn by men at present truly are awful. The dominant one is light turquoise, closely followed by sherbet pink, lime green and robin's egg blue. While women's fashion increasingly suggests work and business, men's fashion has reverted to an almost infantile dream world of play and partying. The leisure look presists, whatever unpleasant or unsocial things its wearer happens to be doing. Men gathering to strike, or shout obscenities at non-strikers, still wear the same jivey, good-time colours, the same twee stripes up the sleeves they are shaking in fury.

An equal role-reversal has occurred in the matter of comfort. It is women no longer but men who buy things too tight under the arms, undo their blouses the better to breathe and stuff their feet into tortuous painted shoes of white or pearlized grey.

While women have enclosed themselves in the billowy comfort of shifts and smocks, men have gone over wholesale to the blouson, a garment as hideously confining as it is unflattering. We have all been forced to witness the blouson-wearer's bend, that parting of garments at the midriff to reveal a length of bare back terminating in underpants-elastic from which the beginning of a bottom may coyly be peeping.

Men now far exceed women in desire to prolong their youth and sex appeal. There is apparently no male torso too withered to don an American college T-shirt, no pair of male buttocks too crabapple-shrunken to be flaunted in faded Levis. Fathers are indistinguishable, at a distance, from their teenage sons. Here and there, one sees a stylish son sweating in the company of a Dad obstinately attired like a pop group roadie circa 1971.

While women look cool and happy in their new-found 'power' suits, male business wear continues the long tradition of purgatory. In vain do men's designers like Willie Smith offer suits as soft and roomy as favourite dressing gowns. The Briton will not be weaned from his waisted two-piece, twin vents straining and flapping over protruding bum. The country's tightest suits must be those worn by Terry Wogan. That prodigious strain on his chest and haunches, even more than his questions, almost bring tears to the eyes. As each of his guests comes on, you see the give-away sign of the agonisingly-dressed man. Before he sits down, he unbuttons his jacket.

As for Bill Giles, I fear his full-frontal Lapp inferno is no longer alone at the London Weather Centre. Ian MacCaskill has taken to appearing in a luminous pink shirt with a matching kipper tie. What will Michael Fish's answer be? The outlook, I fear, is gruesome.

Going Home To Mother

I am lucky enough, when in London, to have my mother living only a street away. She is not always there, spending much of each week as she does with her farming friend in Cambridgeshire, or at the races. On my last return from New York, it so happened, there was a lull in the racing calendar and the farming friend was being 'tense' about his crops. My mother's voice answered her telephone.

The line between Westbourne Terrace and adjacent Gloucester Terrace, as usual, crackled like a bad connection with the Congo.

'I'm very tired after the flight,' I said. 'Perhaps I could come round and see you just for half an hour, then go to bed.'

'What time were you thinking of?' my mother asked.

'Eight o'clock?'

'Oh.' There was a pause.

'Are you going out somewhere at eight, then?'

'No,' my mother said. 'It's just that at eight there's something on television about a big American poker-player.'

'I'll come at eight-thirty then.'

'No, come at eight. After all,' my mother said judiciously, 'I haven't seen you for two months. Will you want anything to eat?'

I felt my stomach curdle at the thought of any food, save that which only a mother can provide.

'A bit of toast,' I said. 'Maybe a poached egg.'

'I could do you scrambled eggs.'

'Oh – yes, *please*!' I said (actually, gasped). 'I'd *love* scrambled eggs . . . nice and soft, on one piece of brown toast, with black pepper. Oh yes please, *please*. I can't *tell* you how much I'd love scrambled eggs!'

'Are you sure you don't want a lamb chop?' my mother said.

It had evidently slipped her mind that, in the 42 years she has known me, I have always hated lamb chops.

My mother opened her front door in a bright blue tracksuit, the sporting impact of which was somewhat qualified by gold Ali Baba slippers. Her hair, newly done in Knightsbridge, had that full golden sheen which has, at various times, proved so fascinating to high-spirited racehorses.

'I jog now,' she said proudly. 'Twice round the top garden, down at the farm. It makes me feel ever so much better.'

'What do you wear on your feet, though? Not *those*.'

'No. A pair of my old wellies.'

'You should have proper shoes, you know,' I said. 'You can do yourself serious . . .'

'I've got everything ready for the scrambled eggs,' my mother interrupted.

'Oo-er!' I said. 'How lovely. I've been looking forward to them for the past two hours. I can't *tell* you how much I want scrambled eggs tonight.'

'Are you sure you don't want a lamb chop?' my mother said.

'We've been through all that,' I reminded her.

'Oh . . . charming,' my mother murmured, much as she does when her farming friend is being 'tense' about his crops.

It must be admitted at this point that my mother and her farming friend own racehorses. You may have seen her on television, at Ascot or Sandown, leading a winner in. She has been interviewed in camera by Brough Scott, and had her observations reprinted in *The Sporting Life*'s 'Sayings of the Week' column. A racing paper recently referred to her as 'the redoubtable Mrs Norman'. Much of her time these days is spent in being redoubtable.

Any conversation with my mother, on whatever subject, swiftly detours to her five-year old gelding, All Is Forgiven, and her farming friend's three-year old, All Is Revealed. Unfortunately, All Is Forgiven got a nicked tendon last year, and is out to grass in Humberside. But All Is Revealed has had a terrific season – four wins, including a course record at Sandown. His is a story to kindle even my severely limited interest in The Turf.

'. . . and he's the one who was no good at all, isn't he?'

'No good at all,' my mother said. 'Whenever he got on any racecourse, he used to sweat.'

'I thought all horses sweated.'

'This was before the race even started,' my mother said. 'He was a bundle of nerves. You couldn't do anything with him. He carried on like that until Dave Thom [the trainer] put a goat in his stall with him.'

'I've heard of racehorses having animal friends,' I said.

'Ah, but the goat wasn't a friend,' my mother said. 'He couldn't *stand* the goat. He'd try to kick it and bite it. That was what made a man of him – bashing up this goat. He was a different horse after that. You should have seen him at Ascot, leaving all those probables for the Cesarewitch behind . . . because he'd bashed up the goat first.'

'A bit rough on the goat,' I said.

'The goat gets its revenge by crapping in the manger,' my mother said.

'So does the goat go everywhere with him?'

'It goes with him to every race meeting, but it's not allowed into the saddling-up box,' my mother said. 'So Dave Thom's made a tape recording of the goat, to get him to go into the box and be saddled. If ever he runs in on his own, Dave Thom makes him go back and listen to the tape recording.'

'Any more press coverage?' I asked.

'They're doing the goat on Anglia Television,' my mother said.

'And when's your next press conference?'

'Ha-bloody-ha,' my mother said.

By this time, the scrambled eggs were ready. The one invaluable piece of advice my mother ever gave me was that scrambled eggs go on cooking after you take them off the stove.

These were as wonderful as I'd hoped. Just runny enough,

with black pepper, on one piece of brown toast. There was nothing left in the world to desire.

'You're *sure* you didn't want a lamb chop?' my mother said.

'I'm sure.'

'Not even some runner beans?'

'Very, *very* sure.'

'Scrambled eggs were *really* all you wanted?'

'Yes. *Yes.*'

'Well, eat them up. Then I'll make you a nice cup of coffee.'

I never drink coffee in the evening. I suppose the fact must have slipped my mother's mind.

My Hero

To this day I doubt I ever had a bigger hero than Brian Read. I remember him in our school singing lesson, a wearisomely chaotic affair in the assembly hall that used to last most of an afternoon. Brian Read had secured some specious quasi-official role which allowed him to walk back and forth in front of us, continually crossing the steps up to the stage. He walked in a humorously disconnected way that flapped his dark hair over his beaky face and windmilled his arms among the loose pieces of his tie. His flat birthday sandals banged like a trampoline each time he hopped over the steps. I thought I had never seen a more dashing or stylish character.

Brian Read became the high point of my 11th year, especially that hot post-Coronation summer when life otherwise seemed to be winding down to a stop. The war between my parents had led both at once to abandon our gloomy seaside flat. I lived there alone with a Siamese cat and an old labrador, subsisting mainly on cherry Neptune and sliced bread.

What attracted me to Brian Read, no less than his debonair walk, was his triumphant normality. His surname was that of a prestigious local charabanc firm. His father was Deputy Town Clerk. He lived in a grey pebbledash villa named The Dolls House, with diamond pane windows and a crazy-paved front path. Not only were his parents constantly and simultaneously at home, but they even seemed quite fond of one another.

He was a year my senior, already long-trousered; an almost uncrossable gulf. At school, I could not presume to address him. Outside, I could know him only by cultivating his younger brother Peter, several months my own junior. On visits to Peter at The Dolls House, I would obtain fascinating sights of Brian's inner life. I remember with what sense of privilege I first glimpsed the large cardboard box on which he had printed DINKY TOYS.

Apart from his black 'All Steel' bicycle, his consuming interest was cars. To win his esteem, I strove to acquire all possible knowledge on the subject. Walking his bull terrier, Brock, across the nearby Recreation Ground, Brian would sometimes genially take me through what I had learned. 'A Vauxhall Velox has got a six-cylinder engine, hasn't it? And a Wyvern's only got four . . .' One day, he explained every stage of building a coach for his grandfather's charabanc firm. I can see his beaky face now, unwontedly serious, his arms for once not flailing through his tie. 'First, you have to get a thing built that's called the chassis. You send that to a firm named Duple, to have the bodywork put on . . .'

My shame was that I could not ask Brian Read to tea, not bear even to let him see inside our deserted, atrophied flat. To compensate, I made wild boasts. 'I'm going to have special visiting-cards printed for the three of us . . .' 'I'm going to have a party soon. With an obstacle-race . . .' As I left The Dolls House that afternoon, I heard Brian through the open kitchen window, washing his hands and telling his mother, 'I've never been to a party with an obstacle race . . .' His trust in my absurd form of words cut me to the marrow.

Then an unexpected thing happened. Crossing the Recreation Ground with Brock one evening, we noticed three girls following us. Two were on foot, the third balanced precariously on a semi-drop handled bike. They were not following Peter or me, of course. They were following Brian, whose reputation as a Romeo I knew to be considerable. Their names were Gillian, Jean and Diane.

For Diane and Jean it was a routine pursuit. But Gillian was obsessed. She had dark curly hair, violet-ringed eyes and a low voice that broke with emotion, particularly in any reference to Brian. Before long, she was writing him extravagant love notes. He showed them to Peter and me with his tolerant smile. 'I like you and love you,' said one. 'I want to go out with you. If it doesn't work, that's life . . .'

The bond between us seemed to grow in satirizing lovelorn Gillian. Once, in an unwise movement on a sea wall, she disclosed a momentary flash of white Aertex pants. Therefore in her company Brian and I would exchange side glances and murmur 'White Aertex pants', not quite inaudibly. The bold but also shy violet-ringed eyes would flutter down in mortification.

Yet I knew her unrequited love and my deferential hero-worship were essentially the same. On nights that Brian wasn't around, I would walk to the seafront street where Gillian's parents kept a tall guest-house. She would be sitting on the stone balustrade, knees drawn up to her chin, affording further hints of white Aertex. It was almost like being with Brian to listen as she poured out stories of her helpless infatuation. '. . . and I used to go crazy if I ever saw him out on the Canoe Lake. But he's high class, isn't he?' she would sigh. 'That's the whole trouble.'

Then another unexpected thing happened. My father returned home for a few days. He had many criticisms of me to make, not least that the routine I had evolved without him, and my mother, neglected almost all the conventional pursuits of boyhood. Before vanishing again, he made a typically radical gesture to remedy this. In our part of the communal garden he erected a tent.

I could not invite Brian and Gillian into the flat. But I could into the tent. And all at once, something in the atmosphere of canvas and trapped grass made Brian relent towards his pursuer. He consented to lie back, her head resting on his arm. 'We're all right, aren't we?' he said, smiling down at her. 'Yes,' she replied, gazing up with those woundable violet-ringed eyes.

I sensed – as she clearly did – that it was a moment of unrepeatable magic. I ran into the flat, made tea and brought it out in the filigree silver pot no one used any more. Gillian knelt forward studiously to pour. Brian stretched out, grinned at me and, in a nasal American accent, said 'Better get some sleep now, you guys . . .'

A couple of weeks later, we quarrelled over some model soldiers. I never spoke to him again.

Touching Up The Verbals

The next public honour given to Richard Branson should be that his accent receives an Arts Council grant. It is the most utterly perfect Sixties period-piece. Mrs Thatcher is only two decades late in creating Britain's first nationalized hippy.

Is there a more nostalgic sound to be heard than that light, faintly lisping tenor voice which, one knows instinctively, issues from someone wearing tennis-shoes, an amusingly-inscribed T-shirt and a beard? The vowels are pure Flower Power, flattened by the necessity of appearing simultaneously mystic and child-like, and never being caught without a smile. When complimented, he says 'Thank yee'. When answering a call of Nature, he goes to the 'lee'. And when faced with any downright question – like 'How many million did you coin last year?' or 'Isn't Boy George's heroin-cure fantastic publicity?' – he stares off, as if contemplating Nirvana, and talks absoleet bloody drivel.

It is the accent which was called 'classless' back in those heady times, 20 years ago, when class truly did seem dead and buried. It was posh people talking down and artisans talking up; earls with Nikons round their necks and East End wide boys sporting names like Justin de Villeneuve. It was hyperbolic towards everything, save that which merited hyperbole. A Sixties person said 'Beautiful' or 'Far out' when offered a cigarette but in the Valley of the Kings would nod omnisciently and say 'Those tombs are really nice.'

Though the idyll of classlessness perished long ago, its vowel sounds go on for ever. Today's young generation filter their hardness, opportunism and social ambition through exactly the same teeth-clenching quasi-hippy smile. The 'ou' sound in our language has, this past decade, become virtually extinct. BBC announcers now read the 'Nees'. Even professional drama-coaches seem to have given up. The finest British film of recent years had its fastidious Edwardian detail fatally marred by its young leading actress's insistence that she wanted 'a room with a vee'.

Sloane Ranger and Hooray Henry talk is also sprinkled with Beatle-ish colloquialisms like 'wellie' and 'photie', bizarrely at odds with the plums in their mouths. I recently endured a train-journey near a party of young blimps, all smoking in the No Smoking area and stridently discussing that afternoon's game of 'footeah'. When a Sloane embraces a Sixties concept, the result can be plain baffling. A high-born girl asked me the other day if I had ever 'done Jaeger'. I thought she ment cardigans and socks. She actually meant Buddha and meditation.

I remain baffled by this new game of turning 'ou' into 'i', as in 'country hice', to indicate one is quality. I hear, though, of a delectable come-uppance suffered by Mark Hamilton, the literary agent, who recently wrote to a publisher suggesting a biography of Sir Walter Raleigh. Unluckily, Mr Hamilton did not notice his secretary had typed his letter just as he'd pronounced it. The fulsome missive ended with a reminder of all the fascinating material that could be included about 'The Tyre of London'.

Why is the whole country suffering this plague of builders? Every street one sees is defaced by scaffolding, debris, dust and filthy skips. The men concerned seem positively to exult in their destruction of the environment. Pavements and roads are scarred for ever by huge spillages of paint. Skips are left rotting until rats appear. The din, both near and far, is purgatorial.

Other than limiting their hours (which lots don't anyway), builders appear at liberty to disturb and pollute us as they please. How is it, in an age of technological miracles, that most builders' engines still emit a noise like massed Stuka dive-bombers? How come that, even when a house seems finished and its scaffolding disappears, men still come daily with hammers and whistle Engelbert Humperdinck's Greatest Hits?

Last month, builders were at work in the flat above mine, and making rather a mess in the communal hall. I went up and asked one of them, quite politely, to lay a sheet down. His response took me wholly by surprise. 'F--- off,' he said, 'and stay outa here, you f---ing arse-bandit.'

I am not, as it happens, the euphemism stated. Most of my life's problems, indeed, have sprung from quite the opposite cause; stranger still, my accuser wore a gold bracelet and several rings, his hair in Byronesque curls and lovelocks and white trousers whose tightness one might have thought would attract widespread comment in the building trade. Today's male homosexuals are more likely to resemble crop-headed 1940s National Servicemen, a conundrum I am at a loss to explain.

Some literal Sod's Law, however, ordained that, every time I saw my accuser afterwards, I should – in his eyes, at least – confirm myself to be an 'arse-bandit'. Next day he saw me waiting outside in a tracksuit, holding a fishing-bag. Just a plain Hardy bag, canvas and leather, full of my writing materials. As I stood there, he came out of the house with a plank, and I saw his face dissolve into a smile saying more plainly than could any words, 'There's that f---ing arse-bandit again.'

It is strange to acquire an instant, implacable foe, deaf to all verbal persuasion, even if one knew what to say. 'Look here, I'm not one, you know ... Ask anyone.' I found myself consciously dressing in a more 'manly' style and leaving the Hardy bag indoors. When I left the house in tweed jackets and cords, Of course, he wasn't about. Then he saw me in my running-shorts, and smiled that smile again. Then, as builders do, without warning, he moved on.

The other day, coming through Covent Garden, I was lucky enough to buy a whole cache of P. G. Wodehouse novels in their original dust-jackets. As I walked home with them in two carrier-bags, I saw my former persecutor approaching. I looked down my manly lapels to my sensible shoes and promised myself that, if he called me it again, I'd threaten to sue him for slander. As he passed me, that same quiet, corroborative smile appeared on his face. Too late I remembered that both my plastic bags were bright pink and bore the bookseller's name: Horace C. Blossom.

Live At The Palladium

He was not just picking staff for his new club, Steve Rubell said: he was casting a great drama.

He sat behind his desk at the still unfinished Palladium, staring with his large, liquid eyes at a young hopeful currently under audition for the major role of bartender. At his side hovered his personnel director, Skip Odeck, murmuring names from a clipboard list. Both, from time to time, looked across at a wall festooned with the Polaroid snaps sent in, with their résumés, by prospective waiters, cloakroom attendants and washers-up. Each boy's and girl's face was sun-tanned and pretty, and contorted into the the desperate New York smile that says 'Hi there!'

Steve Rubell is a frail-looking man of 42, somewhat like Frank Sinatra circa 1960. You feel he, too, would flinch under a strong handshake, yet might punch a guy out for showing disrespect to a lady. Today he wore the same kind of dark suit and white shirt that Sinatra did under sufferance in 'Pal Joey'. On his head perched a white peaked cap, chequered around the base like a British policemen's. The cap concealed the fact that, because of great stress in Steve Rubell's life, all his hair had recently fallen out.

He looked harder at the would-be bartender, a laid-back Lower East Side god in whose cheek faint movement could be discerned.

'Don't chew gum if you work for me,' Rubell said softly. 'You can chew it in here, never out there.'

To Skip Odeck, without varying his tone, he said: 'Why should Andy work opening night?'

'He's easily the best-looking bartender, Steve. Tell me – what am I to say to this girl Brenda? She's been calling me every hour.'

'Do you think Andy's strong enough for the main bar?' Rubell mused. 'I think Reeve knows how to bartend. And what about Yolanda?'

'If Yolanda works there, all the bartenders will be dark-haired, Steve.'

'I don't care if they're all dark,' said Rubell. 'I'm talking about who I think belongs in the Mike Todd room.'

'I think Yolanda's very . . . exotic-looking.'

'I don't like her weight,' Rubell said. 'You'll have to talk to her about that.'

The would-be bartender looked on in awe, his chewing gum carefully immobilized. As minutes passed, he clearly judged he had the audition in his pocket. Shifting his gum, he ventured a question to Skip Odeck.

'He wants to know if he can bring some friends to the opening,' Odekc said.

Steve Rubell smiled incredulously. 'Just worry about yourself,' he advised.

'Don't worry about anybody else,' Odeck agreed.

'Forget your friends,' Rubell said. 'Opening night, there's going to be about 10,000 people out there on 14th Street. Worry about getting yourself in. If your friends fit, they'll make it.'

As the new employee left, Rubell stared thoughtfully after him. 'I'd say he was more of a street type, wouldn't you?'

Skip Odeck made the classic casting director's gesture of tearing hair out by the roots. '*Steve!* He's not the *least* bit ugly. You couldn't honestly describe him as an *ugly* person . . .'

Steve Rubell became famous for being just as choosy about the people he would allow to be his paying customers. From 1977 to 1980, his Studio 54 club was *the* haunt of New York's innermost in-crowd: Warhol, Jagger, Capote, Halston *et al*. No less famous were the nightly scenes on West 54th Street as crowds struggled to persuade Rubell they were fit company for these supernatural persons. Such was 54's power, it frequently could oblige the stars themselves to mill around outside, enduring ritual self-abasement until the right eye was caught, the right list consulted and the scarlet rope grudgingly unhooked.

Since those heady days, Rubell and his partner, Ian Schrager, have run into some access problems of their own. In 1980, they were jointly convicted of evading more than $400,000 in income tax on cash allegedly 'skimmed' from Studio 54's receipts. Each was sent to prison for a year and barred from ever again holding a liquor licence in the State of New York.

This is what's great about the Big Apple, they say. Even if you rescind his liquor licence, you can't keep a good man down. Two years ago, Rubell and Schrager bounced back to the entrepreneurial scene fronting a consortium to build a luxury hotel named Morgans on Madison Avenue. They also announced plans for a new disco club that would be to the Eighties what Studio 54 was to the late Seventies.

For a site they chose the old Palladium Theatre on East 14th Street, a relic of New York's Victorian past that, in its latter days, served as headquarters for the impresario Mike Todd. The neighbourhood could scarcely be less glamorous. Nearby is Union Square with its cheap Asian bazaars and shoe outlets. Two avenues west is a district of narcotics dealing so intense that the innocent pedestrian risks getting high by proxy.

To Rubell, the location is exactly right. 'I always go to bad neighbourhoods. In 1977, they said I was crazy to open up on 54th Street. Shall I tell you why 14th is perfect? It's half-way between downtown and uptown. Manhattan has gotten to be two cities. People from uptown don't go downtown. People downtown don't come uptown. The Palladium will be where downtown and uptown meet.'

The club has been designed with sentimental regard for a great cigar-smoky auditorium that in its time echoed both to Caruso and the Rolling Stones. The dance floor is itself a stage set, flanked by 3-D murals of tenement streets that can be raised to increase space as the crowds expands. New spiral stairways

ascend past gold-wreathed Victorian madonnas into the massive
dress circle, now a sitting-out place for those fatigued by the disco
din. Mike Todd's old office at the top has become a VIP bar,
modelled on Jean Cocteau's designs for 'Beauty and the Beast'.

In place of Studio 54's harsh theatrics and deafening light,
Rubell says the Palladium offers comfort, elegance and together-
ness, expressing the more secure good opinion New Yorkers
have of themselves in the Eighties. 'At 54, we had less than 100
seats. Here we have almost 900. The Palladium is somewhere you
can have a great time dancing, or just come to relax, talk and be
with people. In the Seventies, it was all "me, me, me". Today,
it's "we, we, we".'

Most of all, the Palladium reflects the new kind of stardom
that now obsesses bohemian New York. It is pop stardom or
couture stardom no longer, but *art* stardom. Hockney, even
Warhol at his apogee, scarcely enjoyed the adulation currently
given to young painters like Keith Haring and Kenny Scharf
whose work a few months ago seemed merely impudent addi-
tions to New York's graffiti plague. Haring in particular is
lionized for the child-primitive light bulbs and little running,
tumbling man shapes he used to draw surreptitiously on subway
hoardings. Today, Keith Haring man shapes fetch big bucks in
chic SoHo galleries and cavort across the trendiest posters,
prints and anti-apartheid T-shirts.

Rubell has given over the Palladium to a display of original
work by these wall-daubing wonders. The basement is a
psychedelic grotto, where Kenny Scharf's Cyclops-eyed spanners
and Hoover-heads rear up on every side, and the very pay-
phones are encrusted with entwined purple and green dinosaurs
copulating. In the corridor, where white shirt collars turn
ghastly violet, primeval whiskers seem to sprout between the
strata of luminous lime and pink. Upstairs the dancers gyrate
against a backdrop of Keith Haring manikins. On a quieter wall
by Francisco Clemente, a puzzled-looking mule peers over a
trompe-l'œil stable door. It is a source of much satisfaction to
Steve Rubell that the Palladium is the first New York club to
employ its own full-time art curator.

Eight years have produced no serious rival to Rubell and Schrager as discoland's Barnum and Bailey. Its uptown imitators – like flashy Xenon – never came close to Studio 54's magnetizing pazzazz. Latterly, with the *haute bohème*'s migration downtown to SoHo and TriBeCa, the trend has been to smaller, more eccentric places like the Mud Club, Limelight, Danceteria or Area, on Hudson Street, which kept its edge for almost two years by completely changing its decor every month.

The Palladium's 'door policy' will be the same as Studio 54's – that is, to let in only the kind of people Steve Rubell feels he would like to entertain in his own home. 'To make any club work, you have to have the right combination of people. Some wild, some straight, some uptown, some downtown. You need a mix that's going to work well together. At 54, I'd sometimes split up a couple at the door. Sure, I'd even split up mother and daughter. It's the criterion anybody would use who was giving a private party. When it's put on a commercial basis, it causes controversy.'

This promised re-sorting of social sheep from goats was sending tremors through Manhattan's credulous smart set long before the Palladium's grand opening in May. 'Not to be there,' one downtown *salonier* said, 'will be social *death*.' To work there was equally crucial in a city where bartenders and waiters habitually treat their calling as a pathway to becoming rock singers, actors or musical comedy stars. At Area, Limelight, Kamikaze, Pyramid, as in restaurants like Caramba! and Indochine, key employees prepare to defect the instant they received Rubell and Schrager's call. The auditions for staff would have furnished poignant extra scenes to 'A Chorus Line'. To work at the Palladium, bartenders accepted demotion to waiters, and waiters to lowly bus boys. A qualified female audio engineer willingly became an attendant in the ladies' room.

Elsewhere, sardonic questions were asked about the evident ease with which Rubell and Schrager had bounced back, despite court judgements apparently designed to prevent their ever operating a club again. Their protestations that they did not own the Palladium – but were merely 'consultants' to an anony-

mous development group – hardly allayed suspicion that, somewhere along the way, rules had been spectacularly bent.

The pair had their problems, however. The original grand
opening, set for May 7, was to have been a fashion spectacular
featuring the modelling debut of Princess Stephanie of Monaco.
This had to be cancelled when it was learned the Princess had
entered a 'detoxification centre'. Then, four days before the
rescheduled opening, a court application was lodged by an
outraged private citizen (clearly not on the guest list) seeking an
injunction to prevent it.

Seventy-two hours before opening night, the dance-area was
still strewn with electric drill cables and masked by corrugated
paper. While Ian Schrager talked to lawyers, Steve Rubell carried
on auditioning bartenders like a Broadway producer who, at the
eleventh hour, still hopes to spot his big star in the crowd.

An elderly *New York Times* photographer gazed at the stairways twisting up, through disco hardware, to the soft-lit theatre
heaven. He looked harder at the stairs, which are iron and, in
contrast with all else, severely functional. 'I get a strong jail-type
feel from all this,' the photographer said. His face broke into a
grin, half censorious, half admiring. 'These *guys* . . .'

It is 11 p.m., opening night. The ill-wisher's injunction has not
been granted. East 14th to Union Square is lined by blue police
barricades. Under the old theatre portico – purposely left in its former tattered and discoloured state – the crowd is already such as
would surround a major street accident. To the rear stand squat
policemen, walkie-talkies blaring on their hips. Keith Haring
arrives but, like everyone else, must wait. He is a bespectacled,
fidgety-looking youth in a lemon-coloured suit and hand-painted
sneakers. His presence causes audible gasps of desire.

The minuscule access channel is guarded by about a dozen
stewards, and three rather more unlikely figures. Two are Oriental girls, dressed somewhat like Little Maids from 'The Mikado'.
The third is a young man with tightly-curled hair, voluminous
white satin shorts and a clipboard, ostentatiously flourished.
This is Haoui Montaug, nonpareil among Manhattan club door

managers: the same Hanoui Montaug who, with his mixture of theatrical bravura and implacable firmness, once compelled Mick Jagger to pay a $6 admission charge.

Even entrance to Manhattan's newest club is subject to America's age-old bureaucracy. Arrivals, with their Western Union telegram invitations, first present themselves to a steward, who refers them to a Little Maid, who in turn asks them to wait until Haoui has a moment. If all is satisfactory, Haoui waves them through the channel with his clipboard like a choreographer shooing chorus girls onstage.

A ramp through a white, marbled corridor leads into a vestibule of deep Japanese green where small, black-clad Orientals move round with long-handled brass dustpans, picking up each cigarette-end that is dropped. Through the new carpet-smelling twilight, a British voice resounds. It belongs to Anthony Haden-Guest, New York's most conspicuous expatriate journalist, a man who can convert even his lack of an invitation into strident one-upmanship. 'They told me, "You can come in. But Steve's still *very cross* with you."'

A stairway of garishly-lit glass tiles ascends to the main disco area, already thunderous with drum-machine noise. Behind the long ocean-liner bar, brand-new bartenders hover, stupefied, over brand-new cash registers. The *cognoscenti*, nursing $4 spritzers, swap legends from the dear dead days of 54.

'Do you remember the night they had so much money, they put it into garbage sacks, tied them to helium balloons and floated them to the ceiling?'

'Do you know where the account books were found? Stuffed into a Manila envelope with two ounces of cocaine . . .'

Few recognize Ian Schrager, an unflamboyant ex-lawyer of 37, who describes his role in the partnership with Rubell as 'making the body for Steve to breathe life into'. They met at college in Brooklyn, originally as suitors for the same girl. Through thick and very thin, Rubell has remained the flash senior, Schrager the admiring freshman. 'I'll tell you a Steve Rubell story,' is a frequent line with him. '. . . the other night John McEnroe and Tatum O'Neal wanted to stay at Morgans, but the hotel was all sold out, so Steve gave them his bed, and he slept on the couch. The guy only cares about pleasing other people.'

At midnight, the tenement street stage sets surrounding the dancers are pulled up to reveal a wide area walled by red squares that glimmer on and off in the pattern of a giant Ludo board. A television camera predictably settles on two girls dancing together with identical high-stacked blonde hair and black leather costumes that show more deep fissures of flesh than a hospital operating gown. A preppy in a blazer is pulled across to frug with four wildly jumping breasts. If this is what Steve means by 'a mix', it's certainly happening.

At the front door, some 500 people now shove hard against Haoui Montaug's dozen-odd security men. Those who have made it come up the ramp breathless, dishevelled, some lacking earrings, even shoes. Saris and ratty orange feather boas are much in evidence, both favoured by hairy-chested men. Each intake brings a few undesirables who have somehow slipped through Haoui's net. 'This way, please,' a Little Maid says icily, leading a black teenager out. 'Fellas, we can talk,' a steward says, leading two more black teenagers away.

The crowd now includes Bianca Jagger, Christopher Reeve, designers Calvin Klein, Willi Smith and Halston, art stars Julian Schnabel, Kenny Scharf, Keith Haring. Boy George is there also, in peaked cap and oilskin, looking like a very odd deck-chair attendant. The apotheosis of downtown fashion parading past does not greatly impress him. 'Everyone,' he says scornfully, 'is trying to look *nice*. It's just middle class, and money, money, money.'

At 2 a.m., the crowd outside turns nasty. A hundred or so people who Steve Rubell definitely would not invite to his house break through the stewards' cordon and thunder up the ramp. Heavy main doors are dragged shut and bolted. It is now impossible for anyone to get into The Palladium. It is equally impossible for anyone to get out.

Upstairs, there now hangs over the dancers' heads an object like a railway goods wagon, emitting white steam. Men dressed in white Berber robes or leather micro-skirts gyrate in slow

unison on ledges at either side. For all that, the atmosphere –
especially the constant, pointless movement of overdressed over-
anxious people up the stairs, then down again – most strongly
evokes the QE2's Double Up Room in mid-Atlantic.

Steve Rubell becomes visible, still in his 'Pal Joey' suit and
policeman's cap, standing on the steps near the bar with an air –
peculiar to some impresarios at the birth of great enterprises –
that it is all really nothing to do with him.

He stiffens as an entourage comes through the crowd, usher-
ing Andy Warhol's gold-bleached grey cockade and boyish
death's head face. 'Make way,' Steve Rubell says, as one welcoming his Redeemer. 'Make room for Andy.'

By 3.30 a.m., the crowd outside has dwindled to barely 100.
Beyond the portico stands a group of black men. Not teenagers,
but middle-aged, sardonic black men, residents of East 14th
Street, watching the early homegoers, grinning sourly, hitching
up their trousers and – one might concede, with some point –
spitting on the ground.

London's Purgatory

The signs of plague are everywhere. Monster motor coaches stand nose to tail the length of Park Lane. Figures in fake Burberries cluster at corners, trying to hail taxis not for hire. Student crocodiles shuffle in pursuit of Sixties nostalgia from Covent Garden to the rubbish tip called Carnaby Street. The air scrapes with the noise of blue denim inside legs.

Surely no one can keep up the pretence that tourists bring anything to London but squalor and depression. It's purgatory for us – and not much better for them.

I live in Bayswater, a district catacombed with dingy, uninviting tourist hotels, often given impossibly grandiose names like The Royal Windsor International Hyde Park Towers. Each day I see visitors arriving from the airport to stare bleakly at the pups their travel agents have sold them.

As air travel has grown cheaper, dizzy spirals have continued in the inflation everyone says is only three per cent. I rate London now even over New York as the world's number one rip off capital. Most tourists are little more than camera-toting refugees, dismally wondering when they can afford the next £2 hot dog.

No one denies the benefits of tourism to countries like Spain, where tracts of empty coast lay waiting to be opened up and people were so poor they could not object to being turned into a race of waiters and bedmakers.

It is totally different for a metropolis already burdened with the huge problems and pestilences of London. This further year-round dump of displaced persons, their fingers haplessly stuck in Tube maps, is palpably helping speed us towards terminal collapse.

Other European capitals survive their inundation chiefly through the ubiquitous outdoor cafe, where tourists may linger indefinitely over modestly-priced drinks, and thus be kept from under the feet of people with work to do.

But London simply isn't an outdoor city. I don't know why. I know it more certainly each time I see some foolish cafe-owner trying to turn Marylebone into Montmartre.

Let us deal with the myth that tourism's economic benefits percolate through to everyone. They could do if a direct tourist tax were levied – say a museum tax to stop us having to pay to see treasures that already belong to us.

As things stand, tourism's chief beneficiaries are proprietors of businesses London needs like a hole in the head: rubbish gift shops, hamburger pits, the ever multiplying (and criminally mislabelled) 'bureaux de change'.

Nor does even that arch equivocator Lord Young try to pretend tourism has any noticeable effect on the unemployment figures. The British, for whatever psychological reasons, remain almost congenitally incapable of being waiters, washers-up and soda jerks. Hotel and catering staff have to be imported in quantities almost equal to the visitors.

And all the time, the burden on London and Londoners grows more intolerable. Already inadequate and overcrowded Tube trains are crammed to suffocation. Already fearsome traffic jams are reduced to arteriosclerosis by trans-European coaches. Already dirty, unkempt streets vanish under ankle-deep deposits of cans and Wimpy bags. All nationalities now drop garbage where they will and treat any green open space as a urinal.

As I write, I can hear the pro-tourist argument, so often expounded by PR men in pink ties. We should be glad to share our heritage with the peoples of the world. We should count it a blessing, in these uncertain times, to be able to sell our British-ness to such eager, admiring customers.

But what we are selling isn't Britishness. It is parody British-ness, as cheap and ludicrous as those little Grenadier Guardsmen dolls in plastic cylinders. Our real Britishness is the matchless city we happily lay waste to sell a bit more tat to a few more mugs (or vice-versa).

As for foreign visitors revering our heritage, I have some late news on that. Do you know what is now a popular open-air urinal for tourists? It is on Constitution Hill – the garden wall of Her Majesty the Queen.

Getting Quite Old For His Age

Three events I've attended this past summer suggest that, at the age of 42, I may finally be joining the grown-ups. I will pass over the Royal Wedding and the Private Eye lunch, and tell you how I presented the prizes at my old school's Speech Day. Pardon me while I pull up a stool for my gouty foot and stare reminiscently into my claret.

It was just after the Royal Wedding that my telephone rang and an unfamiliar voice with a familiar intonation asked if this was 'Phil Norman'.

'Could be,' I said.

'Jim Ball here – remember me? I was at Ryde School a couple of forms below you.'

'Jim Ball? Oh . . . *Jimmy* Ball!' I pictured him then, among the smaller boys on our 1958 school trip to Barcelona. I pictured his orange shirt, his box Brownie and look of wonder at his seniors' debauchery.

It appeared he was now a substantial Isle of Wight business-man and friend of our old school, empowered by the new head to sound me out. Would I come to Speech Day at the start of the autumn term, distribute the prizes and afterwards say a few words?

I looked down at myself, then around the room where I was working.

'Are you sure they mean *me*?' I said.

He seemed quite sure.

'Well . . . of course, I'd be delighted.'

'I remember you on the school trip to Spain,' were his parting words. 'When we got mixed up with that girls' school and their teacher, Miss Goss. I remember you saying you'd like to pull every hair out of Miss Goss's bum . . .'

Youth, ah youth!

The small private boys' school I left in 1961 has since become a sizeable public school, fully co-educational, with facilities we never dreamed. It has science labs, music rooms, a swimming pool, computers. But there is still the Victorian seaside mansion above the oval field, the same creosoted wooden assembly hall with the seat outside it where my friend Paul Carlton was caught . . . no, definitely *not* an anecdote for my Speech Day address.

The night before. I had dinner with the new head and his wife, in that iron verandahed white villa on the edge of the school grounds which used to brood like some mystic volcano over our collective consciousness. In my whole school career. I set foot in it only once, to collect my O-level results.

Also present were Jim Ball and his wife – who begged me earnestly not to call him 'Jimmy' – and a boy named Peck I last saw in an Italian box jacket, jiving at the Royal York Hotel. He has recently become a school governor.

'I remember you, too, on that trip to Spain,' I told him. 'We all bought 200-cartons of Senior Service. By the time we got off the boat at Calais, you could hardly croak.'

'Philip . . .' he said tolerantly. 'I've *never* smoked.'

'Quite so, quite so. Silly of me.'

The new head is a man about my own age, not remotely intimidating. His only advice concerning the morrow's speech was that it should be brief. 'The person we had last year was very interesting, but he went on for ages and then spoke individually to every boy and girl who came up on the platform. In the end, his wife passed him a note saying, "If you go on any longer, you'll miss your bloody ferry."'

For dessert there was a choice of cheesecake or pavlova with fresh strawberries. 'I was a bit short of time,' the head's wife, Alice, said, 'so I got the school kitchens to make these.'

'The school kitchens,' I gurgled.

'What's the matter?' Jim Ball's wife inquired.

'Nothing. I was just thinking.'

The platform party assembled in the formal parlour where, in my time, prospective pupils and their parents used to be interviewed. I remember an American boy named Leonard Martinet who thought the expanse of green brocade armchairs and sofas was the boarders' own common room. Not until he arrived for his first term did they show him the basement where we lived our troglodyte lives, huddled round the heating pipes or belabouring each other with wet games socks.

The ceremony was not in the Hall, as I remember it, but in a big marquee down on the school field. We entered amid an intense but genial hubbub, not like awesome dignitaries so much as panellists on 'Gardener's Question Time'. On my chair lay a programme marked 'Mr Norman' in a hand I had last seen tersely commenting on an English essay of mine circa 1959. It belonged to Mr Fenn, a recent Cambridge graduate then, now second master. 'I suppose I can call you Maurice officially now,' I whispered.

'Indeed you can,' he whispered back.

Save that the girls now wear it also, the uniform of dark blue, red and gold is unchanged. The girls are a natural element, long taken for granted by everyone. How infinitely healthier it must be than the fetid monasticism of 20 years ago – the endless, ignorant fantasizing, the misapplied amorousness, the mad annual rush to attend any local girls' school production of 'The Mikado'.

My immediate sightline was a row of very small boys who, during the Headmaster's Report, began to exhibit classic symptoms of Speech Day Syndrome. Watching their coat-collars ride up around their ears and their fingers probing every external orifice, I realized which element in the audience I might best try to win over.

The speaker before me was the Junior School head, a man himself looking scarcely out of kindergarten, so mild and kind and utterly delightful, one almost pined to be back with Old Lob, the tadpoles and tin paint-palettes. Nowadays, I am told, junior boarders cry when they have to go *home*. One recently remarked tearfully to the Junior head's wife how much he was going to miss the school lasagne.

After last year's lesson, prize-giving proceeded with dispatch. The winners lined up in pre-announced blocks to receive books they had chosen beforehand. Frank Herbert, Jeffrey Archer and J. R. R. Tolkien headed the popularity league. Blazers came and went in all sizes, topped by the requisite palsied smile. 'Do you like aeroplanes?' I asked, handing an aviation encyclopaedia to a chunky arrival uncannily like my old schoolfriend Miln. 'Yeh, brilliant,' he rumbled, Miln-like. The last recipients were so small, I had to hoist them into my august presence. The concluding Frank Herberts and Jeffrey Archers scuttled back down the grassy aisle. It had all been accomplished in little more than 15 minutes.

I had decided long before that my speech must be played strictly for laughs. I told them about Mr Savage, the aptly named PT master in my time who used to lift us up by our heads. I told them what Miss Turner, 'The Spitfire', said to N. O. Flux, and how Mr Monk, the octogenarian music teacher used to wear a sheepskin-lined flying jacket as he sat at the piano. I told them about Bungy Millard, a silly boy who, every morning on our way to prayers, used to poke his head out through an empty window-frame, and what happened on the day the glass had been unexpectedly replaced.

At the sherry party afterwards, several elderly and deeply respectable-looking local solicitors and accountants sidled up to me and made the same comment.

'You said we used to call Miss Turner "Spitfire". What we *really* used to call her was "Titsy".'

Another innovation was a black-tie ball in the marquee that night, with a jazz band, a disco and supper provided by school kitchens which have evidently changed beyond recognition. The head himself carved in his shirt-sleeves. 'I particularly remember the cottage pie,' I told him across platters of profuse salad. 'When Mrs Edie used to wheel that trolley into the dining-room at night, I *knew* I could have eaten all 44 boarders' portions on my own.'

The Sixth Form boys wore wing-poke collars, the girls Spanish shawls and mantillas. 'Look at that table,' the head's wife said, indicating a solemn conclave along one wall. 'They all look utterly miserable, but actually they're having the time of their lives.'

Returning from the dance-floor, I met a man called Keith Brading who could repeat every word of my late father's summer loudspeaker announcements to the daytrippers on Ryde Pier. 'We are still serving our special half-crown lunch, with reduced prices for children, Make certain of your meal in comfort before you leave the pier . . .' I thought no one but myself had that sad, unavailing boom graven on his soul.

Before midnight, a boy came with his mother to the head's table to say goodbye. The boy's head was bald in what seemed merely current teenage fashion. In fact, he has spent the past year fighting leukaemia. 'I'll tell you what kind of boy he is,' the head said. 'When he heard about his treatment and what the symptoms would be, he and his brother organized a Hair Fall-Out for charity.'

Towards the end, I took a stroll round the lit marquee pumping out sounds never heard before when I used to lie up there behind that big dormitory window. I looked out beyond the field to the sea and the dark pier where so many sorrowful ghosts of my family linger. I thanked my old school for reminding me that time really does move on; that things can get better than you ever dreamed.

The following week, I saw a woman speaker at the Labour Conference announce – with the vindictive gleam that nowadays seems inseparable from all social phrophecy – that under Labour's intended 1988 Education Act, schools like mine would be abolished as 'immoral'.

Try as I may, I just can't see it.

To Be Or Not To Be An Adman's Stooge

Did you see that sumptuous 'King Lear' on ITV a few weeks ago? After Olivier, the finest performance was John Hurt's as the Fool. But alack, Mr Hurt was not only to be found with Lear amid the storm: he also turned up in the commercial break. The voice that had just riven us apart with pity and pain was suddenly to be heard talking about Conqueror office paper 'with its beautifully-centred watermark'.

Thank heaven Michael Hordern wasn't playing Lear. One can too well imagine how 'Blow winds and crack your cheeks' might inadvertently have dissolved into the great man's current tremulous eulogy to 'lovely soft Kleenex toilet tissue'.

We should not be surprised that so many noble thespians nowadays appear as voice-overs in TV ads. Thespians, however noble, have always been well known to do anything for money. This is quite plainly, and literally, money for jam.

Nor can one begrudge John Hurt, a splendid actor overlooked for years but now bursting out in commercials everywhere. As well as Conqueror paper he is the voice of Spanish wines and Mattesson's cooked meats, and has virtually cornered the market in government health warnings. In voice-over terms, it must have been like a triple Oscar to get the job of warning Britain about Aids.

Yet a feeling of disillusion persists. How can a sensibility schooled in Shakespeare and Ibsen pass on, with no discernible crunch, to Conqueror paper's 'beautifully-centred watermark'? How can the passion of an Oedipus or Antony be poured impartially into lines of stupefying pretentiousness about some mass-produced motor car?

The late Orson Welles never resolved this difficulty. A famous bootleg tape exists of a voice-over session by Welles for someone or other's crispy cod balls. Every few seconds, the sonorous recitation breaks down in nauseated disbelief.

'We know a Scottish fisherman named Angus McTavish who each morn' . . . listen, do you actually expect me to *read* this?'

(Producerish murmurs of 'Orson . . . please. *Please*.')

'We know a Scottish fisherman named Angus McTavish who each morn', rows his coracle out into the North Sea . . . Jeezus this is *chickenshit*!'

No such inhibitions seem to trouble the various British theatrical eminences who have yielded to the lure of the voice-over booth. Jeremy Brett – that definitively cerebral Sherlock Holmes – is content to narrate a storyline for Phileas Fogg tortilla chips that one can practically hear destroying brain cells. Sir Michael Hordern's toilet tissue soliloquy, far from catching him just once with his pants down (so to speak) has developed almost as many weekly episodes as EastEnders.

More and still more heavyweights are selling, not just their voices but their whole selves for the riches and nationwide exposure of total 'brand-identity'. We have had Donald Pleasence for Pils lager, Leo McKern and Simon Callow for Lloyds' Bank, Timothy West for Pilkington glass. Major theatrical names have become an essential feature of what I call adsturbation – that is to say, hugely expensive and glossy corporate ads serving no purpose but to remind boards of directors how much money they've got. Until recently I thought the most boring ad in creation was Hanson Trust's interminable transatlantic cross-talk routine between Joe Don Baker and Denholm Elliott. It has not surpassed itself with an even more fatuous duologue between George Segal and – most disappointingly – Glenda Jackson.

The fact is that ad agencies seldom have any idea what to do with the acting talent they've bought. Plots and dialogue are invariably that substance referred to earlier by Orson Welles. Technique and timing, mastered over decades, are rendered down to a few gestures of pantomime pique or astonishment.

*

Something else about these ads makes them specially repellent, the selling-out of talent and reputation, of course. But also the myth they seek to perpetrate that all great actors and actresses are so very twinkly and smiley. Here is twinkly, smiley Michael Williams, conducting music on the radio with a breadknife. Here is his spouse Judi Dench, even twinklier and smilier as she comes along and snaffles his slice of bread and Clover.

Did anyone else happen to catch this same twinkly pair being interviewed recently by Brian Matthew on Radio 2? Matthew is a late-night disc jockey, chronically infatuated with stage people. But on this occasion with the Denches he somehow kept on hitting just the wrong note.

'Well . . . congratulations, both of you, on the Pooter play, which I loved, whatever the critics may say . . .'

Ms Dench (audibly smiling through gritted teeth): 'It has had *rave* reviews, Brian.'

'Oh . . . yeah. It's *marvellous*. What I meant was, the humour might not appeal to absolutely everyone . . .'

Mr Dench (snarling ditto): 'It has been playing to *full houses*, Brian.'

Now there's a power that could push a product. Feel like Brian Matthew did after tangling with us? Try Alka-Seltzer.

The World's Last Waisted Man

Ask most writers how it feels to finish a book and they'll reply it's like coming out of prison. Even after a modest two-year stretch, the world outside the cell you call your study will have changed in all kinds of ways. There is a feeling near panic as you venture forth again, clad in the tell-tale garments you wore on the day they took your wallet and pen-knife away, and the terrible gates clanged shut.

Clothes, above all, betray the literary recidivist. People who write books as a rule abandon all clothes but slippers, torn sweaters and jogging shoes. The squalor of an author's home life reaches its height in the author himself (this one, anyway) slumped over his desk, in beachcomber garb stained by everything imaginable, including bitter tears. An immemorial cliché comes true on the longed-for day you are free to go out into the sunshine again. 'My God! I've got nothing to wear!'

When I finished my first full-time book in 1981, the problem was minimal. Male fashion since 1979 had not changed that dramatically. Jackets still had the stiff uprightness they first acquired from 19th-century huntsmen. Trousers were still straight and cuffless, aiming – as Jeeves said – for 'that careless break over the instep'. A wider lapel here, a stopped vent there, a cheque for some hundreds made out to Jaeger Ltd, and I was more or less painlessly back in the mainstream.

Different indeed was the posish (Wodehouse is contagious) when I finished my second biography, two years ago. While I had been tapping and cursing, a revolution had occurred in the male silhouette. Trying on my 1982 suits in New York in 1984,

I was dismayed to see myself assume the flares and acute angles of a fatter, more baritone Lionel Blair. Had all my bookish pretensions brought me only to this? I was The World's Last Waisted Man.

It can well be argued, I know, that clothes do not really matter. But if they matter to you, there's no point in pretending they don't. I speak as one who, at school, never had the required number of games shirts and was once called out of the panoramic photograph group for being the only boy in 250 without a badge on his blazer.

Uptown New York is not a good place to begin the nervous, tentative process of changing one's whole shape. At the best man's shop, Paul Stewart on Madison, the assistants spring on you like ravening Dobermanns. 'Can I help you, Sir?' a dozen or more barked at once. 'Yes,' I replied. 'You can give me a chance to get inside the store.' 'The gennelman wants to be left alone,' I heard a floorwalker bellow with the contempt of a Goldwyn for a Garbo. The gennelman browsed indecisively, then departed with nothing but a suppressed longing for a ludicrously-priced English golf umbrella.

My first, deeply dubious experiment with the Eighties line was a suit from Agnès B's shop on Prince Street, way downtown. Agnès B is a wonderful Frenchwoman who makes shopping even in New York pleasant and civilized. At Agnès B, there are no security doorbells, disco soundtracks or suede coats in chains. Quiet lights shine on plain pine floors. Men's and women's clothes are displayed together, straightforwardly priced, on shelves apparently made from Meccano. You change more or less in the open, as if for a dance-class. The assistants are not yapping dogs but gentle, amused cockatoos.

The suit from Agnès B was brown herringbone tweed with a short jacket, long lapels and trousers front-pleated and willowy. I put it on at home and spent some time studying my new silhouette, restless in the unaccustomed spaciousness, wondering why, for all its dramatic difference, it seemed so oddly familiar.

Then I understood. The man looking back at me was almost exactly the shape of my late father. I remembered how long and fruitlessly, 20 years ago, he tried to get me to wear trousers that billowed exactly like these. I remembered the horror on his face when he saw my first-ever pair of khaki drill drainpipes, and the depth of damnation in his comment: 'You look just like a chorus-boy.'

The suits I currently own are less like the ones my father wore 20 years ago than those he got on Demob in 1945. It is hard now to recollect the era when 'wearing a suit' was a penance, grudgingly borne for others' sake. Now, it is more like slipping on a favourite dressing gown. My suits envelope me as totally and naturally as the one-piece garments worn by Lord Snooty's pals, Snitch and Snatch. I buy from stores no longer, but from designers – Agnès B, Jean-Paul Gaultier and, especially, Willi Smith, a black New Yorker who combines the crushed non-colours I like with the generosity of Omar the Tent-Maker. My only caveat with Willi Smith is his label. It is disconcerting to have to go round asking for 'Willi Wear'.

The fabulous comfort of 'unstructured' clothes brings some disadvantages. In Agnès B's summerweight suits, the shoulder-pads are peripatetic: after drycleaning, one must knead and pummel the jackets arduously back into shape again. And wearing zoot-style, ankle-hugging trousers – especially with the addictive, all-purpose French lace-up canvas boots – means relinquishing a male prerogative, taken for granted from childhood. One can no longer, in an emergency or moment of high passion, take one's trousers off over one's shoes.

There is also, from the unconverted, some ridicule to be endured. 'Are those for hiking?' people ask of the French canvas boots. Attending an old school friend's party in my Max Miller-style blue, orange and purple checked Willi Wear suit, I was aware of a definite hush when I came in. 'Did you knit it yourself?' my old school friend asked, with the endearing candour of old school friends.

Though I miss New York for very little, I do miss it for the clothes. London still has to catch on to the SoHo style of individual shops, reflecting individual tastes. The big stores in which I used to trust, like Austin Reed and Jaeger, all seem on the same downward path to cheap anonymity. What used to be called boutiques now cater mainly to the Third World. My best buys in London have been at Jones (it may be Zones, the carrier-bag is so unclear) where French clothes are sold in American surroundings by diamanté-wearing punks. It turns out that diamanté-wearing punks can also be salesmen as impeccable as even Wooster could wish.

I urge a similar change of shape on all my fellow Britons – especially those I see about me still with flapping double jacket vents or, worse, the ghastly little leather-patched tweed blousons sold by shops like Next. There are few things less attractive than the average British male bottom. I comfort myself mine, at least, can no longer offend, hidden as it is under yards of glorious Willi Wear.

Annoying The Chef

'You must go to Alastair Little's,' people kept saying. 'Alastair's this *marvellous* young chef who was at the Zanzibar and the Escargot and has now got his own place in Frith Street, which is wonderful. You must go.' So, a couple of months back, I and a publisher friend decided to lunch at Alastair Little's.

We found it a smallish place, rather Japanese in design, crowded with fashion and PR people, many of them holding lighted cigarettes aloft. A woman in a print dress greeted us pleasantly and showed us to the table beside the open kitchen door. From here we could see a fair-haired young man, evidently Alastair Little himself, going about the work that once shed lustre on the Escargot and the Zanzibar.

We ordered vegetable soup and, since neither of us was very hungry, asked if we could have the 'seasonal salad' hors d'œuvre as a main course. The woman in the print dress said this would be quite all right.

The vegetable soup was very pleasant. As we drank it, we could see Alastair Little throwing lettuce leaves on to two plates with what we took to be merely the born craftsman's energy and passion.

The woman in the print dress took our soup-bowls away. Simultaneously Alastair Little himself strode from the kitchen and crashed our salads down in front of us with a fury that made the cutlery rattle.

Our waitress was as taken aback as we were. '*Alastair!*' she protested, as he slammed back into his kitchen again.

The experience made me realize how sick I am of these

restaurant superstars and prima donnas. From now on, I patron-ize only establishments whose proprietors have taken an oath of invisibility.

There was, admittedly, a time when I held restaurateurs in awe and, indeed, could think of few compliments more desirable than to be greeted by them personally and be visited by them throughout the meal for assurances that everything was to my liking.

Now and again would occur what I considered the supreme compliment. The restaurateur would sit at my table, talk to me, perhaps even deign to partake of something like coffee or dessert.

My naive wonder disappeared the first time I visited Leith's, and Prue Leith had her dessert at my table. I remember the dessert clearly – a sort of patch-work tart. I also remember the price, since it was subsequently added to my bill.

Since then, too, I've got to know Peter Langan, and been joined by him many times, both head first and on all fours. Once after joining me, he did not sit but knelt on the ground, his chin wedged in an avocado shell like some ghastly Egyptian mummy as he offered his usual detailed speculations about my companion's anatomy.

I also spent two years in New York, where fashionable restaurateurs are not so much tyrants as terrorists. I've eaten at Elaine's and Elio's and Nishi's, the Upper West Side Japanese place where, if Nishi likes you, he sends you his special hot chocolate and pineapple dessert. Each night the place is crowded with yuppies of all sexes, rigid and sweating with desire for Nishi to like them.

I discover, though, that we are now even more ingenuous about food and restaurants than New Yorkers. If we were not there surely would have been an outcry against Nouvelle Cuisine, that totally shameless method of charging double price for half the portion, floating in useless coloured liquor and garnished with crystallized lemon. Yet still when these travesties arrive one hears the same cries of 'Ooh' and 'Aah' and 'Isn't that pretty'.

There is a wise old axiom 'Never eat at a place called Mom's or play cards with a man called Doc.' To that I would add 'Beware all restaurants that are eponymous.'

A Passage to Piss Poor

David Lean's film adaptation of A Passage to India is showing exclusively at one of New York's smarter cinemas, the Ziegfeld on West 54th Street. As we had decided to see it on only the second night of its run, and being somewhat hardened to Manhattan moviegoing, we arrived a full hour before the scheduled performance time. Already, two queues stretched almost the full block to Sixth Avenue. The first queue was for ticket buyers. The second consisted of those who had paid their $5 each and, with New York's characteristic regard for paying customers, had been herded to wait behind a blue police barrier.

It took 20 minutes in the first queue to reach the single ticket window, in a foyer easily able to accommodate all those outside, were it not 'policy' (a word never challenged here) that movie and theatre audiences may not await the performance on the premises. Some effort, however, had been made to fill the empty space with uniformed ushers bawling 'Have your money *out* when you reach the window!' and 'No standing inside. The ticketholders line is *outside*.'

The ticketholders line waited 50 minutes, as meek in that penitential darkness as it would have been in a rainstorm or snow shower. Around us, we noticed the faces of prominent journalists, publishers and members of other opinionated professions. All shuffled together obediently when a guard with a loudhailer passed by, barking, 'Close up that line, folks. Close it up.'

Eight minutes before performance-time, permission was given for the customers to come in. The ticketholders line surged forward like wagons in a 19th century land-rush. The over-corralled, over-policed queue, of course, was instantly beyond control. In front of us, a further guard reared up, shrieking 'Hold the line here!' We just got by. Our friend – visiting New York from Buckinghamshire – was left behind. 'Please,' we cried, 'he's with us.' Our friend somehow slipped through. 'I said "Hold that line!" the usher spat at the next person. 'Don' move till I tell ya to move! Got it?'

We arrived by packed escalator in an upper foyer whose pandemonium surpassed all Forster's descriptions of the Chandrapore bazaars. There were frantic queues for the popcorn stand, the ladies' room and – more inexplicably – the telephones. More ushers moved against the tide, helpfully saying, 'Showtime in less than one minute!'

In the auditorium, the lights were already dimming, even though hundreds of people still had not found themselves seats. We had been lucky to spot five together – two for late-arriving friends – in an area which British cinemagoers once used to call 'the ninepennies'. Thick plastic debris and old popcorn, left by the previous house, crunched under our feet. As the credits rolled, the frantic scurrying and pleas of 'Are all these taken?' grew more piteous. Our friend from Buckinghamshire was heard to remark, 'It's never like this at the Regal, Marlow.'

'A Passage To India' itself is a terrible disappointment. David Lean, above all directors, has proved it is possible to bring great literature to the screen intact. Here he was working with a book which, for all its subtle metaphors, is never less than utterly cinematic. Hollywood market forces, presumably, are responsible for the gratuitous shots of lancers and night mail trains, and the stubborn misrepresentation of Forster's characters and their motives. Thus, Adela Quested and Professor Godbole become major characters while the relationship between Aziz and Fielding shrinks to a mere vignette. Two or three of Forster's lines survive in a script whose lameness hardly matters since, to suit the American attention-span, most scenes cut as soon as they have begun. The ending has been moved from Mau to scenic Srinigar. Gone is the wonderful coda where Aziz and Fielding try to embrace but their horses swerve apart like their cultures. In David Lean's version, Aziz writes sentimentally to Miss Quested; so glad all that unpleasantness at the Marabar Caves is over.

Because we were an upmarket audience – and because this had been called 'a dark comedy of manners' by the *New York Times* – the auditorium was relatively free of talk. Most movies here play against an uproar recalling the Saturday morning matinees of my boyhood. There also was no detectable marijuana smoke. Upmarket New Yorkers, however, still drink noxious brown fizzy drinks and consume popcorn from outsize tubs, imparting to the most hushed onscreen moments a sound like armies advancing over gravel. Being an upmarket audience, there was also an intermittent 'beep' as someone's jogger's stopwatch alarm accidentally went off.

When I get back to England, I know the first thing I'm going to do. I'm going to book a season ticket in perpetuity at the Regal, Marlow.

Dakota Days

My first visit to Yoko Ono was in April 1981, four months after John Lennon's death. The circumstances were sadly ironic, given my previous unsuccessful attempts to interview Lennon for my Beatles biography. I was in New York publicizing the book and, on a morning TV show, happened to say that in my view Lennon's talent represented three quarters, not one quarter, of the Beatles. As I walked off the studio floor, I heard there was a phone call for me.

'Hi,' a voice said. 'This is Yoko. What you just said about John was very nice. Maybe you'd like to come over and see where we were living.'

Late last century, when an eccentric Gothic apartment house appeared on the then countrified western margin of Central Park, New Yorkers joked that it might as well have been built in far off North or South Dakota. Hence the Dakota Building – more correctly 'the Dakotas' – traditional Upper West Side eyrie of actors and bohemians, scene of the Polanski horror classic 'Rosemary's Baby', and John Lennon's last home.

One presumes he was attracted by its resemblance to sootily-grand old maritime insurance buildings in the Liverpool of his childhood. New York for Lennon was always a heftier surrogate Merseyside with its wharves and piers, its muddy sea and salty wit. Especially Downtown, where cobbled lanes stretch between iron fire escapes, he could almost have been finding his way back to teenage at the Cavern Club.

Everyone who enters the Dakota nowadays walks over the spot where Mark David Chapman waited with his John Lennon LP and his gun. Past the copper sentry box, under the Germanic arch, a notice on a stand still insists, with futile formality, that 'All visitors must be announced'.

You announce yourself at a desk where some old Scouse porter in brass buttons might preside but where, instead, a black guard watches a bank of electronic monitors. Identified, you pass through a buzzer door, down a hall that could belong to an ocean liner but for the trapped, malty smell of New York interiors. At length you reach the reception area for Studio One, where Yoko's two assistants sit talking on phones in low, obsessed voices like negotiators doing deals in high price real estate. Before proceeding further, you are asked to remove your shoes.

Yoko's inner office is an immense, eerie chamber, lit by Art Déco lamps and the soft diffusion of half a dozen white sculpted palm trees. At the end, crosswise, is a mahogany desk, inlaid with ivory symbols of ancient Egypt, and a chair said to be a replica of Tutankhamun's throne.

The 20 years since she took Lennon from the Beatles have changed Yoko almost beyond recognition. One remembers the shapeless little Japanese skittle who seemed to shadow him everywhere, doggedly yet passively. One remembers in particular a face pinched between curtains of hair that seemed incapable of smiling. Today she wears white shirts, black slacks and silver-laced vaquero waistcoats. Her hair is tied back. She smiles often, in a shy, even self-deprecating way.

That first two-hour talk for me ended the always questionable myth of Yoko Ono as The Woman Who Broke Up The Beatles; the remorseless self-promoter who dared muscle in on their sacred 'White Album' sessions, not letting John alone even when he went out to the Gents'.

'Do you know what the truth of that was? He *made* me go to the men's room with him. He was afraid that if I stayed out in the studio, one of the others would try to get off with me. Jealous! My God! He wrote a song, Jealous Guy, that said it all. He even forbade me to read books or newspapers in Japanese because that would be a part of me separate from him.

Her version of their life together at the end I found totally convincing. After all the madness, and one long, serious separation, they were together for good, looking forward to old age. The joy of their life was raising their son, Sean. They preferred New York to anywhere because it left them alone. Though John would never return to England, he could never get it off his mind. On Sunday nights they always watched Channel 13's *Masterpiece Theatre*, showing English classic serials like 'Rebecca'.

After our talk, Yoko suggested that I might like to see the seventh-floor apartment where Lennon and she spent their final years of 'role reversal'. By a further irony, my guide was the same male secretary from whom I'd received all those polite formula refusals to my requests to interview Lennon. His name was Fred Seaman, a soft-voiced, soft-footed young man, the perfect confidential clerk.

I saw the small side room where Lennon escaped from rock'n'roll lunacy to sit on his bed and look at the trees change colour in Central Park. I saw the long Victorian kitchen where, watched by baby Sean, he learned to bake bread, much surprised when his first successful loaf didn't receive a Gold Disc. I saw the triangular room, like some weird frozen boutique, where he stored every garment he ever owned in two decades at fashion's sharp end, with their attendant cloaks, scarves, floppy hats and Cuban- or wedge-heeled shoes. I saw his gold Egyptian mummy and, next to it, the English bentwood hatstand wearing his cap from Quarry Bank Grammar School.

My judgement of the secretary Fred Seaman as soft-footed was to prove all too accurate. It later transpired that within hours after Lennon's murder, Seaman had begun methodically stealing his diaries and drawings from the Dakota and feeding them to an accomplice stashed in an uptown apartment with a typewriter. The aim, already touted among New York publishers, was a book that would 'blow the lid off' John and Yoko's private life.

Though Seaman's literary plans were aborted by prosecution for theft, books on that theme have appeared regularly through the Eighties. There was 'Loving John' by May Pang, the Chinese girl with whom Lennon spent his 'lost weekend' in the mid-Seventies. There was 'The Love You Make' by Peter Brown, the

Beatles' former factotum, an odd mixture of uninformed venom and heavy dredging from my book, *Shout!* There was *Dakota Days*, a suitably fantastical account by the Lennons' former astrologer, John Green. Finally this summer there was Albert Goldman's ludicrous biography, portraying Lennon as a concatenation of sickness and madness almost exhausting the medical dictionary, Yoko as a black-hearted witch and their married life as a cynical PR charade.

When each grubby volume appeared, Yoko's only response was steadfast silence. As she told me at the time of the Goldman book: 'I'm in the position of someone who's been punched 500 times. There are so many allegations, I could never deal with them all in one interview. If I answer one, people might say, "Hey, what about the other 499? Maybe those are true."'

An answer does now exist, however, in a voice that could never help but be heard. Two years ago, Yoko authorized the TV producer David Wolper to compile a movie biography of Lennon from her vast film and video archive and an accompanying book from the many hitherto unpublished photographs in her possession.

Though film and book ostensibly trace Lennon's life from Liverpool suburbs through Beatlemania, their main focus is his time with Yoko, first as the Sixties' most unpopular lovers and notorious media-baiters, then as the Seventies' least likely Darby and Joan. The film starts and ends with video sequences Yoko directed for Lennon's definitive post-Beatle song, 'Imagine'. The book's chief interest are pictures she took of Lennon around their various Manhatten hidey-holes, and with his multitudinous in-laws in Japan.

The use of Lennon himself as sole narrator reminds us of something possibly obscured by Albert Goldman's ordurous prose. He was in many ways an impossible human being, with most of the rock superstar's worst traits. He also was a man of unique talent, charm, still resonant wit, but above all, scathing honesty. In John Lennon's lifetime, nothing could be said against him that he would not clamour to say against himself.

Last month – having never expected it – I found myself back

at the Dakota: passing the murder-spot under the arch, going through the high security door, along the marbled passage and, without shoes, once more into that long, eerie office with its illumined palm trees, its inlaid Egyptian desk and pharaoh's throne.

Yoko is slightly changed in that she now has a man friend, and chain smokes again. Her speech is still full of Lennonisms, like 'choked up' and 'cuppa tea'. With her sat her son Sean, now 13, a John lookalike but for his dark Asiatic eyes and the gold stripe through his hair.

The quality few suspected in Lennon was his kindliness. In the film, he discovers a bedraggled hippy sleeping rough in the grounds of his stately home, 'to get close to the songs'. 'The songs are just words,' Lennon explains patiently. 'They're just me saying "I had a good shit today, and I love Yoko . . ." Are you hungry?' The hippy nods miserably. 'Okay . . . let's give him something to eat.'

'When I first me John,' Yoko said, 'it seemed that the whole world didn't understand me, but he did. I was timid – not about my work but about my appearance. I had this strong jaw that I was hiding with my hair. And I had bony, tiny hands and legs that I thought were too short and knobby.

'John would say, "Look. You've got beautiful hands. And your legs are fine. Put your hair back and show your face.' He made me feel I needn't feel ashamed of how I looked. Just be myself and it'd be all right.'

Affirmation is there on the film soundtrack, in the sandpaper voice that couldn't lie: 'I don't believe in Beatles . . . I don't believe in Bobby Zimmerman . . . I just believe in me. Yoko and me.'

Mrs Gandhi's Great Escape

Shall I tell you the habit I'd most like to lose? It's pulling That Face when I look into a mirror. You know the face I mean – cheeks hollowed, mouth tautened, eyes half-closed to give a soft-focus effect. And, floating above, a thought-bubble of idiot self-deception. 'I'm really not so bad looking after all.'

I've been trying the same con-trick on myself in mirrors since the age of 10, when I would flatten my hair with water, arrange pens and a pen-torch in my blazer-pocket and walk down to Ryde beach, certain that today Jean Black, who helped at the donkey-stand, must finally fall for me. I can see That Face 30 years ago, peering back at me in just the same hopefully deluded way from shop window reflections, car wing-mirrors, the shiny chromium of automatic weighing machines.

Oddly enough, I always knew that I was kidding myself. I suppose that, in my entire life, I've never looked more totally repellent than the day I appeared on my father's Ryde Carnival float, dressed as a roller-skating Scotsman. I kept my eyes shut throughout the parade rather than even risk looking down and seeing my ghastly little rabbit-fur sporran. But once, as we passed a traffic mirror on a dangerous corner, I couldn't help glimpsing myself. There it still was, looking at me even from underneath an unspeakable tam o' shanter. Oh God . . . That Face!

It also got into photographs, creating anything but the desired effect. All pictures of me as a child have the same sidelong, wall-eyed look – the look that was what Jean Black, at the donkey-stand, actually beheld. So marked was it in one school photo-graph that my housemaster took me aside later and asked if I was worried about anything. I was but, alas, could not summon up any words to advantage. Thereafter he, and most of the house, took to calling me Parrot Face.

We none of us really grow up, however desperately we try. I know That Face will accompany me to the end of my life, along with every fear and superstition rooted back in the long days when reason had no power and thoughts couldn't be articulated.

A nonsense word that occured to me at the age of two still frequently rackets round my head. As long as I live I'll loathe the woman who held me up to ridicule when I was four, on the balcony at Ryde Rowing Club. I've never really stopped giggling at the wonderful new joke passed on by my fellow six-year-olds as we knelt on the summer grass behind Partlands School. Why did the lobster blush? Because it saw the Queen Mary's bottom.

I'll always be furtive about reading in the lavatory, even though the prohibition has not applied for 30 years – even though most of my friends have lavatories done out like small lending libraries. At home alone, I still find myself smuggling the book in. I still, in my innermost heart, believe that if I start the project in hand before I've found a semicolon, I'm going to be overtaken by a nameless catastrophe.

Jean Black's only public observation about me used to be 'He's mad'. Sitting there, holding my breath and racing to find a semicolon, is just one of the times in my adult life when I feel she may have had a point.

For instance, do you ever get, as I do, an overpowering urge to wreck your whole existence just at the moment when it's going most swimmingly? In Underground lifts, on my way to pleasant meetings or meals, I have to fight a perennial temptation to put my right hand between the steel gates as they crash shut. During interviews I've longed to do, at the point where I realize my interviewee is telling me all, I suddenly want to leap up, kick over the tea things and show my bare behind.

The worst of these urges to self-sabotage occurred when I was interviewing the late Indira Gandhi, and had special permission to be with her in her garden while she greeted political deputations from all over India. Standing just behind her, I saw with terrible clarity the way to ruin my life for ever would be to wait for the next time she bent forward in the sign of *namaste*, then give her the most terrific goosing. I could visualize every dreadful consequence – the rush of guards, the prison cell, my picture back-projected behind Sandy Gall on 'News At Ten' (probably pulling That Face). I could see my own footnote in history – not as author or journalist but simply The Man Who Goosed Gandhi.

Jean, you were right in 1954 when you would stare at me, then look at your friends round the donkey-stand and pityingly tap the side of your head. But I bet you never thought I could make a living out of it.

The Wild Witch of the Waldorf

My halcyon fiction-writing summer on Shelter Island – off the east coast of Long Island – was interrupted by only one formal social event. It came about through my friend Angela Miller, the New York publisher with whom I shared the big house on Menantic Avenue. One Friday afternoon, Angela appeared at the screen door of my garden study and said she was driving out to have dinner with a literary agent friend in Bridgehampton. The literary agent friend had kindly extended the invitation to me.

'She's called Ros Cole,' Angela said. 'She's quite a famous agent; she owns racehorses and an apple farm upstate. When she's in New York, she lives in the Waldorf Tower. She's so *awful* on the phone, the Waldorf keeps a special operator just to deal with her calls. In the book trade they call her The Wild Witch of the Waldorf.'

I heard more about our hostess as the little car ferry bore us across to Sag Harbor, that once great whaling town, now a summer ghetto of authors and *New York Times* executives.

'. . . She has some interesting clients. She represents Andy Warhol, Sheilah Graham and the estate of Brendan Behan. She has a Stanford White house, right on the beach, that used to belong to Harry Truman . . .'

'And she doesn't mind you bringing me along?'

'No, she's delighted. She just said she hoped you weren't fancy.'

Skirting Bridgehampton, we drove out among the twilit dunes and scattered lights of multi-millionaires' ocean-front bungalows. We stopped at the end of a dirt road, behind a haphazardly-parked orange Cadillac. The house beyond was obscured by brambles and low-hanging foliage. 'Can you make it?' a voice called to us through the undergrowth in the accents of Ethel Merman. 'I had Gene out there this afternoon, cutting you a path.'

Waiting for us on the sundeck was a raven-haired woman in her sixties, bound into a bright yellow batik version of the sarong worn by Dorothy Lamour in almost every 'Road' picture. Behind her loomed an immensely tall man, probably in his late seventies, wearing a blonde Beatle wig and a psychedelic shirt, high-collared and puff-sleeved, whose gruesome striations of pink, silver, mauve and lime imprinted themselves on the retina for ever. This gentleman was introduced by Ros Cole as her friend, Colonel Gene Ryan, ex-United States Air Force.

They led us round the sundeck to the ocean front. Overhead shone the eerie blue light of an insect death-ray. When an insect crosses the ray, it is zapped to death with a noise like an elephant crashing through dry brush.

I studied The Wild Witch of the Waldorf covertly while Colonel Ryan was fetching our drinks. She was indeed, ferocious-looking, with her tousled black wig and Cleopatra black eyes. But the sarong disclosed a girlish waist and glimpses of long, slender legs. On her feet she wore plastic mules, the type you can buy for $5 at any Lamston's drug store.

I had been looking forward to some literary discussion with the agent of Sheilah Graham *and* Brendan Behan. Eventually, she turned to me and asked what I was doing out on Shelter Island.

'Writing a novella.'

'Oh, well,' she said. 'I guess you have to get it out of your system.'

She disappeared into the house, followed by Angela, to see how dinner was progressing. I found myself alone with Colonel Gene Ryan and his retina-ravishing shirt.

'You've got a beautiful place here,' I said, fixing my attention wholly on the Colonel's face. Under its Beatle fringe, it looked as remote and impassive as a presidential profile on Mount Rush-more.

'Yes,' I heard him say – the first of his only two intelligible utterances that night. 'It's pleasurable.'

The house where Harry Truman had spent his leisure hours consisted of one large ground-floor room stuffed with objects that did not exclusively evoke ocean-front life. Among the inflatable mattresses, sunshades and deep-sea fishing rods, I noticed a scallop-shaped music stand and a white grand piano wrapped in thick transparent plastic. Many of the ornaments, ashtrays – even cushions – were shaped like whales. 'I never could resist a garage sale,' our hostess said as she led us through to dinner.

Dinner was jambalaya, and the best pecan pie I had ever tasted. I sat next to Colonel Ryan. The flaxen-fringed Mount Rushmore being inclined in my direction, I made a further attempt to induce small talk.

'When you were in the Air Force, did you fly jets?'

A watery look, like a far-off subway train, came into his eyes.

'Four hundred miles an hour,' he said. 'You know – I always hoped I might find the end of the rainbow. I tried it once, in my plane. But even at 400 miles an hour, I couldn't catch it.'

We returned to the main room for coffee. I sat on a blue chaise-longue, toying with a tartan whale-shaped scatter cushion. The noises of surf and the insect-zapper mingled with vintage big band music from the radio. It emerged that, before becoming a literary agent, our hostess had sung with a big band in New York.

'I was never as big as your Staffords or your Whitings,' she admitted. 'But I did okay. Everyone knew me as a chantootsie.'

'You could be discovered all over again,' I said. 'Look at Margaret Whiting.'

'What I need is a Walter Winchell,' she said. 'You know who Walter Winchell was? As well as his newspaper column he had this radio show which he always introduced with the words, "Good evening Mr and Mrs America and all the ships at sea . . ." Now if Winchell said you were it, you were *it*.'

She jumped up and climbed the first few steps of the exposed spiral staircase.

'I used to do a great entrance.' She began to come down sinuously, one slim leg peeping from her sarong. 'Then the band would start my number . . .' She flung out both arms and filled her lungs. For a moment, she seemed about to give out with something on the scale of 'There's No Business Like Show Business'. Then she thought better of it, dropped her arms, came down, resumed her seat and frowned at Colonel Ryan, who was worrying the remains of the pecan pie.

'Gene!' she said, in a tone not at all like a torch singer's. 'Leave the pie *alone*!'

Slumped against the tartan whale cushion, I began to be overcome by the early fatigue of beachcomber life. Our hostess was recollecting Brendan Behan and the alcoholic binges from which she sometimes had to retrieve him.

'. . . Once, his wife had no milk for his tea, and that started him off on an *enormous* bender. Ah, but he liked me,' she added nostalgically. 'He used to call me Rosheen.'

At midnight, to my intense relief, Angela put down her coffee cup.

'Well, it really *has* been fun . . .'

Colonel Ryan barred our way in a fresh tumescence of ghastly stripes and indistinct speech. 'Before you leave . . .' he protested. 'You *must* . . .' He lunged through the chairs and canoe-paddles to the plastic-wrapped white piano and began tearing opaque layers from it with the frenzy of Christmas morning.

'Gene – now stop!' commanded The Wild Witch of the Waldorf.

'*Can't* I?' he entreated. '*Won't* you?'

'No, Gene. *Stop*!'

He sighed deeply and wrapped the piano up again.

When I pass the Waldorf now, I often look up and picture its Wild Witch in her strawberry boudoir, waiting for the word from Winchell to become a chantootsie again. And to this day, if I shut my eyes, Technicolor liver lines remind me of Colonel Ryan's shirt. I suspect he *had* found the end of the rainbow after all.

His Way

Its most famous concert hall bears out the truth that New York is a city without style. Do not expect an evening of Drury Lane, or even Bolshoi elegance at Carnegie Hall. The building on West 57th Street has the quasi-Gothic glumness of a Victorian furniture depository. European concert-goers, accustomed to pleasant preludes in gracious foyers or cosy crush bars, can forget all that at Carnegie Hall. The front steps lead straight into the harsh white, cheaply-lit, smallish auditorium.

We are here for a performance by, unarguably, the century's greatest popular singer. Carnegie Hall labours to make every preliminary joyless. The usherettes have thrown the programmes under the seats rather than have the bother of distributing them. On the stage – beneath the name *Sinatra*, back-projected in cheapo italic script – perhaps two-thirds of the orchestra are desultorily tuning up. At five minutes to showtime, the audience is still arriving. Carnegie Hall greets them without enthusiasm. This nine-concert season has attracted mainly what Manhattan-ites call 'The Bridge and Tunnel Crowd' – from Brooklyn, Queens and, of course, New Jersey. They have not dined at Lutèce, but shared pastrami sandwiches at Wolf's deli. There are many teased-tight coiffures and shirt collars thrown recklessly open on gold-charm-tangled chests. There are those familiar New York faces, artificially tanned, agonizingly vigilant lest one more particle of youth should slip away. Anxiety fills the air, strong as the aftershave and too-musky scent. Will he still be able to make their age seem as irrelevant as his? Will he still recognize them, one and all, as 'swingers'?

New York's stylelessness comes, above all, from an ability always to strike precisely the wrong note. The opening act for Frank Sinatra at Carnegie Hall is a stand-up comic named Pete Barbutti whose speciality, the programme tells us, is 'turning unusual objects into musical instruments'. The singer of the century is thus heralded by a desperate clown, thumping a kitchen broom on the stage in time to the theme from 'Love Story'.

There is an uncomfortable hiatus. Then, without any announcement, an elderly man in a grey flat-top toupee walks onstage carrying music, like a schoolteacher, under his arm. He acknowledges the standing ovation with an ironic bow, sets down his music, puts a hand-microphone to his face and begins: the song they so much want. The applause momentarily becomes something more like a collective fit. *'It seems we danced . . . like this . . . before . . . We looked at each other in the same way then . . .'*

Age has blunted the famous cheekbones, melting them down to an extra fold between his chin and butterfly bow. But the shoulders are still lean and fidgety, reminding us of the bobbysox idol who so hated to be touched. From the grandfatherly face, the same lop-sided grin can flash that made girls in ankle socks scream at the New York Paramount, and girls in English wartime boarding schools sit in bed, hugging their knees, while the wind-up gramophone played.

'. . . that smile you are smiling, you were smilin' then . . . But I can't remember where . . . .'

The slightest of his gestures have defined performance the world over. In the million nightclubs from Macón to Middlesbrough, you will see singers use a hand-mike exactly like that, nursing it against their shirt-fronts, flicking the loose flex away. What balladeer in any language has not drawn that same horizon with the flat of his hand, then closed his eyes as Sinatra does, and pulled thin shoulders up to signify love lasting for ever? Any man who would seduce by music has at some time slipped into the Sinatra stance: the hard-bitten romantic, the knowing fall-guy, mocking his own susceptibility through a whisky quizzing-glass.

And what of the voice and its supposed embarrassing decline? In its essentials it remains. There is still the rise, in a single phrase, from curt growl to feathery tenderness. There are still the schizophrenic Sinatra vowels: the punctiliously-formed 'you-oo' and 'beau-oo-tiful', the Hoboken upstart's 'toon' and 'stoo-pid'. There are still the extra syllables, pushed in everywhere to make each song peculiarly his, and no one else's, ever afterwards. At full strength, surfing on crests of trumpet and trombone, he seems not to have aged a day since the mid-Fifties Pan Am chic of Come Fly With Me. Only on some last notes do you realize anything could be wrong, when the voice cracks dry and the spotlight goes off, hurriedly.

As sole concession to the years, he makes his performance part-seminar in the works of America's lesser-known major poets. His speaking voice is pleasantly businesslike. '. . . Here's a great song by Harold Arlen and Johnny Mercer . . . A terrific song by the master of them all, Irving Berlin . . . fabulous arrangement by Don Costa . . .' An unheeded shout of 'My Way' comes from the balcony. As the next song begins, there is a clatter of applause, followed by a widespread, urgent 'Ssh!'

'It's the wrong game, with the wrong chips . . . Though your lips are tempting, they're the wrong lips . . . They're not her lips, but they're such . . . good lookin' chops . . .'

The style that was absent from this New York night now fills it as a tangible presence, seizing the brass, concentrating the spotlight-beam, pulling the darkness taut. Everything that was so wrong has come right. No note is struck except with utter appropriateness. For an hour and 15 minutes, everyone here knows who they are.

At the age of 70, Frank Sinatra would seem to have every cause to be at peace with the world. His supremacy as a performer is undisputed. As well as a singer of genius, he has proved himself a screen actor of distinction. He is a spectacularly successful impresario and businessman with an estimated annual income of $3.5 million. He has been honoured as a notable philanthropist, raising millions of dollars through benefit concerts for such charities as the American Cancer Society. His health is excellent, his many appetites all remain undiminished. He lives on a boulevard named after himself, in a mansion whose guest quarters display a plaque inscribed 'John F. Kennedy slept Here.' From his four wives to his 60 toupees, America can show no other son whose every high, apple-pie-in-the-sky hope has been so bountifully gratified.

For all that, Frank Sinatra seems only marginally more at peace with the world than he was 25 years ago, when *Mad* magazine published its famous spread of the supposed contents of his wallet. The principal item was a California court summons. 'Type of violation,' the joke summons said – 'Parking in illegal place. Illegal place parked – On top of newspaper reporter.'

Sinatra's hatred of the American Press continues, unabated. True, he no longer stuffs small bills into the handbags of female journalists he regards as 'two dollar hookers'. It remains, however, war to the knife, waged on Sinatra's part with a ferocity often far exceeding the provocation and heedless of the blots it may drop on his ascent through the social register.

The November before last, for instance, Sinatra received the greatest public accolade of his career. He was invited to organize the gala concert that followed the Inauguration of his old friend – and maturing asset – Ronald Reagan. The two-hour spectacular, beamed from the White House, featured Sinatra as compère, conjuring forth a phalanx of Hollywood buddies, among them Dean Martin, Bob Hope, Joey Bishop and Don Rickles. The Press previews, predictably, were not all starstruck, the *Washington Post* in particular casting readers' minds back to an earlier epoch when Sinatra's good buddies got involved in presidential affairs. The story was caustic, its headline still more so: 'The Ratpack is Back.'

Just before the gala, Sinatra was approached by a female TV reporter and asked to say something to the camera. He made as if to turn away, then rounded furiously on her. 'Listen, I wanna tell you something,' he shouted. 'Did you see the *Post* story today? You're dead. Every one of you! You're all dead!'

Two sharply different images remain of the White House

night of the stars. The first is of President Reagan, those ever-ready tears in his eyes, paying tribute to Sinatra as a great artist and American. The second is of the great artist and American seemingly threatening his nation's media with mass assassination.

His 70th year has been punctuated with such instances of Sinatra on the one hand gaining great respectability and on the other, just as determinedly, throwing it away. There he was at one moment receiving a Presidential Medal of Freedom in company with Mother Teresa. There he was again, branded an 'obnoxious bully' by a New Jersey gaming board official after video cameras had caught him swearing at a blackjack dealer in an Atlantic City casino. The paradox was perfected last spring, when Sinatra received an honorary doctorate at a college in his native Hoboken, emerging in gown and mortar-board, surrounded by ugly bodyguards. 'This isn't Nazi Germany, Mr Sinatra,' one photographer remarked as he was elbowed aside.

What enrages Sinatra about photographers, reporters, TV interviewers and, especially, would-be biographers, is their incorrigible interest in an aspect of his life at the furthest possible extreme from Medals of Freedom and Mother Teresa. It is an allegation never proved and latterly further rebutted by the tacit assurances of his President. The allegation is that, throughout his 50 years as a nonpareil, Frank Sinatra has mixed on friendly terms with America's most notorious mafiosi.

It must be said at the outset there is no evidence that Sinatra has ever had any but the most perfunctory, accidental links with America's underworld. The evidence is that he is of Sicilian origin, has led an exotic and often intemperate life, has made many enemies in the Press and has, in his years as a nightclub singer, met very many shady types. We are dealing with the stuff of legend, gathered in impenetrable clouds around a man who, long ago, decided to let people believe what they want. The legend has relevance, though, both to Sinatra's own personality and to the teetering line, in America's most cherished folklore, between the famous and infamous.

The Sinatra/Mafia legend has, over the years, competed in

fictional luridness with the best of Damon Runyon and Dashiel
Hammett. It goes back to his beginning as a teenage vocalist in
the early Thirties, singing with a ukulele at cheap New Jersey
roadhouses and on radio amateur hours. A Sicilian boilermaker's
son, derided in adolescence as 'a skinny kid', he is said to have
hero-worshipped local mobsters like the avuncular 'don', Willie
Moretti. America's best writer on such subjects, Gay Talese,
believes Sinatra's whole character can be explained by a lifelong
wish to be regarded as a Sicilian *padrone*, or village chieftain. His
generosity, no less reckless than his temper, his need to be
surrounded by bodyguards and sycophants, even his lavish
charitable gestures, all, in Talese's view, recall traditional attributes of the 'man of respect'.

Pure as his talent was, it allegedly received a leg-up from
gangland in 1942, when Sinatra quit Tommy Dorsey's band to
begin his tumultuous eight-week solo season at the New York
Paramount theatre. Dorsey still had him under contract, and
continued to take a lion's share of his earnings. The legend has
it that Willie Moretti visited Tommy Dorsey and asked him
nicely to relinquish Sinatra's contract. When Dorsey refused, a
Moretti bodyguard pushed a pistol into his mouth.

Four years later came Sinatra's famous trip to Havana – then,
in pre-Castro days, a boom town for the American mobs.
Sinatra travelled with Al Capone's two cousins, Rocco and
Joseph Fischetti, and, later, appeared to be part of a gangland
summit conference organised by the exiled Mafia monarch
'Lucky' Luciano. It was even claimed by Narcotics Bureau
agents that Sinatra had acted as 'bagman' for the Fischettis,
carrying $2 million in a suitcase to add to Luciano's exchequer –
a claim which Sinatra has successfully rebutted.

The legend shadowed Sinatra, not always unbecomingly,
through the Fifties, from his slump in fame as a crooner and
anguished break-up with Ava Gardner, to his Oscar-winning
performance in 'From Here To Eternity' and the airy, sharkskin
panache of 'Songs For Swinging Lovers'. Especially after he moved
his court to Nevada, and sang, lived and had his being in the all-
day dark of Las Vegas, rumours grew and multiplied around his

supposed links with 'Joe Fish', with New York 'Family' heads Louis Pacelli, Carlo Gambino and, most notoriously, and disastrously, for him, with the Chicago syndicate's boss of bosses, Sam 'Momo' Giancana.

Giancana was the undoing of a heady moment in Sinatra's career when he might have been appointed to a high diplomatic, even governmental position. In 1961, American's swinging balladeer was on intimate terms with America's swinging young President, John F. Kennedy. Sinatra had raised $1.5 million for Kennedy's election campaign. He had escorted Jackie Kennedy to the Inaugural Gala. His 'Ratpack' clique of Hollywood playboys were practically related to the Kennedys, via Peter Lawford's wife, Pat Kennedy. Duetting with Sammy Davis Jr on Me and My Shadow, he sang, 'We're closer than smog when it clings to LA . . . We're closer than Bobby is to JFK . . .' At Kennedy's Camelot, Sinatra was troubadour-in-chief.

The Ratpack earned Kennedy's friendship, it later transpired, chiefly by ministering to the young President's well-camouflaged randiness. At a Ratpack party, just before he took office, Kennedy was introduced – supposedly by Sinatra himself – to a 26-year-old good-time girl named Judith Campbell. Shortly after Campbell became Kennedy's mistress, she began a simultaneous affair with Sam Giancana. The dual affair continued after Kennedy entered the White House – until, indeed, an FBI wiretap revealed America's President to be rogering (sometimes in his official aircraft) the moll of America's bloodiest racketeer. At Robert Kennedy's insistence, JFK abruptly severed all connections with the Ratpack, cancelling a weekend visit to Sinatra's California home, where a new wing had been built especially to accommodate him.

Sinatra paid a further heavy price for his alleged association with Sam Giancana. In 1963, he fell foul of Nevada's State Gaming Commission after Giancana was spotted at his Lake Tahoe casino, The Cal-Neva Lodge. The Commission accused Sinatra of playing host to Giancana, who was at the time prohibited from even entering Nevada. Sinatra afterwards sold his part-share of the lucrative Sands Hotel in Las Vegas and, for

18 years, held no gambling interests in the glitzy desert kingdom he had largely helped to create.

These past three decades, his answer to the Mafia charges has remained the same. If he does know any gangsters, it is by the purest accident. How can he be expected to tell them apart from thousands of people who have come backstage, wanting to shake his hand? Especially in the world of casino showbiz, who can be sure where entrepreneurship ends and extortion begins? Some of the legends are clearly laughable, and Sinatra, in public, has resolutely laughed them off. He was said to have flown to Cuba in 1947, carrying Lucky Luciano's $2 million 'in small bills'. Has anyone, he once asked, ever tried to fit $2 million in small bills into a suitcase? When he met Luciano in Havana, he insisted, it was at dinner 'with some other people'. He did not think it polite to get up and leave.

Privately, there is less amusement on the subject. There was evidently none whatever when Mario Puzo's Mafia novel 'The Godfather' portrayed an Italian crooner named Johnny Fontane, down on his luck and whimpering to his Mafia don for help in getting a plum Hollywood film role. The parallel was obvious with Sinatra and his surprise casting as Maggio in *From Here To Eternity*. The difference was that, whereas Johnny Fontane gets the part by Mafia terror – a horse's head dumped in the studio boss's bed – Sinatra convinced producer Roy Cohn to let him play Maggio by his acting ability and by offering to take only modest wages.

Some years later Mario Puzo found himself placed next to Sinatra at a Hollywood dinner. The usual gratification of people fictionalized by 'The Godfather' did not apply on this occasion. Sinatra broke into a flood of abuse at Puzo, and refused to sit at the same table with him.

In 1981 Sinatra was declared *persona grata* again in Las Vegas gambling circles. The Nevada Gaming Board granted him a 'key employee's license' to act as consultant for Caesar's Palace after receiving a written deposition from President Reagan that Sinatra was 'an honourable person, completely honest and loyal'.

The hearing provided a rare opportunity to cross-question

him about Mafia stories right back to Willie Moretti and the pistol allegedly pushed into Tommy Dorsey's mouth. Sinatra cut a dignified figure, in pinstripe suit and professorial glasses, testifying that his Mafia acquaintanceships, if they ever existed, were all the purest accidents. Did he ever know Willie Moretti? Only slightly. Why did this backstage photograph show him in a pose of apparent amity with New York godfather Carlo Gambino? He was posing with a little girl when, suddenly, three strange men muscled into the picture. Most vehemently did he deny any business association with Sam Giancana, and an earlier alleged financial interest in a Mafia-owned New Jersey racetrack. 'I haven't in my life, Sir, received any illegal money,' he told the hearing's chairman. 'I have had to work very, very hard for my money, thank you . . .' The commission ruled there was no evidence to connect either his career or his business with the Mafia.

Sinatra's mistrust of journalists extends even to those who suspect he may have been persecuted by the Press barons, hounded beyond endurance by paparazzi and slurred largely on the hearsay evidence of convicted criminals. Journalists who approach his Hollywood friends for background find them to be bound almost by the Sicilian law of omertá.

The Sinatra legend is in danger of becoming less interesting than the measures he adopts to prevent anyone from penetrating it. In 1983, his latest unauthorized biographer, the gossip writer Kitty Kelley, found herself hit by a $2 million lawsuit before she had written a word. The suit was not for defamation but for 'misappropriation' of Sinatra's name and likeness for commercial purposes. The lawsuit was later withdrawn, having given massive publicity for Kitty Kelley and her project. It is sad that such a towering 20th-century figure will probably never get the biography he deserves. He clearly cannot comprehend that coming clean about his life might actually make people like him.

His existence at 70 seems little different from that suggested by his mid-fifties album sleeves. There are still the sharky suits, the too-loud ties and rakish little hats. There are still the parties, private jets and bodyguards. There are still the sleepless nights, spent prowling through casino darkness with his old Ratpack crony, Dean Martin. There is still the private language, distilled from old jazzmen, with a twist of Runyon. Women are 'broads'. Good things are 'a gas'. Drinking is 'soppin' up the sauce'. He does as much of that as ever, though not as much as he would like people to believe.

He has admitted many times that he finds it difficult to talk to women. The enduring love of his life is said to be Ava Gardner, who long ago abandoned Hollywood for the quiet purlieus of South Kensington. Someone else who came close was Marilyn Monroe – another player in that bizarre 1961 drama of swinger, gangster, boy Attorney General and oversexed President.

His brief marriage to Mia Farrow in the Sixties seems to have been Sinatra's last desperate attempt to swing before succumbing to the elder-statesmanly aura of Ol' Blue Eyes, and turning Republican. In 1976, after a long affair, he married Barbara Marx, ex-wife of Zeppo, the Marx Brother.

He has three children by his first marriage, to his childhood sweetheart, Nancy Barbato. Relations between them have been uneasy since 1979, when Sinatra persuaded the Vatican to annul the marriage. His elder daughter, Nancy, once said of him: 'He has everything, he cannot sleep, he gives nice gifts, he is not happy, but he would not trade – even for happiness – what he is.' There seems, even now, to be only one place on earth where he feels at ease.

'I don't know if I made any mark,' he muses in the spotlight at Carnegie Hall, and the lop-sided grin briefly flashes. 'I know I made a mark on some *people*. You don't get hands like this for nothin' . . .' To an audience he can even joke about his premature exit from Australia in 1974 after a famous temper tantrum. '. . . There's so many places we can't go. Australia, we can't go . . . France. It's easier to keep a list of places we *can* go.'

He confides in them for almost half an hour, about growing up in Hoboken; about days with 'The Clan' in Vegas, and the jokes they used to play on Sammy in the steamroom. His reminiscences are directed partly through a tall glass of amber and ice.

'. . . Some people ask me if I got ginger ale in here. Ginger ale!' he echoes, amid a ripple of laughter from all those sympathetic swingers. 'There's a $7,000 reward for anyone who ever catches me drinking ginger ale. Jack Daniel's and water – *that's* what I got in here.'

He raises his glass at the tautened darkness, left and right. 'A toast to you all. Happy, good thoughts . . . warm feelings. Everything you wish for yourselves and people you love.'

Tonight, only one thread in his life story matters. '. . . Another great song, lyrics by Sammy Cahn . . . Lyrics by Ira Gershwin, a wonderful arrangement by Nelson Riddle. This next song, a tribute to a great artist, Judy Garland. A friend and a fabulous, funny person I still miss . . .' He loops the hand-mike flex away, as they are doing in that million other spotlights. 'This song always has very special meaning for me . . .'

He passes over 'My Way', choosing for his farewell what he calls, simply, a 'saloon song'. It is the number with which he closed the Presidential Gala last November – in five minutes redeeming the whole two-hour orgy of wrong notes and stylelessness. It is not so much song as short story: an American classic identified for all time with Sinatra's voice, portraying him in his art so completely, one can cease to care what murky, neurotic reality he may or may not have lived.

The scene is a bar room in the early hours. A bony young man, the synthesis of Maggio, Pal Joey and Tony Rome, sits with collar loosened and hat aslant at the end of the counter, nursing his Jack Daniel's and his shattered heart. A tinkling piano, somewhere, plays the blues. A sleepy barman dries glasses and receives the soliloquy with a long-suffering, all-knowing eye:

'*It's quarter to three. There's no one in the place . . . 'Cept you and me. So set 'em up, Joe, I got a little story, I'd like you to know . . .*'

The piano tinkles to a stop. The bony young man slides down from the bar-stool, shrugs and hooks his raincoat over his shoulder.

The septuagenarian, his music under his arm, walks away, until the next time.

Wizards of the Cliché

I've just been trying to watch a 'Newsnight' report on the decline of trade union influence in Thatcher's Britain. It was a worthwhile subject, explored with 'Newsnight's' customary fair-minded diligence. So why, after a couple of minutes, did I leap to switch off my television with something approaching a scream?

It was the usual reason. The clichés used by the reporter – in this case one Gavin Esler – were the kind that cause actual physical pain: 'The wheel of industrial relations has turned full circle . . .', 'The strait-jacket of declining membership . . .', 'The boiler-makers are boldly going where no union has gone before . . .', 'They are hoping to reach the parts other unions cannot reach . . .'

Why *is* English on television so abysmally bad? And why is everyone so resigned to it? On the slackest newspaper, such a parade of ninth-hand, clapped-out usages would be cut to extinction. Television, for some reason, allows them to be uttered, not merely without shame, but with the triumphal smugness of fresh-minded, Swiftian aphorisms.

It isn't merely that television constantly pumps out diseased English in the form of cliché-leaden banality and near-cretinous mixed metaphor. It is also achingly devoid of good English. In all four channels' news and documentary output, is there a single presenter or reporter whose words leave behind the faintest resonance of originality, stylishness or wit?

Television people will no doubt reply that language is the inevitable casualty of a medium growing daily more breathtakingly instantaneous. When pictures of war, riot and pestilence can be flashed across the world into our homes virtually as they happen, who can be bothered with nuances of thought or expression?

The answer is one accepted by all television's inspirational talents, from Grierson and Jennings to Weldon and Isaacs. There never was an onscreen image that did not become a hundred times more powerful with the right words to complement or challenge it.

Indeed, as pictures bombard us from every side, subject to every kind of manipulation and distortion, sensible and sensitive words are more important than they've ever been. Who by now has any idea what is happening in Ulster, the Lebanon or our own blighted North? They are the horror stories of the century. Yet they wash out of our screens over our heads in the same featureless, colourless verbal tide: not news any longer, but Newsak.

Twenty years ago, television journalists were iconoclastic figures, expected to flavour their dispatches with their own highly personal, even eccentric humour, passion and morality. One need not mention only the dapper jewels like James Cameron and James Mossman. A whole range of unique voices powered by unique sensibilities, from Richard Dimbleby to Fyfe Robertson, made the news more compulsively watchable than all today's powdered and bouffanted, deskbound glamour boys.

The last of that great line, I suppose, was René Cutforth, before he sold out to Krona margarine. I remember a wonderful commentary by him over a film about the 1914–18 war. When top-hatted statesmen were shown, Cutforth merely quoted the T.S. Eliot poem, *'We are the straw men, the stuffed men.'*

Today's television reporters, by and large, are a dismal breed, chosen for insipid good looks and conventional dress sense rather than any palpable journalistic talent. Television reporting consists merely of recycling Newspeak metaphors, often in addle-brained unawareness of their cumulative effect: 'This package paves the way for a long-running government cliff-hanger . . .' 'There's a groundswell of opinion that the SDP is running into troubled waters . . .', 'After the bubble burst, a lifeboat operation was launched to shore up the system . . .'

The habit has grown of speaking with condescending slowness, like nanny reading stories to recalcitrant toddlers. The viewer is treated as a near imbecile, unable to assimilate any statement that is not supported by a picture or by the tiny-tot graphics that break out at the slightest excuse.

This dread of the simple spoken word now extends to the most upmarket, intellectual programmes. I recently saw Joan Bakewell – that monument to broadcasting wit – deliver a BBC2 item about the Royal Shakespeare Company in which it had to be mentioned that the RSC now operates seven theatres.

Could we simply be told that fact? Of course not. We had to see a filmed sequence of each theatre with Ms Bakewell outside it in her big boots and polo neck, frowning roguishly.

As for wit and humour, one might suppose them to be incapable of existence under studio light. Humour on television is a tongue inserted noisily into a cheek, an eyebrow winched up like a creaky crane, then a pun of the kind that makes your sphincter cringe. Let us say we have seen an item about Neil Kinnock ending with film of Kinnock in a rowing boat. 'Will it be all plain *sailing* for Labour now?' the voice-over will say. 'Or could there be *squalls* ahead?'

Such occupational wits as television can produce tend to be practitioners in dated facetiousness like Alan Coren, Barry Norman or the unspeakable superannuated fixture of 'Call My Bluff'. Even those with reputations as writers clearly take no trouble with their television scripts. Would Barry Norman dare to write, as he said on 'Film 87', that 'The Mission' was 'a little gem . . . a real epic'?

Twenty years ago they had James Cameron. Today we have Russell Harty saying things like, 'When God made Paradise, He kept a bit over, like a cook saving pastry from an apple pie, and called it Yorkshire.' A moment later he was talking about flying over this paradisiac apple pie for 'a Bird's Eye view'.

That's the only real pleasure to be had from language on television – seeing it occasionally blow up in a twerp's face.

Return to Liverpool

Going to Liverpool by train is cheerier than it used to be. The new Merseyside Pullman (hauled by the locomotive *L. S. Lowry*) serves afternoon tea in a setting of beige herringbone that seems a genuine atonement for the Maxpax era. The staff are smart but unoppressive, handing out embossed menus but saying on the quiet that you don't *have* to order anything. Why, in all British Rail's prodigal advertising, has none of this been mentioned?

It's five years since I saw the black stone canyon that leads into Liverpool Lime Street. Since 1981, I've seen only the TV news picture of Liverpool – the depression, the ruin, the ranting, snub-nosed demagogue in his horrid little pastel suits. I feel guilty for having shunned a city that gave me a best-selling book as well as laughter, fascination and enduring friendship.

Lime Street also looks decidedly cheerier with its new glassed-over concourse and computerized signs. Outside, St George's Hall still looms, a sootier Parthenon, girt by pale green buses and rattle-trap taxis. Away to the left, the Adelphi is still there, less hotel than ossified luxury liner. Even under Militant, it seems, life has managed to carry on.

I'm met by Joe Flannery, one of the mainsprings of my Beatles biography. Joe was Brian Epstein's first love and his confidant in early days when no one south of Manchester wanted to know the Beatles. As they all sat around depressed in Birkenhead pubs, Brian would get Joe to come in and tell him, 'Elvis Presley's manager's been trying to get you on the phone from Memphis.'

He is now a tall, quietly hilarious man in a brown Regency

suit and tinted spectacles, and shy as he is, and as I am, we always seem to greet one another by hugging.

Driving out of town with Joe, the cheerier feeling persists. There are green verges and bushes where I remember waste ground or dead canyons for abandoned motorways. The city feels faintly resonant again, thanks to the new Maritime Museum, the Albert Dock condominiums and, in another way, to lusty new Liverpool pop groups like Frankie Goes To Hollywood.

But the Hatton Age still casts a long shadow. Among Militant's last educational improvement was the closure of Liverpool Institute, the Victorian high school which both Paul McCartney and George Harrison (not to mention Hatton himself) attended. As someone said, inaudibly, at the time, if Ford or Bird's Eye want to shut a factory on Merseyside, no one can stop them. 'But for *us* to do away with something like the Institute is just like shooting ourselves in the foot.'

Two years ago, when the city teetered at the edge of bankruptcy, Joe was stopped in the street by two old Liverpool ladies, clearly never in personal debt in their whole lives. 'They were asking me if Liverpool going broke meant they'd lose their furniture. They thought they were going bankrupt, too, and someone was going to take all their things away.'

We drive up through Toxteth, which I last saw in a summer when police stood across Upper Parliament Street, facing rioters massed like the Zulu armies before Rorke's Drift.

Even today, you can see the respectable area it used to be. We pass a little old 'High Class Family Butcher', next door to a black-fronted funeral parlour.

'Did you know some the rioters broke in and stole a body from that funeral home?' Joe said. 'Then they took it next door and left it on the butcher's slab.'

Joe lives in Aigburth not far from Otterspool Promenade, that unlikely beauty spot along the Mersey front. I remember a Beatles employee, driven to distraction by his masters' wild whims, manically typing the ultimate Fab Four day's task list. '. . . Two Turkish dwarfs dancing the Charleston on the side-

board? Certainly, John. A sock full of elephant-shit on Otterspool Promenade? Give me 10 minutes, Ringo . . .'

After helping Brian with the Beatles, Joe migrated to Hamburg, becoming a father figure to other Liverpool groups who
followed them out to play on the Reeperbahn. He took me back
there in 1980, while I was researching 'Shout'! As we walked
through the strip-joints and mud-wrestling booths, he told me
how he used to encourage all the groups to cook in their rooms,
saving their money for new amplifiers or to send home to their
mothers.

Joe's younger brother, Lee Curtis, used to be a lead singer
with the All Stars, a group which Liverpool once rated almost
equally with the Beatles. Lee himself was so good-looking that
Paul McCartney would never appear on the same bill with him.
When the Beatles sacked Pete Best for his too-good looks, Brian
Epstein gave him the job of drummer with Lee Curtis and the
All Stars. Alas, one beat group could not stand two good-
looking boys, and that was the end of them.

My first evening, we go to see a friend of Joe's named Kenny
MacMillan whose night club, MacMillan's, is among the biggest
in central Liverpool. On the way we call for a laughing, blond
boy named Ian who, until only last week, ran a country pub out
in North Wales. Told my name, he replies, 'All right' in that
tolerant Liverpool way.

It emerges that, in fact, his country pub accidentally burned
down around him. Humorous reference will be made to this
throughout the evening, not least by the dispossessed publican
himself.

Kenny MacMillan lives in an opulent bungalow with a suit of
armour in the front hall. He joins us in his Bel-Air style living
room, a short, rubicund man with straw-coloured hair, dressed
in pale turquoise and white.

'I've just been saying,' Joe tells him, 'that what you really
need over in that corner is a nice grand piano.'

'Aye, that'd give it some point,' Kenny MacMillan agrees.

'The Brazilian Ambassador's got two,' Joe says, 'and I know
he can't take *both* of them back to Brazil. Isn't it depressing,' he

adds. 'Even the Brazilian Embassy in Liverpool's shutting down.'

Ian, Kenny, Kenny's friend Mark and I pile into Joe's car and set off down the East Lancs Road, which can take you both to slums that eclipse Belfast's and restaurants more impossibly pretentious than Midtown Manhattan's. On the way, we sing Diana Ross' 'Chain Reaction', then listen to private tapes of a club comic wildly popular in Liverpool, despite the fact he's from Newcastle.

'The wife comes in and says, "Guess what's different about me." I says "New dress?" She says "No," I says "New shoes?" She says "No." I says "I give up." She says "I'm wearing a gas mask."'

We go to a pub owned by a friend of Joe's called Norman, a phone-in show host on Radio City, the Liverpool commercial station. Norman takes us upstairs to see his new wine bar, whose Victorian embellishments include the head of a stuffed fox peeping roguishly out of an airborne fire-bucket.

'There's a bloke near here who cuts up stuffed foxes for places like this,' Norman says. 'He can do you a head like that or a back part with a brush to stick out of the skirting-board.'

The talk is mainly of night clubs in Warrington, Wigan and St Helen's, with names like Cindy's, Crystal's, Mr Smith's, and of the bouncers protection war now raging. I myself fall into conversation with Kenny's friend Mark, a saturnine boy in white shirt and bootlace tie who could instantly fit into any Mersey beat group of 25 years ago.

It turns out his father was in the Mojos, yet another band who should have made it but didn't. 'They really got ripped off, my Dad and the Mojos,' he says loyally. Indeed – apart from the Beatles – who didn't?

As well as running his artists agency in Liverpool, New York and Hamburg, Joe takes in paying guests. He cooks for them himself, just like he used to for the teenage Beatles after their dance-hall marathons. Then John, as leader, would appropriate the couch, leaving Paul to push two armchairs together, while Joe took George out in his car for an all-night driving lesson.

The only boarder who has given trouble was a Greek in the

shipping business – such a chain-smoking handful that after two
weeks Joe had to evict him. But they have stayed good friends.
On my second day, indeed, the Greek rings up to tell Joe he's
now got a place in Garston and would like us to go over there
for some 'traditional food'.

Garston used to be a fearsome part of Liverpool docks with
its Teddy Boy gangs and the infamous Saturday dances at its
swimming baths – otherwise known as The Blood Baths –
where many a beat group, the Beatles included, had to use
guitars and hand-mikes as defensive weapons. Today, its back-
to-back streets are quiet and bijou under the gasometers. Garston,
even, is getting gentrified.

The address we are bidden to is a small, timber-fronted fish
and chip shop. We arrive just before opening-time. In the back
room an elderly Cypriot is peeling potatoes into a plastic pail, a
look of gentle bewilderment on his face. At the nearby pay-
phone, evidently placing calls all over the world, is Joe's ex-
boarder.

He has a black moustache, a striped fitted shirt, much chest-
hair, an open executive briefcase and a total inability to keep still
or stop talking. After Joe threw him out, he walked to Garston,
lit on this poor little Cypriot chippie and, before they knew it,
moved in.

In a spirit of true Greek friendship, after he has shaken my
hand, he shows me the contents of his wallet. 'This is a photo of
me in the army . . . My brother . . . My father . . . My second
wife . . .' Diving to his executive briefcase, knocking salt-pots
and vinegar-shakers right and left, he produces a panoramic
picture of an oil tanker. 'My whole life,' he declares fervently,
'is chips!' The old Cypriot shakes his head and smiles over his
peeling. 'Yes, chips!' the Greek cries. 'Merchant chips! Passenger
chips! Container chips!'

In the evening Joe is visited by an American girl doing
research on mid-Sixties culture for her university in Oregon.
There are always such students around Liverpool, visiting Penny
Lane and Strawberry Fields, interviewing Allan Williams about
how he gave the Beatles away, pinpointing the precise location

of Brian Epstein's record shop in Whitechapel and the Cavern Club in Mathew Street. The three of us go to a restaurant in what is Britain's oldest Chinatown. As long as the Chinese stay, no city needs lose all hope. Through our window we can see The Nook, a pub where 'time' is called in Cantonese.

Joe has been sent tickets for the first night of a new city-centre disco club, Snobs Take Two. We find it at last among the cobbled back lanes, its pink and silver neon sign wagging wildly at the end of a wartime Anderson shelter. We are admitted through a mock-Georgian town house door by a bevy of men with squashed noses, wearing wing-poke collars. This is a city where privilege cannot be too surreptitious or well-guarded.

The air-conditioned phantasmagoria within reminds one, as do all today's great new disco clubs, of a wartime Anderson shelter. Joe leads the way through, resplendent in his white blouson and turquoise satin shirt.

The difference from Limelight or Studio 54 is that girls are dancing alone, each one moving in a circle round what looks like a small, shiny cowpat on the floor. As at the Cavern a generation ago, they prefer to leave their handbags where they can see them.

Next morning on our way to the station, Joe stops at a village florist's to collect two bouquets he's ordered. One, I know, is for Cynthia Lennon, John's first wife, whom Joe is escorting to a James Last concert in Liverpool tonight.

'Who's the little posy for?' I ask.

'Don't you know what day it is today?' Joe answers.

We drive to the Jewish cemetery in Long Lane where Brian Epstein is buried. On each anniversary of his death 19 years ago – that lonely, confused death amid prodigal wealth, Indian yogis, flowers, beads, suicide notes and murder threats – Joe has had special permission from the rabbi to put flowers on Brian's grave.

We stand for a few moments before the black marble head-stone. 'They wouldn't bury him next to his father,' Joe murmurs. 'His mother's always felt so unhappy about that.'

I say goodbye to Joe outside the Adelphi and pop in for a

quick drink with Bob Wooler, the Cavern Club's original disc jockey and another unacknowledged maker of the Beatles. It was Bob Wooler who said they should begin playing even before the curtains opened, and who lent them rare American import discs, later mistaken for Beatles originals, like Chan Romero's 'Hippy Hippy Shake'.

He is a dignified man with a Roman senator's haircut; bearing up well – I'm happy to see – after his recent stroke. We sit in the Adelphi's downstairs bar, once a domain of walnut wood and pewter, now converted to yet another Studio 54 lookalike with lights that flash in lines, floors that change colour and pumping soul music, even at lunchtime on a Tuesday.

At ledges round the empty, cacophonous disco floor sit half a dozen elderly drinkers for whom this is evidently just another pub. They are my last view of Liverpool – straightforward old men in raincoats and flat caps, sitting over their pints in the ever-changing rainbow din, past caring what to make of it.

Ruby It's You

Life can have odd ways of making amends. Eight years ago I lost a live-in girlfriend and, the same day, acquired a black and white female cat. When I first picked her up, she twisted and tried to put her front paws round my neck.

I live in a west London basement flat with a large courtyard at the back. She had come over the right-hand wall, down the long iron fire-escape. She was barely more than a kitten, nervy and tentative. But her face even then had a stare guaranteed to catch the Speaker's eye at 200 paces.

After her, to my dismay, came a circle of male admirers – a handsome tabby, a red-collared black, a moon-faced marmalade. Typically, she had rejected these in favour of a sinister customer with her own black and white marking, plus a toothbrush moustache, a withered back leg and the general air of a tango champion in reduced circumstances.

On her early visits I would find the fur at the back of her neck damp and bitten, presumably by the tango champion's ardour. My initial concern was to prevent, or at least limit, a case of child abuse. I bought a collar, put it on her and attached a jocular note to her owner, mentioning the number of her male followers and asking if she'd been neutered yet.

The following day I was rung up by someone called Francesca in neighbouring Cleveland Terrace. To my surprise, the call was anything but jocular.

'Have you been feeding her?'

'Yes . . . a little.'

'Well, what do you *expect*?'

Next time she appeared, I resolutely picked her up and carried her round to Cleveland Terrace.

Francesca proved to be a patrician-looking girl, wearing a lot of purple. Behind her I glimpsed the kind of flat where young stockbrokers call at 6 p.m., holding bottles of claret.

After I'd handed over the squirming truant with profuse apologies, there was a slight thaw.

'I brought her up from the country last weekend . . . her name's Rhubarb, by the way.'

Next time she came down the fire-escape, I kept my study window firmly shut. Heart-rending cries came from below. After about 10 minutes I opened the window. And that was it.

She has never been conventionally beautiful. The black cheeks and white jowls bear too strong a resemblance to Sylvester in the Tweetie Pie cartoon, especially during our intense eyeball-to-eyeball confrontations over timings of meals. In repose, the black arcs round her eyes become bland and expressionless as outsized sunglasses.

Nor has she ever been a paragon in matters of personal hygiene. Though the bib under her chin is always fresh and fluffed, there have been the same two oval patches of grime behind her white back legs as long as I've known her. And of all the pleasant places I provide for sleep, her favourite is still a dirty old earth-filled plant pot.

Unable to stand 'Rhubarb', I shortened it to 'Ruby'. I could visualize those white paws as dimpled fingers, burdened with cheap rings, rootling among the papers in a chocolate box.

In that era, going out daily to work, I saw her only in the mornings and at night. I knew she had adopted the rear court-yard as her domain, seeing off even the tango champion with amnesiac ferocity. An occasional spot of blood on her nose was my only clue to this vigorous other life, though Mrs Burgess, my cleaning lady, saw somewhat more. I remember once saying to Mrs Burgess that I had to go away for a few days and wondered what I should do about Ruby.

'Shall I tell you?' Mrs Burgess replied with sudden spirit. 'Wring her neck!'

In 1983 I went to live in New York. It was a confused time, when the last thing on my mind was a black and white cat. I left her lounging in the plant pot, with hardly a backward glance.

The emigration to New York wasn't a success. One night as I lay in my Canal Street loft, listening to trucks roar past to the Holland Tunnel, an unexpected thought came into my mind. I remembered the sound of small teeth crunching up Meow Mix and in that moment I realized I did have a home to go back to.

Since then we've lived together in great amity, making allowance for each other in remarkable ways considering both our natures.

She, of course, is getting on now and has a tendency to shrewishness, confronting me when I fail to come up to scratch, her arms as nearly akimbo as a cat can contrive. Green gimlet eyes glare through the outside shades, their expression saying, plainer than any words, 'Just *what* do you propose doing about this?'

Nor is she the scrapper she once was. Recently I awoke to find a strange orange cat with a white barn-owl face actually in the room. Ruby crouched nearby, showing all the trauma of an elderly spinster on finding a man under her bed. Yet in middle age she remains the same utterly amiable, docile, malleable being whose every part can be ruffled, rolled and stroked the wrong way, and whose purr operates by hair-trigger.

I have made it plain that, since living in New York, I abhor all kinds of overt hustling. At mealtimes, therefore, she comes and sits demurely, front paws together, eyes downcast, as if food were the very last thing on her mind. It reminds me of people on the 'Antiques Roadshow' when the expert asks whether they've ever wondered how much their ancestral china or glass might be worth. 'Has it – ah – ever remotely occurred to you to eat Whiskas?' I sometimes say as I open the tin.

For all this time I've gone on carefully explaining to people that she isn't really my cat. I always half expected Francesca to come and restore her to that other world of Sloanes and stockbrokers. An ingrained adolescence in me still resisted full responsibility and commitment to anything.

Then, the other week, a vet had to call and give her a flu jab. The vet was young and very nice; she greeted him with her invariable purr. When the needle went in, she didn't struggle, only uttered this one low, sad little wail . . .

Just let anyone try to take her away from me now.

Sticking To A Buddy

July 1987

Sit alone in Pizza Express, Bayswater. Toy with mozzarella and tomato salad. Feel lonely and under-appreciated.

Maudlin thoughts lead, as usual, to childhood on end of Ryde Pier, Isle of Wight. Recall hearing news of Buddy Holly's death in plane crash on February 3, 1959. Reflect how 'That'll Be The Day', 'Peggy Sue', 'Rave On', 'Words of Love' and other Holly songs virtually only things made 15 year-old life worth living.

While eating cassata, remember excellent BBC2 Arena documentary on Holly's short career. Fume at 30 year-old parental propaganda that rock and roll stars all shiftless con-artists, unable to sing or play guitars. Wish had known at time Holly not only gifted musician but also decent, attractive human being.

Get sudden wild idea could write short story about Holly's death in Iowa and self on end of Ryde Pier. Become so entranced with own audacity, cannot finish cassata.

August

After three weeks, produce 7000 word story, 'Words of Love'. Often tempted give up, as when take four days to write third of page. Spurred on by thought that, if unsuccessful, can never enjoy Buddy Holly music again.

Take precious single manuscript to Bayswater photo-copy shop. Watch in anguish as grubby-fingered operative instantly dog-ears first page. Almost die of apoplexy when operative returns from machine with puzzled look and says 'Does this really start on page 4?'

While grappling with operative for re-possession of manuscript, decide this probably moment go in for word-processor.

September
Grit teeth and phone agent to ask if story safely received. Agent
says yes. Hating own indelicacy, ask if any magazine sale likely.
Agent says story not most magazines' kind of thing, but has
tried it on *Harpers & Queen* and *Granta*. *H&Q* say No. *Granta*
has not even bothered to send acknowledgment.

Hang up feeling short story writing practice akin masturba-
tion.

October
Show story to Brian Eastman, independent film producer and
friend. Do not feel much better when receive note he likes it.
Wish *Granta* would even acknowledge receipt of MS.

In depths of gloom, get phone call from Brian suggesting
turn story into one-hour play for him produce in BBC2 'Screen-
play' series. Agree to try, but privately sure will never work out.

Go with Brian to see Brenda Reid of BBC2 Drama department. To amazement, am subsequently offered total of £5,000
for rights in story and dramatizing it. Not fortune, admittedly,
but five or six times amount paid for fiction by even best magazine.

Thought repeats in head like joyous refrain: 'Screw you,
Granta'.

December 1987–February 1988
Take six weeks to turn story into play. Explaining all in dialogue
heavy sweat for prose-writer, used to hiding under blankets of
description. Start to feel profound envy of TV soap-authors
permitted lines like 'You're forgetting that I am your mother'.
Oddly, find it harder to write scenes about adolescent self in Isle
of Wight than about Buddy Holly on tour in Iowa. Knowing
too little on subject far easier for writer than knowing too
much.

In astonishingly few days, hear from Brian that Brenda Reid

likes script, but must submit for final approval to BBC2 Head of Plays, Peter Goodchild.

March
Await Peter Goodchild's decision.

April
Await Peter Goodchild's decision.

May
Await Peter Goodchild's decision.

June
Await Peter Goodchild's decision.

July
While still awaiting Peter Goodchild's decision, have lunch with Brian and Colin Nutley, his choice as director. Nutley pleasant, fortyish with fringe and Marc O'Polo sweatshirt. Discover he grew up in Gosport, just over water from self on Ryde Pier head. Discuss topics of inexhaustible fascination such as Gosport ferry and Isle of Wight steam trains. Colin Nutley evidently one of best.

Ask Brian when Goodchild likely give final go-head to production, and receive useful TV industry maxim: 'The secret of this business is not to want anything too much.'

August
Spend month in room overlooking English Channel, writing novella about Edwardian music hall. Pass spare time watching badger-headed blue tits spin in and out of sunny foliage around windowsill. When have almost ceased to care one way or other, receive call from Brian in London. Peter Goodchild says 'Go ahead'.

Am asked, by the way, did I realize that February 3, 1989 will be 30th anniversary Buddy Holly's death? Confess that had no idea.

September

Go to BBC-TV Centre for talk with Brian and Colin Nutley.
Discover large office suite given over to 'Words of Love', and
team of high-powered women working round clock on finding
cast and locations.

Learn of major change to script. Ryde Pier too dilapidated to
use as location, so must be content with Cromer Pier. Undertake
to change all Isle of Wight references in script to East Anglian.

Make first acquaintanceship with marvellous minutiae of BBC
drama shooting-schedule, providing information down to high
and low tides at Cromer and phone number of local vet.

Discover standards of research in BBC drama put print journalism to shame when subsequently rung up by Assistant Floor
Manager, Suzannah MacLean.

'Philip, you've written a line about Buddy Holly's Guild
guitar. We've discovered that by February 1959, he'd got rid of
the Guild and bought a Gibson. All right make that change?'

Same week

Sit in at auditions of young American actors reading for Buddy
Holly, Ritchie Valens, Big Bopper and other members fateful
Rock 'n' Roll road show. Agonize over choice between Pancho
Russell, who almost Holly reincarnated, and Gary Kemp of
Spandau Ballet pop group, better bet publicity-wise.

Meet Charlie Creed Miles, obvious choice to play sensitive,
vulnerable 15 year-old self. Unanimity reinforced when picks up
guitar and plays wonderful Blues riff. Only wish had been half
good that at 15.

Walk into room at BBC, Acton, to be confronted for first
time by full cast, production team, makeup, properties and
wardrobe, in all some 50 people.

Feel knees go weak. Think 'Oh my my God, what have I
started?' Half wish could all go back being just nice cosy little
manuscript.

October

Attend first day's shooting at BBC Ealing Studios. Marvel at set for American road-side diner, perfect down to period chewing-gum in display case. Get inkling why BBC drama best in world.

Receive first exposure to film set language: 'Red light and bell ... turn over ... sound running ... Go!' Notice penchant of film technicians for tailored designer jeans.

Lunch on stuffed peppers in BBC canteen. In afternoon, become prey to fearful stomach gurgles audible to sound-boom even when retreat 30 yards from set.

Attend shooting of classroom scenes at Emanuel school, Wandsworth. Agree to play part of teacher, cycling up to front door. Consent to be wardrobed in hideous sports jacket and orange wool tie, and given haircut. Pull off scene in only three takes.

Told by Colin Nutley must write additional dialogue for schoolmaster teaching causes of Crimea War. Realize know nothing additional about subject, and spend anxious evening ringing round historically-minded friends. Sit up late, trying produce humorous lines about 19th century Russian expansionism and French colonial rule in Syria. Tricky.

Next week
Attend shooting of American backstage scenes in underground bay at old Hoover factory, Western Avenue. Watch uncanny growth of Pancho Russell into character and psyche of Buddy Holly. At moment he leaves for fatal plane trip with Ritchie Valens and Big Bopper, feel both sadness and twinge self-disgust. Am, after all, exploiting death of three young men for gain.

Next week
Take Third World commuter train to Cromer, Norfolk, for filming of pier scenes. Find there almost eerily perfect reproduction of own childhood environment. At pier gate, facsimile of grandmother's sweet and rock kiosk. At pier head ditto father's ill-fated pleasure dome. Every detail perfect down to his Series E Morris van with carnival loudspeakers. Recall how used to hide from van after dark, flitting one doorway to next like French Maquisard.

Arrive too late to see Liz Smith play scene as grandmother,

nursing cat in sweet kiosk while liver boils malodorously on gas-ring. But receive full force of Tom Bell, bringing father back to life in all quixotic menace. During some scenes, cannot stand it. Have to go outside and gulp sea air.

At intervals, walk round Cromer. Notice Post Office due to close. Feel hatred well up afresh at Thatcher Can't-Be-Bothered culture.

Become hooked on cuisine of location caterer. Wonder what will do when can't mount wooden block at end of silver lorry and receive free goulash or apple strudel on paper plate.

Realize with some emotion that entire unit, not only director, cameraman and lighting cameraman but also 'grips', 'sparks' et al working to utmost to make play good as possible in every tiny way. Reflect how different from most experiences in news-paper offices.

As final writing job, am prevailed on by production manager Ruth Mayorcas to write song lampooning principal unit mem-bers for her and Suzannah perform at last night party. Make verses fit tune of Buddy Holly's 'Not Fade Away'.

Leave location at surreal moment. Half-way along pier, four burly men making up single bed, neatly tucking in blankets, arranging pillows and smoothing coverlet as waves thresh under planks and seagulls cry. Think to self how far situation has evolved from few pages of typing.

Travel back London, feeling bit flat.

November
Ring up editor of *Male & Femail* magazine. Ask if interested in short story coincide with 30th anniversary Buddy Holly's death. Sell immediately for £1500.

Remember still awaiting acknowledgment from *Granta* for MS sent July 1987.

Realize only one thing remain say.

Screw you, *Granta*.

The Casting of Clouts

There are two terrific things about London at present. One is the blooming of horse chestnut trees. The other is a sexist comment, but who cares? Life always picks up for me when women start to go about in fewer clothes.

Unfortunately, men also are going about in fewer clothes.

The summer so far has shown me quite enough scraggy torsos, pigeon chests, brewer's goitres, milk-white biceps, old ragged vaccination marks and grimy tattoos. The more unimpressive the male physique, the likelier it is to be flaunted in a display of imagined animal magnetism. Hipster trousers are as much in evidence as ever among those having no hips. In Paris or Rome, summer is the signal for males to put on crisp white linen suits. In London, it is the signal for them to show you their yellow underpant rims and coyly-peeping bottom cracks.

While women in summer garb just go on with normal life, men get overwhelmed with some woozy notion that everything is now a party. You see them all afternoon round here outside the shut pubs, lolling on those Swiss-style wooden benches in every degree of incapacity and villainous undress. Hyde Park is littered with their prostrated forms, like the Harvest of Death after Gettysburg.

At my local stationer's there is a youth who, on hot days, serves customers stripped to the waist. He is – as they say in Liverpool – 'built like a racing tadpole'. His nipples are small, flat, brown and very nasty to behold. I do not want to see them ever, but somehow least of all when I'm buying Pentel pens and Oxford 200-sheet writing tablets.

Under sexual equality, why should not men's nipples be subject to the same protocol as women's? It would be a swift step to a more beautiful world, particularly for customers at Globe Stationers.

Most unwelcome male nudity, of course, belongs to the builders who continue to lay London waste without apparent constraint. There is scarcely a street not somewhere polluted by scaffolding, sand-heaps, filthy skips and the din of ghetto-blasters accompanying work seldom in progress.

The trail of their nonchalant wrecking grows even wider. In Westbourne Grove some cretin-gang has lately spilt white paint all down the centre of the road. Don't worry, lads – it's only going to be there for ever.

In my neighbourhood there is a small florist's shop racked on both sides with exultant gouging, smashing and hammering. It's heartbreaking to see the rubble and dust rain down on the heads of potted palms and daffodils.

The owner pleaded for consideration in vain, until his mother had the brilliant idea of photographing everyone on site. For some mysterious reason, this makes builders deeply nervous, and thus more amenable to suggestion they might act like human beings. Remember it if you, too, are being plagued.

I am currently compiling a book of notable insults and abuse. Like for instance what the Hollywood press agent said of Orson Welles: 'There but for the grace of God goes God . . .' Or Dorothy Parker's epitaph to an obnoxious movie idol, drowned off Malibu: 'How do you send a telegram of congratulation to the Pacific Ocean?'

The best matched crotch-kickers were probably Hedda Hopper and her arch-rival gossip columnist Louella Parsons. Hedda once called Louella 'a has-been practising to be a never-was'. Louella replied that Hedda was 'just a little hiccup from Hicksville who's somehow got her butt into the butter'.

The veteran British actress Coral Browne proved her supremacy in this line when a young Hollywood producer was wearisomely giving her his views on plays and writing.

'Don't talk to me about writing,' Ms Browne said crisply. 'You couldn't write f--- on a dusty Venetian blind.'

The Master and Colonel Mad

Few modern masters of literature have proved so unsatisfactory to the biographer as P. G. Wodehouse. So far as anyone can see, all the man did for his 93 years, apart from some golf and transatlantic travel, was sit and hammer out his books. As a person he was unflamboyant, unsociable and – save to a very few – almost pathologically uncommunicative. One just cannot fathom the connection between that benign, smudgy face and that stupendous body of work.

The work is what has engaged biographers, a Wodehousian sub-species in themselves. Richard Usborne, author of the definitive critique, ended up even resembling his idol – same bald head, prep schoolmasterly air and flannel bags. A delightful lunatic named Geoffrey Jaggard out in the shires devoted his life to cross-indexing Blandings Castle and the Drones Club. After Wodehouse died in 1975, Usborne got the job of editing his last, unfinished Blandings book from the outlines and notes he left behind. I remember meeting Usborne at the time, creeping along with the incredulous stealth of one who had just re-split the atom. He alone knew the answer to one of the great debates among Wodehouse addicts: whether Lord Emsworth's revered pig expert was originally named Whipple or Whiffle.

Now here is N. T. P. Murphy, described on his publisher's handout as 'Colonel Murphy', and evidently barmier, in a nice way, than all previous Wodehounds put together. He contends that Wodehouse did not spin pure dotty make-believe, as is generally thought, but that all the major characters – and not a few of the plots – derived from people Wodehouse knew or knew about. To this end, the Colonel has apparently checked every word of Wodehouse's 100-odd books against contemporary newspapers, Somerset House records, *Burke's 'Peerage'* and *Kelly's County Directories*. The results are impressive. Bertie Wooster, Stanley Featherstonehaugh Ukridge, aunts, clerics – and, finally, Elysium in the form of Blandings Castle itself – are each run to earth by Colonel Murphy, often with almost audible whoops and yips.

He turns up gold in an early chapter about the London Wodehouse knew as a young gossip columnist – the London of Seymour Hicks, Romano's in The Strand and, especially, the Pelican Club, whose membership mixed bookies, showgirls and disreputable dukes very much as Wodehouse novels would mix them unchangingly over the next half-century. Lord Emsworth's brother Galahad was always proud of having been a Pelican. Evan Gally, though, scarcely matched the hell-raising of true life Pelicans like Hughie Drummond or the famous 'Brer Rabbit', who once outsmarted a debt-collection agency that was dunning him by joining its staff and pursuing himself with writs all over England for best part of a year. That was a plot even Wodehouse dared not try on the punters.

A hater of smoking-room life himself, he clearly drew on his youthful fascination with the Pelican in creating the most famous men's club in literature. Bertie, Bingo, Pongo et al at the Drones, albeit dressed for the Twenties, are much closer in spirit to 'knuts' and 'mashers' of the Nineties. I knew that Oofy Prosser, the Drones' richest, meanest member, took his first name from the Victorian schoolboy's 'oof', for money. Colonel Murphy adds the savoury fact that, in Pelican circles, a 'prosser' was both a borrower and stingy bird.

He finds the most likely model for Bertie Wooster in George Grossmith Junior, a musical comedy star renowned for 'dude' roles like 'Lord Percy Pimpleton' when Wodehouse was starting to work in the theatre. Ukridge – whom Wodehouse told me was based on his friend Craxton – seems drawn as much from Herbert Westbrook, an early collaborator who treated Wodehouse rather like Ukridge treats Corky, on one occasion purloining his only dress suit, on another pawning his banjo.

Aunts provide a rich seam of investigation. Well might Wodehouse have described 'aunt calling to aunt like Mastodons across a primeval swamp.' Colonel Murphy has discovered he had 20 of them – and, consequently, as many nephews as Mr Mulliner. One Wodehouse aunt outdid even Aunt Agatha in villainy, having written the original 'Types of Ethical Theory', which eggheaded Florency Craye urges poor Bertie to read instead of 'Blood on the Banisters'.

The Colonel's tone is like Aunt Dahlia's on the hunting field, whether hacking through *Burke's 'Peerage'* or rummaging round the grounds of Hunstanton Hall to find the very octagon mentioned in 'Jeeves and the Impending Doom'. The spirit of Wodehousian metaphor is ever on him, as when he describes 'working round Bush House' to reach the office for perusing death certificates. Here and there, his appetite for discovery carries him away a bit. I baulked at recognizing the prototype for Bertie's childhood Nemesis, the Rev. Aubrey Upjohn, in a deeply circumstantial Victorian headmaster named Henry Hammond. Nor do I think we can trace the Efficient Baxter to a 17th century Puritan preacher, Richard Baxter. Where, pray, was *his* marcel wave?

The Colonel confesses sorrowfully that he has been unable to pin-point the exact whereabouts of the Wooster flat, or add much to existing data about Jeeves. This is more than offset by his 600-mile trek round England's stately homes, culminating in his positive identification of Blandings Castle at Sudeley Castle, Gloucestershire. Not Shropshire or Wiltshire, whatever the evidence of railway timetables left at the bedsides of ill-behaved young men, with the 8.30 'highly recommended'.

It is all great, slightly crazed fun, though I would have liked more about Wodehouse himself as the model for Lord Emsworth ('happy as only a fluffy-minded man with excellent health and a large income can be') For future Wodehounds, let me add a topographical note of my own. I have just spent two years in Downtown New York, close to where Wodehouse lived in 1916 when the Jeeves-Bertie saga began. To get from Canal to Houston, you go along a little thoroughfare called . . . Wooster Street.

Springsteen's Blazing Summer

Live Aid was Bruce Springsteen's generosity of spirit, catching on.

Why was rock, at its earlier apotheosis, so seldom generous? Why was it so much more often tainted by reluctance, condescension and niggardliness? As usual, we find an answer in the Beatles, who, by the time the world adored them, passionately hated concert performance. Along with everything else, they bequeathed the conventions of disgraceful lateness and shilly-shallying contempt for paying customers. To go to a Dylan or a Stones concert was usually to fear the worst – perhaps, to dissolve into enraptured surprise if the performers deigned to be adequate. Those, like Rod Stewart, who most ardently styled themselves men of the people, ended up covered in just the same vainglorious conceit. At their most brilliant, most giving moments, you always felt the greater allure of the world waiting for them in the wings.

Bruce Springsteen has no world in the wings. His completeness as a performer, I think, stands comparison only with Charles Chaplin. Like Chaplin, Springsteen's whole life seems to be the one he lives for us, with every heartbeat, muscle, sinew and fibre. And, after the dizzy climaxes of his adventures, there is the same sad moment, for us and him, because it must all end. The little, unkempt figure sets off alone down the road. But we need not worry. The road leads only back, and ever back, into the rapt eye of his audience.

I'll describe my one and only encounter with Springsteen because it was so ludicrously unmemorable. It occurred in 1975, the year he was all but smothered by record company hype. I was covering pop for *The London Times* and *The Sunday Times Magazine*. Skeptical as I felt about the 'new Dylan' tag, there was no resisting the breathless, panoramic excitement of Born To Run. Springsteen had just arrived to begin his first British tour. CBS Records in London asked if I'd care to spend the day with him.

We met in the depressing coffee shop of a West End hotel. Springsteen wore a cracked black doublet and a grimy beard. He was, in fact, a different creature from the cleancut, marvelous boy who would later be reborn. With him sat a publicist whose defects included the most appalling stammer. Springsteen seemed morose and bewildered, and spoke only in monosyllables. The publicist did not supply a compensating fluency. At times, his stammer became so bad, he could break it only by pounding himself violently and at length on the letter of his Yale football shirt. I would not wish to make fun of anyone with such a handicap. But for PR purposes, it would have been just as sensible to retain a Trappist monk.

Then we drove in a limousine . . . guess where. We drove to Harrods. Springsteen wanted some new woollen hats, and the publicist thought they might stock Rasta fashions in this terracotta haunt of shopping Royalty. I remember standing in Harrods menswear department, amid the tweeds and silk smoking jackets, while Springsteen leaned, silent, against a display case and the publicist, pounding his chest, attempted yet again to explain why I was in the presence of someone special. When we looked round, Springsteen had slunk off alone.

What Springsteen gave at the beginning seemed generous enough. What he gave us until 1975 was the most colossal public love affair with pop music in its simplest, most joyous forms, orchestrated by a performer whose voice was as warmly intimate as Buddy Holly's, who possessed Chuck Berry's gift for turning the minutiae of his life into narrative poetry, all allied to a gusto, good humour and hurtling energy that made other early seventies rock demigods seem, by comparison, geriatric dwarfs.

Then Springsteen disappeared in Harrods menswear department and, two years later, reemerged minus the hype and *Time* and *Newsweek* cover stories, shorn of his beard and biker's slouch: an open young face, a clean white T-shirt, and quietly passionate songs about the new urban melancholia that awoke echoes of Spector no longer, but of Steinbeck.

I cannot say what impact Springsteen's albums 'Darkness At The Edge of Town' and 'The River' had when first released in America. I know what their effect was in Britain in the late seventies on a generation freshly weaned onto the expectation of nothing. To young men in blighted urban areas like Greater Manchester or Merseyside, Springsteen's elegies of dignified labour and small hope, and sad resignation to the wrinkles around his baby eyes, were nothing less then fatherly lullabyes.

Then came the reports of concerts such as no rock audience had seen before – reports, not from the hype factory but from independent critics, galvanised out of the seventies' pent-up torpor and cynicism. Then came realisation that, if anything, the reports had understated matters. I saw Springsteen at Wembley Stadium, London, in 1981. Half an hour into the show when he did the Mitch Ryder medley, it seemed impossible that he could go on surpassing himself. An hour later, I was ready to reel home satiated, for ever. 'I'll just take a break for a few minutes,' Springsteen said. 'Then I'll be back to play another little set for you.'

We saw the rise, to unprecedented height, of a star who forswore stardom. His concerts were not just feats of strength – they were feats of simplicity. From all those hours in the audience's eye, can anyone remember a single garment Springsteen has worn? Can anyone instance a single night down all those sold-out roads, when he was late or moody, or walked off-stage, or succumbed to any of the thousand vices rock 'n' roll flesh is heir to? Even his all-conquering title, 'The Boss', is one that could be bestowed only by brothers.

The feeling that has waxed stronger than ever on this last Springsteen tour is something infinitely more than mere fan worship. It is more even than love. It is *trust*. Not only in pop, but in any realm where people gaze longingly upward, Springsteen stands for strength, for hope and – most important – for consistency. He cannot speak, any more than he can sing, a lie. He seems almost Jesuitically immune to corruption. The paramount object of Madison Avenue's commercial lechery, he steadfastly refuses to endorse anything but conscience and good cheer. Those millions who flocked to his concerts did not do so just for the marvellous music and miraculous energy. They also were going to meet the most reliable man they know.

Such a being, clearly, could not be allowed to exist without interference from the most pervasive of all today's hype machines. Just the same, I felt my heart giving a sickening downward lurch last November, when Ronald Reagan took to informing his re-election campaign-trail audiences that Bruce Springsteen's music pretty well summed up the values of the Republican Party and that, if one thought about it, The Boss and Ronnie believed in the selfsame America.

Springsteen, at the time, angrily rejected any notion of such blood brotherhood. Since then, the political hype has gone on more subtly. It is suggested that the songs on his last album – songs, like 'Glory Days' and 'Born In The USA', which shout out Springsteen's euphoria at the apogee of his powers – are, on the contrary, anthems to Ronald Reagan's America, partaking in the same jingoistic upsurge that cheered Grenada's 'liberation' and now thrills to the screen exploits of such an old-fashioned nationalistic 'hero' as Sylvester Stallone's Rambo.

Stallone's mesmerically repulsive humanoid, indeed, is the epitome of patriotism as Mr Reagan (and his great fan, Mrs Thatcher) would have us understand it. That sort of patriotism swings, apelike; kicks doors in; remorselessly mows down anything unlucky enough to enter its gunsight; and spends the intervals between bouts of homicide in preening itself before a full-length mirror. It is patriotism attainable only through terrible vacuity round the eyes and brain; the kind of epidemic brutishness that Stallone's creation is even now unleashing, and passing on to children via such play aids as 'Rambo's Black Flak Bubblegum'.

I can think of no greater affront to Bruce Springsteen than placing him in even the remotest cultural juxtaposition with this muscle-oiled onanist. In any case, Rambo and the half-wit patriotism he embodies are phenomena of the most fleeting moment. Springsteen, for the past decade, has been patriotic in the purest simplest sense of loving his native land so much, he can make others love it also. How the Reagan government's propagandists must wish they could catch even a hundredth of the unaffected joy in being American which his every production naturally exudes. Look at the video for 'Glory Days'. Springsteen is seen, just playing knockabout baseball with a boy, a son or kid brother. At the end, they pick up the stray balls, then walk over to a young wife – maybe, a sister – waiting beside her ordinary car. Where are the narcissistic mercenaries, the gunfire and marching bands? What else could make even this cynical Britisher almost wish he had been born in the USA?

Yet how far Springsteen is from being just a joyful all-American consumer. At his Giants stadium concert, pausing in that column of rare, quiet light, he wondered aloud what had become of the flag he himself once looked up to as a guarantee of fairness to all. No one else could have stopped a 65,000-strong audience dead in its hurrahing tracks, to talk seriously and at length about two local organisations for feeding the hungry (which, he did not mention, would receive a substantial portion of his own concert earnings). The high point of the show was his performance – with great passion, and with reproach – of Woody Guthrie's 'This Land Is Your Land'.

Some people wondered why Springsteen did not appear in the Live Aid concert. But in truth, his gift pervaded it. The minor miracle of famous bands starting on time, playing a disciplined span, then retiring – the almost total lack of amour propre among the massed idols – could have derived from no other example. It was fitting, too, that Bob Geldof, who began by mimicking Springsteen's music, should have found his vocation in writing a Springsteen conscience across the sky of two hemispheres. One notices more and more performers following Springsteen's path away from the old rock attitudes, the myopia and selfishness. Dire Straits' Mark Knopfler is another such quiet hero and firm friend to an audience, as he proved at

Wembley by refusing to let even Prince Charles's heavies push people around. One thinks also of Sting, Phil Collins, Chris Rea ... The modern world's most powerful alchemy seems to be falling into responsible hands, at long last.

While writing this essay, I have been listening to New York's station WNEW play all Springsteen's recorded songs, in alphabetical order. The one that made the happiest, silliest grin appear on my face was Springsteen, onstage with the E Street Band, singing 'Santa Claus Is Coming To Town'. I realize there is another gift to acknowledge. It is an ironic one for an artist whose cover versions only ever sought to draw homage to the original. Like Crosby, like Sinatra, like Presley and like no one else. Bruce Springsteen can sing *any* song and make it belong to him forever.

I know a publisher in London – a woman of 35 who has followed pop since the late sixties, and seen the folly in most of it. At her age and level of disillusion, she says, it feels wonderful to be in love with a rock star again.

It is the same for us all. And, as with true love, it never felt quite this way before.

Cold Turkey

The thing I most wanted for Christmas in my whole life I actually did get. It was a black *papier mâché* pirate galleon, laden with red crackers. I can still feel my fingers ransacking the pillow-case and see its dark prow wedged among the New Berry Fruits and netted chocolate money. That was the last truly magical Christmas I can remember. Since 1951, with a few freak exceptions, the whole thing has gone steadily downhill.

The main jinx on Christmas throughout my childhood was our involvement in the licensed trade, which meant lunch could not be thought about until after closing-time, with the glasses all washed, the floors swept, the last noisy customer persuaded to depart. Many, of course, were not persuaded, and joined us at our bleary five o'clock repast. The other jinx was the sea, threshing and moaning around my father's pierhead pleasure dome. It is hard to feel Christmasy at twilight at the end of a half-mile long seaside pier. Then at six we had to open the bar again, for Portsmouth ferry passengers and Trinity House pilots putting out to bring the transatlantic liners past Spithead.

Even after my father left Ryde Pier to operate fruit machines in rural Berkshire, he contrived to remain an honorary publican. Probably my most gruesome Christmas of all came in this year, at a pub run by a friend of his named Ivy – an idyllic-looking place, as these hell-holes so often are – with a log fire, horse-brasses, hunting horns and a Stilton on the bar.

Having helped wash and dry the glasses, vacuum the floor and seats and cover the beer-taps with teacloths, we adjourned to a festively-laid table in the back bar while Ivy and her bearded boyfriend went into the kitchen to finish preparing lunch. A very few moments later, Ivy was carried out unconscious, knocked cold by the bearded boyfriend after some culinary tiff. I can picture her now, laid corpse-like along three chairs, under three vintage car placemats, wineglasses and crackers. Quickly recovering, she began to pelt her bearded boyfriend with presents from under the tree. An early direct hit, I recall, was scored with a gift pack of Max Factor aftershave.

'We must get out of here,' I kept whispering to my father.

'No, we can't,' he said, as more presents wizzed back and forth. 'It wouldn't be fair.'

We finally left – still minus lunch – at about 5.30, to go and repair a fruit machine at a working men's club in Reading. Our black-eyed and battered hostess's last words, as she shut us out into the pitch-black, sleeting car-park, were, 'Are you *sure* you wouldn't like a mince pie?'

All of us know the surest way to spend a happy Christmas. It is to please ourselves how we keep it or – in Scrooge's perfectly reasonable phrase – how we leave it alone. But for that fragment of undigested potato, Scrooge would have had a perfectly pleasant holiday. Could anything be better, especially after the office party season, than a night-cap, a fourposter and a bowl of thin gruel?

What generally happens at Christmas is that everyone thinks they are sacrificing personal pleasure for everyone else's sake. Resentful martyrdom is as much to blame as bilious anticlimax for the upsets that ensure. Over the years I have kept a list of things one only ever hears said by people in funny hats, proffering crackers or wishbones:

'You've always hated me, haven't you? Ever since the day I was born.'

'Now now . . . we don't want old scores dug up at a time like this.'

'I never thought I'd hear words like that from my own daughter . . .'

'You've only been here five minutes, and you've upset everyone.'

'I'm only an old woman, and the sooner I'm dead the better . . .'

There are those who can wipe out Christmas in a single sentence, like the mother of a former girlfriend who welcomed us in to lunch with the words, 'There you are . . . from now on I'm on strike.' Or the terrible old gran in John Osborne's memoirs who, at five o'clock, would gather up all the Christmas paper, sigh deeply and say, 'Thank goodness *that's* over for another year.'

The wife of a friend of mine, having been on chronically bad terms with her in-laws, decided to make peace by having them over Christmas. She put on a magnificent lunch which her mother-in-law received without comment until the very end, when she nodded judicially and commented, 'Yes . . . I think we can give you back your stripes.'

During the Seventies I used to inure myself against Christmas by voluntarily spending it in the most unseasonal, implausible place possible. It became almost a tradition on *The Sunday Times Magazine* that in early December I would begin to trump up journalistic assignments in Bali or the Spanish Sahara. My sole criterion was that it must be at the very opposite end of the earth from pubs with log fires, horse-brasses, hunting horns and Stiltons on the bar.

Christmas Day in 1972 I spent in Calcutta, watching Indira Gandhi address the Indian Congress Party conference. The next year I got to Bali; the next, to Leningrad, on a package tour entirely made up of people running away from Christmas.

In 1975, apotheosis of my Yuletide masochism, I went to Lapland to meet the *real* Father Christmas. I spent three days on an icebound fell, looking out of my window like the Prisoner of Chillon. There were but two hours of light each day. The hotel staff had all left the premises to celebrate Christmas. The sole sign of life was in the yard outside the sauna hut, from which every few minutes a steaming pink figure would emerge with wild Finnish cries and roll flourily in the snow.

Eventually I threatened to complain to the Finnish government if I were not immediately introduced to Father Christmas. I was taken to a log house and shown an old man in a sage green pixie hood, slumped at a table and staring with almost homicidal boredom at a group of picturesquely-attired little children dancing ring-a-rosy round a heap of presents on the floor.

Father Christmas plainly was in the condition of nearly all Finns throughout their country's everlasting night. After a moment he rose unsteadily, picked up his sack and stumped outside to where his sleigh stood, hitched to a single tiny, shivering reindeer. At the first tug on its bridle, the reindeer jerked its head reluctantly. Whereupon Father Christmas got its head in a double arm-lock and half-dragged, half-carried it off into the fairytale maze of snow and conifers.

What changed my attitude to Christmas was living for two years in New York. Nothing previously recorded was in the same league for stomach-churning as that season they call 'the Hallidays' (which, among other things, decided me I could not love in a country where people cannot pronounce the letter 'o'). Such is the New Yorker's sincerity and attention-span that, quite early on Christmas night, people uptown are already putting out their trees for the garbage man.

Since coming home I am mellower about Christmas, as about so much else. Now when I see it coming, I just lie down and let it roll over me. Last week, I gave a coin to a busker playing White Christmas on an electric guitar in the Underground.

Benign as I am – Brownlow now, not Scrooge – I still fondly remember my final *Sunday Times* Atticus column, published 10 years ago this week and largely devoted to essays by readers on the subject The Worst Christmas I Have Ever Spent.

The outright winner had to be disqualified on the grounds that he *gave* a terrible Christmas rather than suffering one. That was the man who dressed his recently-amputated big toe up as a fairy and put it on top of his family's Christmas tree. During lunch, no one could understand why the dog was repeatedly sick and the cat kept scrambling up among the presents and the tinsel.

I can see that on Ryde Pier head, with those melancholy foghorns and drunken Trinity House pilots, I might have been rather fortunate.

And the World was made Horrid

Certain words, of outwardly innocent intent, fill me with paralysing gloom. For instance, 'welcome', as in placards that say 'Welcome to Waterloo Station'. When I am welcomed at Waterloo Station, I'm fairly sure it's going to be after some piffling cosmetic change which in the process will have reduced all genuinely welcoming aspects, like seats and washroom facilities, almost to zero.

In America, 'welcome' is still more deeply suspect, turning up as it does in contexts like 'Welcome to the Army', even 'Welcome to Tennessee State Penitentiary'.

Another word invested with deep gloom for me is 'hour'. As a trainee journalist, I used to have to report the gruesome weekly doings of something called The Vicar's Bright Hour. Similar heart-sinking despair engulfs me, contemplating 'Woman's Hour' or 'Children's Hour', or when I hear a BBC TV announcer say, with that ominous toothsome jollity, 'An hour of comedy now . . .'

Now, too, of course, we have Happy Hour, when yuppies sit around charlatan wine bars, furtively lusting after one another and looking miserable as sin.

So many once decent, explicit words have been bent and twisted into meaning their exact opposite. Merely reflect what we actually visualise when we talk of a football 'supporter'. Or a 'loyalist' in Ulster. Or a 'Christian' militia in Beirut.

When a trade union is said to be taking 'action', we know it is embarking on a period of destructive inaction. When action is said to be 'stepped up', we know inaction is about to grind down to atrophy.

Then there is the much-parroted 'Keep politics out of sport'. What that really means, is 'Keep morality out of business'.

The nastiest deception curled up in a single word that I ever met was 'emergency', as used in Emergency Income Tax. When I drew my first-ever pay packet, I was told it had been subject to Emergency Tax, which had a rather comforting sound, like being given a hot drink and told not to worry. Little did I know that 'Emergency' referred to the Inland Revenue's ungovernably frantic desire to take away virtually all my pathetic three pounds, fifteen shillings.

Under our present glorious Prime Minister, language has been twisted and inverted to a degree George Orwell scarcely envisioned. 'Strong' government means toadying to America and frantically selling off every public asset in sight. 'Caring' government means Mrs Edwina Currie. Those in Cabinet who show the smallest trace of backbone by objecting go down in history ignominiously as 'wets'.

Indeed, in Mrs Thatcher-speak, it is Britain's whole headlong slide into meanness, pettiness, half-wit chauvinism and reptilian greed that tells us we are 'great' again.

Some years ago, as a colour magazine journalist, I interviewed Michael Jackson on the beach at Malibu. He seemed a nice, straightforward, happy little boy. I shudder to think what's happened to him since.

Not content with keeping a permanent suite at Disney World and trying to buy the Elephant Man's carcass as an ornament, he now seems to be bombarding learned medical institutions with multi-million dollar offers for the nastier things in their black museums. What can he get up to in his little candy-coloured bedroom overlooking Snow White's castle?

An English actor playing on Broadway recently received a backstage visit from Michael. 'Loved the show,' he said. 'I wanted to bring Bobo, but he couldn't come. Still, I'd love you to meet him. Why don't you come to my hotel. I know Bobo'd love to see you.'

So the honoured actor went with Michael to meet Bobo, who turned out to be a chimpanzee.

Absolute Baloney

Just one throwaway line of dialogue in *Absolute Beginners* shows its authentic Fifties atmosphere to be counterfeit. When Suzette meets Colin at their Soho coffee dive rendezvous, she leans over the transparent espresso cups and tells him, 'I can't make it for dinner tonight.'

Absolute baloney! No working-class boy and girl circa 1958 would ever make plans for dinner. They would each have had their high tea before they went out. Later, to prolong the coffee bar vigil, they might order a hamburger or buy fish and chips to eat on the top deck of the bus home.

'Dinner' in the late Fifties was still something the majority of British people took at 1 p.m. It did not replace tea in the general vocabulary for at least another 10 years. The silly scriptwriters have their Fifties teenagers speaking in the idiom of early Seventies Artisan Chic.

'Absolute Beginners', to be fair, was scripted by a committee of amateurs working under hideous transatlantic pressure. But howlers in alleged period dialogue can be as easily committed by masters, working without constraint. Dennis Potter's 'Dreamchild' has little Alice Liddell speaking in mid-Victorian dialogue so bogus one can practically see the lines of word processor type.

At one point, Alice is overheard giggling in the schoolroom with her sister over what might seem a wonderfully observed bit of Victorian governess lore. 'Don't say "don't",' she insists hilariously. 'It's not good manners.' The line is thought so much of, it recurs through the film as part of Charles Dodgson's erotic reverie.

Total piffle, Potter! 'Don't' was perfectly good manners to genteel Victorians, if used in a foppy, Prince Regent-ish manner, viz: 'He don't care for it', or W. S. Gilbert's 'Every fairy shall die who don't marry a mortal'. Everyone has been falling about because Suzette in 'Absolute Beginners' invented the mini-skirt about eight years too early. I found it more ludicrous, in this alleged Potter masterwork, that a mid-Victorian little girl, apotheosis of her type, had short hair, cut, shaped and fringed à la Vidal Sassoon.

Period anachronisms in old Hollywood movies can be enjoyed for their own ingenuous sake. I treasure the memory of Jack Palance as Attila the Hun, urging on his wild hordes and showing all the fillings in his teeth. Or Alan Ladd as a medieval swineherd saying to a wondering friar: 'This Christianity – can anyone join?' Or, the moving coda to 'Quo Vadis'?: 'If you folks ever get to the Land of Canaan, be sure and look us up.'

The worst bungles occur when scenarists try to write in the Victorian idiom – the process which, they believe, can be achieved merely by the use of long, unfamiliar words. There is now a recognisable Victorian parody language, invented by Harold Pinter for 'The French Lieutenant's Woman', raging on pub signs or Phileas Fogg tortilla chip packets. I have here a classic example, from the side of a box of Country House herbal bath sachets:

'After an arduous day supervising the running of the great house, the Mistress would retire to her room to prepare herself for the formalities of the evening. At this juncture, the prudent lady's maid would pour a copious bath in which she would steep various relaxing and softening herbs to induce a sense of ease and encouragement.'

It is a rare scriptwriter who understands that Victorians spoke a dense mixture of slang, shorthand and allusion, just as we do ourselves. John Hawkesworth was such a shining exception in his early TV dramas. Victorian society women, for instance, said 'deevy' when they meant divine. Not that every such detail could be picked up, even by me. A good script is like the double bass in a band. You need not notice it, but you always know it's there.

Still less attention is paid to the question of accent in period. Even 25 years ago people spoke with quite different voices, aspiring to upper classedness as generally as our voices now do to classlessness. Before the Second World War, everyone on £1000 a year and above tried to speak like royalty. That recent (and unquestionably loving) TV recreation of Elizabeth Bowen's 'Death of the Heart' foundered because both its junior leads played their 1938 characters in the tone of 1980s youth – dropping 'g's and 't's from word ends, turning 'ou' vowels into 'ew'. The proper Bowen voices would have been as closely clipped and taut as topiary hedges.

In 'Dance with a Stranger', Miranda Richardson got precisely the right vulgar-refined mid-Fifties nightclub voice for her portrayal of Ruth Ellis. The more I see on film and television, the more I wish I were watching Miranda Richardson.

Rocker of Ages

My one and only sight of Little Richard onstage was at Wembley Stadium in 1972, when he appeared in the Foulk Brothers' Rock 'n' Roll Revival Jamboree with Chuck Berry, Bill Haley and Jerry Lee Lewis. It was an event richly illustrating the whims and caprices of rock 'n' roll giants. Chuck Berry refused to perform until he had received £30 in cash to cover bank charges on the cheque for his fee. With £30 in his hand, half-way to the stage, he stopped again. 'Supposing the limo' doesn't pick me up tomorrow morning,' he said. 'I'll have to pay for my own cab out to the airport. Give me another thirty pounds.'

With Little Richard, the difficulty was more cerebral. He believed that someone in the audience was out to assassinate him, and so refused to appear until after the sun had gone down. 'It's gone down now, Richard', the promoters kept shouting untruthfully through his locked door. At last he consented to walk onstage, dressed in a yellow suit sewn with tiny mirrors, and accompanied by two black bodyguards who had evidently been having some private disagreement. As the Wembley crowd roared for Richard, one bodyguard sprang on the other and their two suède maxicoats rolled together, grappling, towards the footlights.

The sound system was chaotic but it hardly mattered, this being an occasion – back in what Richard now calls his 'slippin and slidin' years – when he would do nothing for his fans but shout 'I am King!' and take off his clothes, deaf to boos, catcalls and pleas for 'Tutti Frutti'. Rock's great primal scream had apparently vanished into clouds of megalomania purer than the cocaine he gourmandised. At some concerts he would appear in a crown and ermine robes, attended by *ersatz* Grenadier Guardsmen. Flunkeys used to carry him round on a litter, kohl-eyed, bejewelled, gracious and horrible. The accepted form of greeting from servants and admirers was to kneel and kiss his foot.

The excesses were ludicrous but, in a way, understandable. More than any other founding rock 'n' roll star, Little Richard had to struggle to surpass the shock of his first arrival. What could ever surpass that unearthly pair of lungs, bellowing 'Long Tall Sally' or 'Rip It Up' from the wobbly plastic turntable of a £15 Dansette? What could surpass the spectacle of Little Richard in 'The Girl Can't Help It' in 1957, a crazed urchin with a shock of hair like wet liquorice, shrieking the title song to the Pygmalionis-ation of Jayne Mansfield? What could possibly surpass a white drape suit, a piano keyboard played with the heel, or the sheer idiot joy of that phrase (or is it ejaculation?) 'Awop-Bop-a-Loo-Bop Alop-Bam-Boom'?

I met Little Richard by accident last October, on a 40-minute shuttle flight from Philadelphia to Washington. Sitting in the departure lounge, I watched a fretful black man in white trousers wander unsteadily up and down, followed by a silent black boy with a plastic suit-bag. As he passed me the third time, I recognized the almond eyes, the manic cheek dimples, the Clara Bow mouth with its slippery little toothbrush moustache. He smiled at me in the same instant and murmured 'How you doin'?' I boarded the plane with the expression I always wear remembering the intro to 'Good Golly Miss Molly' – a lop-sided, silly grin.

Little Richard chose the seat across the aisle from mine. He then went forward – it was a very small plane – and opened the cockpit-door. 'Hi, I'm Little Richard . . .' I heard the lisping voice say to the pilot and co-pilot. He returned to his place and sank down in a state of visible terror, mopping at his brow with paper handkerchieves. 'Man, I hate these things,' he murmured. As the engines started, Little Richard looked Lucille-wild and exclaimed 'Lawd have *mercy*!'

It emerged that he was on the road, not to make yet another comeback but merely to do press and TV interviews about his forthcoming autobiography, 'The Life and Times of Little Richard'. I saw him on Washington local TV later that night, still in the white trousers, telling what is, to American ears, a familiar hard luck story.

'See, I was the first to do the flamboyant type of singin'. Ever'body who got big, I mean *big*, in the business all took something from me. Elvis Presley. Buddy Holly. Everly Brothers. The Beatles was *my* group. They played with me over in Liverpool, England. The Rollin' Stones was *my* group. James Brown worked for me. Jimi Hendrix worked for me. Billy Preston . . . I showed 'em all the way. So many big stars up there now is up there 'cause of me. Only, I ain't got all the millions they got and the big, fine houses they got. I ain't even got the money folks owe me for the songs I wrote. I'm not bitter, though. I wish 'em all joy of it. 'Cause what I got from my career was Jesus Christ the Lord. I had to go through rock 'n' roll to find the Rock of Ages.'

If 'The Life and Times of Little Richard' were not a fascinating autobiography, it would still testify to an influence over pop music and style that even its author cannot exaggerate. Paul McCartney contributes a foreword recalling that his first ever performance to an audience, in 1957, was singing 'Long Tall Sally' at a Butlins holiday camp. Sixties and seventies superstars, among them David Bowie, Paul Simon, Smokey Robinson and Bette Midler, fill an entire glossary with their accolades. Even Mick Jagger, nonpareil among egotists, readily acknowledges on the front cover that 'Little Richard is King.' If these names seem to constitute too old a pop generation, look at the photographs of Richard in the late sixties. Do the pompadour and Beau Brummel frills seem at all familiar to teenage fans of Prince?

Little Richard's life story, however, is only secondarily that of an aural anarchist. It is primarily the story of a bizarre human being, bizarrely cursed and blessed; told (to his English disciple Charles White) with the total honesty that is the only true measure of charm.

Ricardo Wayne Penniman was born on December 5, 1938, in a poor black suburb of Macon, Georgia. His father, Bud Penniman, was a stonemason whose spare time activities as a bootlegger frequently brought police into the house, tearing off the bedclothes of Bud's 10 children to see if he had hidden his moonshine whisky there. Bud Penniman's industry, however, bought his family what were considered luxuries for black people so far below the Mason-Dixon Line. Richard – as the local white registrar decided he had better be called – was an extrovert almost from babyhood.

'My mother had all these kids, and I was the only one born deformed. My right leg is shorter than the left. The other kids didn't realize I was crippled. They thought I was trying to twist and walk funny. But I had to take short steps 'cause I had a little leg. I used to walk with odd strides, like long-short, long-short. The kids would call me faggot, sissy, freak, punk. They called me everything.

'I was always singing, even as a little boy, or I'd beat the steps in front of our house and sing to that. You'd hear people singing all the time. The women would be singing outside in the back, doing their washing, rubbing on the rub-boards. There'd be guitar players playing on the street – Old Slim, Willie Amos and my cousin, Buddy Penniman. I remember Bamalama, this feller with one eye who played the washboard with a thimble. He had a bell like the schoolteacher, and he'd sing "Abamalama, you shall be free, and in the morning you shall be free . . ."

'See, I was raised in prejudice. In Macon, black people weren't allowed into most public places, the same as in South Africa today. There were signs on the water fountains, "coloured" and "white". The white fountain would be electric and have cool water. The black one would be rusted, 12 or 15 years old, no cooling. Just an old thing. You mother and father didn't want no trouble, so they used to tell you your place and how to stay out of trouble.

'We used to have a group called the Penniman Singers, all of us, the whole family. We used to go around and sing in all the churches and we sang in contests with other family groups in what they called the Battle of the Gospels. Right from a boy I wanted to be a preacher. I wanted to be like Brother Joe May, the singing evangelist, who they called The Thunderbolt of the West.

'I always loved Mother more than Daddy. I loved her so much, I idolised her. I used to just love it when she put powder on her face. I used to watch her, and later I'd sneak into her bedroom and sit there, putting rosewater and stuff on myself. I just felt I wanted to be a girl more than a boy. Daddy would get real mad at me. He'd say, "My father had seven sons and I wanted seven sons. You spoiled it. You're only half a son". And then he'd hit me.

'My first homosexual experience was with a friend of my family who the local gay people called Madam Oop. He worked on the railroad. He'd tell you he had a vagina and if you'd be nice he'd let you get some of it. Some white men would pick me up in their cars and take me to the woods and try to get me to suck them. A whole lot of black people have had to do that. It was a sickening thing to me. I was scared.'

At the age of 14, he ran away and joined a medicine show, selling snake oil to the gullible at carnivals and county fairs. He sang with itinerant bands and minstrel troupes round the 'Chittlin' Circuit' of segretated black dance halls, and in Atlanta's gay red light district. They called him Little Richard because he was, indeed, just a child. He learned to dress in wild colours from a singer called Billy Wright and to pound the piano from a crazed boogie-woogie wizard named Esquerita. When he was 18, his father was shot to death in a Macon bar after ordering the local bully not to put firecrackers into the stove. Richard returned home to support his family, and took a job as a dish-washer at the Macon Greyhound bus station.

In 1955, aged 22, he wheedled a recording session in Hollywood for Art Rupe's Specialty label – named after the 'race' or 'specialty' music then considered too indecent for white people's ears. A classically trained musician, Robert 'Bumps' Blackwell, was given the job of producing the outlandish youth with his marcel-waved hair and a shirt, Blackwell recalls, 'that looked as if he had drunk raspberry juice, cherryade, malt and greens and then thrown up all over himself.'

The session featured conventional rhythm and blues songs, and was uninspired until Richard started hammering the piano and singing a lewd ditty from his gay repertoire. 'Tutti Frutti/Good booty/If it don't fit/Don't force it . . .' Blackwell, recognising gold dust, brought in a girl named Dorothy La Bostrie to write some clean lyrics. The opening line was lightly amended from its original to "Awop-Bo-a-Loo-Bop A-Good-Goddam.'

'Tutti Frutti' was a hit for Little Richard first only on the black R & B chart. White rock 'n' rollers, Elvis Presley and the anodyne Pat Boone, both released more successful 'cover versions'. His next release, 'Long Tall Sally', co-written with Blackwell, was deliberately in a tempo too fast for any white boy to manage. In February 1956, 'Long Tall Sally' reached the top of the American national charts. It was the end of apartheid in music.

In the dizzy speedball ride of mid-fifties rock, no newly-arisen god was louder, wilder or more fatally upsetting to teenage glands. Little Richard concerts unleashed displays of sexual dementia that even Elvis Presley could not. As he sang, he would be bombarded with girls' panties, nude photographs, pornographic drawings, telephone numbers. Mayors and police chiefs across America shut down his shows for indecency. Other great music extroverts like Chuck Berry and Jerry Lee Lewis admitted they learned their stagecraft from standing and watching him. His songs were covered, but never bettered, by Presley, Bill Haley, Buddy Holly, the Everly Brothers.

His offstage life was a whirl of Cadillacs, pink suits, curling-tongs and sex with any partner in any possible or implausible position. He encouraged his girl friend, a stripper named Angel with a 50-inch bust, to have sex with other musicians in front of him. He was famous in the touring package shows for being able to masturbate seven or eight times a day. 'I'd feel bad after I did it, though. I'd think "Why did you do it. You crazy? You could have . . ." Most gay people fall in love with themselves.'

He was notoriously improvident with the thousands of dollars he earned. Bobby Byrd, of James Brown's Famous Flames, remembers: 'We were stranded in New Jersey once. We asked Richard for a loan. He opened the trunk of his car, reached in and scooped out a handful of dollars without even looking. The trunk was *full* of loose notes.'

In 1957, he was visited by Brother Wilbur Gulley, a missionary for the Church of God of the Ten Commandments. Shortly afterwards, playing an open air concert in Australia, he saw the Russian Sputnik shoot through the heavens, and interpreted it as a summons from the Almighty. Next day, he announced his retirement to his band by throwing a diamond ring into Sydney harbour. He cancelled his tour, returned to America and enrolled at theological college in Huntsville, Alabama.

During the next five years, his fortunes steadily sank. The church he had chosen rejected him because of his homosexuality. He abandoned his studies, made a disastrous marriage, was beaten up by police for loitering in men's lavatories. He refused to sing anything but gospel music – which he did with a power and conviction that impressed even Mahalia Jackson. But he was still the same old Richard. He would keep a full gospel choir waiting for 10 hours, then calmly announce, 'The Lord doesn't want me to sing today.'

Rock 'n' roll had all but died out in America, thanks to establishment disapproval and the furore over disc jockey payola. British ravers however, stayed true to all their gods. In 1962, a London promoter named Don Arden offered Richard a comeback tour with Sam Cooke and the 16 year-old Billy Preston. Richard accepted, stipulating he would sing only gospel. Rumours of his piety grew so alarming that Don Arden had to take out newspaper ads promising the fans that Little Richard would be doing all his old hits. Fortunately for Arden, Sam Cooke also knew how to tear up an audience. When he saw Cooke's show, Richard could not resist the challenge of going one better.

During the tour, a young northern impresario named Brian Epstein had the idea of promoting a Little Richard show to draw attention to the group he had just discovered in a Liverpool dive. Richard was induced to appear at the Tower Ballroom,

New Brighton, with Epstein's discovery, the Beatles, as support-
ing attraction. The Liverpool boys were at first too thrilled by
the presence of their idol even to go near him. Paul McCartney's
brother photographed Richard from one side of the stage while
the Beatles stood on the other side, all trying to squeeze into the
shot.

His infatuation with Brian Epstein brought Richard back to
Merseyside for two more concerts with the Beatles. At one
point, Epstein offered him a share in them if he would take
tapes of their early songs back to his record company in America.
'They hadn't any money,' Richard says, 'so I used to pay for
their food. I used to buy steaks for John. Paul would come in,
sit down and just look at me. Like he wouldn't move his eyes.
And he'd say 'Richard, you're my idol. Just let me touch you.'
He wanted to learn my little holler, so we sat at the piano going
'Ooo, ooh' till he got it."

A year later, Don Arden persuaded Richard to tour England
again, headlining over Bo Diddley and the Everly Brothers. At
the bottom of the bill were a group of surly R & B purists
called the Rolling Stones. Their vocalist, a self-conscious ex-
student, stood in the wings each night, absorbing Little Richard
into the mimic's patchwork that would soon become Mick
Jagger. To this day Keith Richards says 'The most exciting
moment of my life was appearing on the same stage as Little
Richard.'

For the rest of the sixties, he laboured with only partial
success to make an American comeback, billing himself as 'The
Bronze Liberace' or 'The Living Flame', spending fortunes on
costumes and stage effects, playing any kind of venue from
shabby Midwest cocktail lounges to Las Vegas megahotels.
Bumps Blackwell was ditched in favour of younger record
producers with misguided notions about bringing Little Richard
'up to date'. Nothing he tried – not even re-hiring Bumps –
could bring back that first giddy run of hit records. Yet no one,
through the sunburst eras of soul funk and acid rock, ever
thought they could ever hold a candle to Little Richard before
an audience. He upstaged Janis Joplin, Ike and Tina Turner,

Jerry Lee Lewis, John and Yoko at the Toronto Peace Festival.
In an average show he would sweat off six pounds in weight.
Between sets he gulped salt pills 'to stop dehydration' and bottled
oxygen, to slow down his heart.

The singer who had opened the pop market to black artists
now, ironically, found himself criticized for not declaring solidarity with the black political movements. '*People* were always
important to me, whatever colour they were. When I would go
to Madison Square Garden, I would have about thirty-five
thousand whites and about fifty black people in the audience.
But it didn't make me no difference. A scream and a holler's a
holler to me. I just love 'em.'

In the early seventies, finally, the excesses began to tell. The
makeup, and megalomania, grew thicker. He became alcoholic
and acquired a $1000-a-day cocaine habit. Returning to England
after the Wembley Stadium *débacle*, he was nailed by the Inland
Revenue for alleged non-payment of tax on his fee. Rumours
got about that he had cancer of the stomach. His sex and drug
orgies began to dismay even his most mindless companions on
the road. The 'downs' after his cocaine sprees made him moody,
paranoid, sometimes violent. He would lock himself in an hotel
room all day, brooding and mumbling alone until it was time to
leave for the concert. 'Every time I blew my nose, there was
flesh and blood on the handkerchief, where the cocain had eaten
away the membranes.'

One day, as he was flying off for an appearance in Miami, his
brother Tony asked him for $200 to buy a station wagon.
Richard said he would send the money on. He spent that night
licking cocaine from a groupie's naked body. The next morning,
he was told that Tony had died of a heart attack. There and
then, Richard quit the music business for the second time and
for the second time resolved to find God. He was next heard of
in 1977, when he turned up as a travelling salesman for the
Black Heritage Bible Company.

The second conversion proved a lasting one. Since 1979,
Little Richard has worked as an evangelist, preaching the parable
of his own redemption to congregations almost as spellbound as

those which once bopped to 'Lucille'. No longer a drug-user or a homosexual, he believes God's rewards to him have even included 'a different walk'. Between crusades he lives quietly in Riverside, California, still grief-stricken by the recent death of his mother, Leva Mae Penniman; still breaking into occasional protest about all the millions his music earned for other poeple. A TV news programme recently showed him with a striker's placard, picketing the office of the music publisher he claims to be his biggest debtor in back royalties. The TV reporter held up a microphone tolerantly for that familiar hard luck story. 'The Beatles was *my* group. The Rollin' Stones was *my* group. I showed them the way. James Brown worked for me. And Jimi Hendrix . . .'

Earlier this year, a late night TV talk show persuaded him to come on and do a gospel number with Staple Singers. There was Pop Staple, like an elegant old pew-opener, with his opulent daughters. And there, as of old, were the headlamp eyes, the manic dimples, the Clara Bow mouth, the tooth-brush moustache, and the roaring artistry. No one ever got it more right about Little Richard than Little Richard himself. 'My music can make your liver quiver, your bladder spatter, your knees freeze. And your big toe shoot up in your boot!'

Adsturbation – It Makes you Just As Blind

You've probably seen the latest British Telecom posters on the Underground. They feature a series of American showbiz names including George Burns and that woman with the peroxide and acne from 'Hill Street Blues'. Each has a jokey monologue by the celebrity about British Telecom, which you can read as you wait for your train.

The purpose is to show what a fun crowd they all are at British Telecom. The effect is to make one, even more than yesterday, hate their blasted guts.

The traditional purpose of advertisements is to persuade people to choose this or that product over its competitor. But as we know (to our ever-increasing cost) British Telecom have no real competitors. Their strangle-hold, arm-lock and double Nelson on the ordinary telephone-user could not be bettered by Jackie Pallo or Giant Haystacks.

So what are these glossy, expensive Tube ads telling us? That there are such things as telephones. That you can ring people up on them, in or outside Britain. That British Telecom have got your money and don't care to what ludicrous lengths they go in squandering it.

There are many such effusions currently to be seen both on billboards and television – not advertising so much as adsturbation.

You doubtless have noticed the television ad for electricity. The budget of a small feature film has been expended to remind us all how wonderful electricity is, how it powers both industry and homes, and what a sorry pickle Britain would be in without it.

To get the full effect, a certain amnesia is necessary. One must forget that electricity has been in general use, powering industry and homes, for something over 100 years. And also that, when regarded as a normal element of life rather than an ad agency's meal-ticket and a film director's ego trip, it was massively less expensive to the consumer.

For sheer pointlessness allied to mind-boggling expense, the prize must go to a new TV ad extolling The British Airports Authority.

This is adsturbation aspiring to soap opera. Three men and a woman, in 1940s aviation kit, are shown walking through a postwar wilderness of mud and Nissen huts. 'Some day,' their leader, a Biggles-like figure, tells them, 'all this will be a great international airport.' And lo! the glories of Heathrow take shape before their eyes.

I am as open to such suggestion as anyone. I would gladly change my brand of airport authority if someone would please tell me how to do it. I'm ready to accept George Burns – the entire Hill Street precinct-house – as mascots for British Telecom phones, if the damned things would only learn how to work.

But, of course, adsturbation has almost nothing to do with me or you. It is principally about guiltily large corporate profits and chief executives who think they ought to call a meeting after lunch. It is about advertising men in pink socks earning vast salaries for thinking up puns that would disgrace a 10-year-old child. Above all, it is about the great British art of adding insult to injury.

There are signs that the public may be getting wise at last. The British Gas 'Tell Sid' campaign provoked audible revulsion, within the ad business as well as outside. And indeed, for prodigal extravagance and bowel-shrivelling feebleness, it probably represented the nadir.

At the time, having written as much, I was invited on to Robert Kilroy-Silk's 'Day To Day' programme to confront the two 'creative' people responsible. They proved to be a girl in a hat and a youth in blue denim. Neither could tell me who 'Sid' was, whether it had been a joke or not a joke. Altogether,

worthy stewards of a campaign budget cautiously estimated at
£18 million.

'Tell Sid' came from the agency Young and Rubicam, lately
awarded the multi-million pound account to promote British
Gas heating. Look for more garbage soon on the subway wall.

Mother's Day At Hollywood Park

The week I was to meet my mother in Los Angeles, my landlord in New York commenced proceedings to evict me. This is quite common in New York and it was ultimately no cause for alarm; still, there were things I could have been doing more usefully than sitting in TWA Business Class, heading over the Grand Canyon to the City of the Angels.

My mother's foreign travels come about mainly through an organization called The Racegoers' Club. Under its auspices, people who enjoy racing or betting – or both, as in my mother's case – can go to race meetings in exotic countries, visit stud farms, meet trainers and owners and, often, enjoy handsome hospitality from the freemasonry of the turf.

This present trip was to Hollywood Park races to see the $3 million Breeders Cup – an event which the *Sports Illustrated* in my lawyer's waiting-room described as 'an equine Olympics Superbowl'. 'There are some wonderful horses in it,' my mother said over the transatlantic phone, and I thought I could hear her reaching for the form book. 'Don't tell me now,' I said hastily. 'Wait until I see you.'

At the LA Downtown Hilton, I was met by my mother's great friend Joan, a woman whose sticky meringues are among the fonder memories of my boyhood. 'Mum's not feeling too good,' Joan said, guiding me through the uproar of Japanese package tourists. 'Bit of tummy trouble. It came on yesterday while we were in Las Vegas.' She added that it had not deterred my mother from spending eight continuous hours at roulette, blackjack and other games of chance.

Upstairs in their double room, I found my mother looking wan but resolute. She said her stomach upset was all the fault of some 'fishy orange juice' sent up by room service. I suggested she would feel much better if she stopped saying and thinking the words 'fishy orange juice'.

'It was definitely fishy, wasn't it Joan?' my mother replied. 'It was orange juice with a fishy taste.'

I decided to say nothing about my impending eviction. One's mother does not come stateside to hear such dreary news. I settled her down with Pepto-Bismol, Perrier and the form book, and went off to telephone my lawyer.

The fishy orange juice, mercifully, was dispelled by two good nights sleep and a weekend promising to satisfy even my mother's appetite for glamour. On both days of the Breeders Cup meeting, the Racegoers were to be entertained in a brand new VIP enclosure called 'The Pavilion of the Stars'. My visit being so short, special dispensation was given for me to spend the first day with them there. 'Only, darling . . .' Joan said tactfully. 'You'll have to wear a tie.' For the thrill of rubbing elbows with Fred Astaire, Paul Newman and Daryl F. Zanuck at the paddock-rail, it seemed the least I could do.

Afterwards, we had been invited to visit an old friend of my mother's in Westwood. The difficulty was that the Racegoers' bus would not be passing near Westwood on its way back to their hotel.

'Don't worry,' I said. 'We'll go on to Julia's from the racetrack by cab.'

'You said there weren't any cabs in Los Angeles,' my mother objected.

'Not on the *street*,' I said, 'but one can always phone for them.'

'Where will you phone from?' my mother demanded.

'This is America,' I said patiently. 'There are telephones *everywhere*.'

On the bus journey to Hollywood Park, we sat with a baronet. He was quite young, very rubicund and extremely attentive, though whether to my mother or Joan in particular, one could not be absolutely sure. If it were the former, I hoped he did not make the mistake of thinking her wealthy and susceptible.

We had, rather naturally, supposed the Pavilion of the Stars to be a pavilion frequented by stars. It was in fact a pink concrete hangar fronted by clear plastic that excluded all sound from the course, and situated about a quarter of a mile on the wrong side of the finish-post. Despite the dire warnings about dress on my gold-embossed admission-card, there were men sitting all around us in cowboy hats, jeans or checked Bermuda shorts.

'It's a right rip-off,' my mother observed with her usual point-fulness.

We watched the nine races in an atmosphere as stimulating as that of a Boeing 747. From time to time, we trekked to the winners' enclosure, through a far more appealing non-VIP grandstand, full of fast food stands and Pat Hobbyish bad characters. My mother formed a belief that the endmost clerk at the Off Track Betting counter had a lucky face, and with his help managed to finish up $20 or so in profit. The baronet sat with us, excusing himself intermittently for what he called 'a reccy'.

At 6 p.m., the Racegoers adjourned two levels up for a rather grudging cocktail party. After half an hour, I went outside to phone for our taxi to Westwood. Only now did I discover that, though there may be telephones every few inches throughout the rest of America, there are, for some obscure ethical reason, no telephones whatever in the precincts of the Hollywood Park racetrack.

I further discovered I was locked out of the Pavilion of the Stars. Everyone else had left the track; the forecourt and car parks were deserted. Rattling one rigid glass door after another, I remembered I ought to be 5,000 miles to the east of here, fighting eviction.

I finally got back inside with a cleaner through a service-door, pounded up the four escalators to the cocktail party and, with some difficulty, prised my mother and Joan away from their plastic beakers of gin. 'I can see a hotel across the car park,' I said. 'We'll walk across and phone for a cab from there.'

'Brian's coming with us,' my mother said, indicating the baronet.

In America – and especially California – never suppose anything you can see to be within walking distance. The car park merely took us into another car park, twice as enormous. Our progress was slow owing to the vulnerability of my mother's hair-do and the mirth into which her friend Joan frequently dissolved. To me, in my agitation, the two of them seemed like those little plastic figures one had as a child, that would walk unsteadily down a gentle slope. One or the other was always wobbling off in the wrong direction. '*Please*,' I entreated. 'Watch out for the potholes.' Back in New York, US marshals were probably breaking in and impounding my furniture.

We finally reached a busy highway which showed the hotel to be a mile or so further on than I'd estimated. Across the highway, I spotted a neon sign reading 'Leroy's Cocktails & Grill'. Depositing my mother, Joan and the baronet on a roadside bench, and forbidding them to wobble off anywhere, I plunged into Leroy's Cocktails & Grill to beg use of a telephone.

I found myself in a Stygian wilderness of latticed disco light and juddering bass music. Around the bar sat a dozen of the biggest, most frightening black men I had ever seen. 'Hey, honky . . .' several voices growled. While telephoning I judged it wise, both for politeness and safety, not to turn my back on the company.

I emerged from Leroy's intact, and rejoined my mother, Joan and the baronet on their bench.

'I've managed to call a cab,' I panted. 'It'll be here in ten minutes.'

My mother looked at Leroy's Cocktails & Grill with an expression I can only describe as petulant.

'Oh . . .' she said. 'Can't we wait in the cocktail bar?'

This story has a happy ending. I refused to let my mother wait in the cocktail bar. Our cab did come. We reached our friend's in Westwood. I was not evicted. The baronet did not press his suit. It remained quite crumpled when, three days later, he, my mother and Joan, with their form book and Scrabble board, jetted onward to Hawaii.

My New York Bower

The first artist's loft I rented in New York was a grimy industrial space above a cobbled rat-run for Tropicana orange juice trucks to and from the Holland Tunnel. This time, I have been far luckier. Bob and Eve's loft is light, clean, airy and hung with just enough of their respective painting and photography. From a purely status angle, it does have one disadvantage. It is on The Bowery.

Directly across the street is the Fulton Hotel, 'for transients', where luckier down-and-outs can spend the day, feet propped along the serried window-ledges. 'It's a dollar a night,' Eve said.

'No – it's more now,' Bob said. 'It went up to a dollar and a quarter.'

'We once saw someone try to commit suicide from the roof,' Eve said. 'This man was standing on the top ledge there, swaying to and fro. The police brought enormous inflatable cushions to break his fall. People crowded round, not to see the man on the ledge but to watch the police bouncing around on these pillows.'

'. . . and there'll probably be a fire,' Bob continued.

'Expect a fire at least once a month,' Eve concurred. 'There was one recently in the hardware store right below us. I went to the owner's wife and said "I'm sorry to hear you had a fire." "Oh, never mind that." she said . . . I guess she couldn't have been that unhappy about it,' Eve added with a guffaw and a wink.

Even Skid Row is getting gentrified, its human flotsam squeezed into even smaller pockets by the encroaching, unstoppable industry of Chinatown. On the corner, where a man lies all day like a corpse in Vietnam, Chinese and Italians use the same bank, with multilingual cash-dispenser, to pay in their wealth from the restaurant and garment trades. Further along is a lighting showroom, currently throwing reject stock out onto the pavement. 'People come from uptown in BMW's and Audis, just to grab the stuff,' Bob said. 'Rich people picking over garbage on The Bowery!'

Americans are far better than we at making sub-tenants feel instantly at home. While I am here, I have free run of Eve's art books, Bob's electric guitar, their drop-handled bike (for getting to Farmer's Market at Union Square on Sunday), their Thermos mugs, sunglasses and umbrellas. Bob has thoughtfully left me a small transparent packet of what I take to be herbal tobacco. There is also a South American hammock that can stretch right across the main room. 'Shall I tell you how to get *really* cool?' Eve said. 'Bring the big fan up close and lie in the hammock with a tray of ice cubes on your stomach.'

'You may see the occasional roach,' Bob said. 'Or the occasional mouse.' He made it sound no worse than an occasional table.

One block north is Grand Street, beginning as Chinatown, then melting into the pastry and espresso scent of Little Italy. My local shops are Di Palo, the world's best for cheese, Alleva for smoked mozzarella and prosciutto bread, and Piedmonte, for home-made pasta shells. I can walk to Umberto's Clam House, a no-hope place until a well-known Mafioso was shot there, since when it has had queues every night.

To the south are Canal Street's flea markets, Chinatown proper (where the police's 'Jade Squad' are out in force after a spate of Tong slayings) not to mention wacky TriBeCa haunts like Area, a disco club whose decor changes completely every month, and a new eaterie, highly recommended, name Exterminator Chili.

I shall, of course, exercise constant vigilance, always look where I'm going, carry a ritual $20 dollars in my wallet for muggers and come in through the street door at night with the dispatch of an SAS man. I shall also, in this ultimate city, paradoxically become a beachcomber, wear little but shorts and T-shirts from the Canal Jean Company, jog without attracting ridicule, and eat hot dogs and ice cream outdoors as if I am on the prom at Shanklin.

Two flights up, a vertical iron ladder leads to the roof. You can see right uptown to the Empire State; across to the World Trade Center in one direction and Confucious Plaza, the massive Chinese tower block, in the other. You can see turrets and cupolas of wonderful New York Victorian follies, and the frontier-looking black water towers that seem to be expecting Apache attacks from the sky. Eve has made a garden, with morning glory and sunflowers nodding in the sweltered breeze of laundering and noodle-cooking from the street below.

Bob and Eve have left helpful tips about where to buy 'French heros', how to find the Chinese store that sells every known European beer, and which subway line to take to Far Rockaway. ('Great beach. Empty. Big waves. You'll need no. 6 suntan lotion.') And one quite unlooked-for Bowery bonus: 'Mint on rooftop is for your Pimms.'

I awaken under pleasant gusts from the big propellor fan, to the sound of Norm N. Knight on CBS-FM. After coffee, I undo the front door locks, ascend two flights, raise a trapdoor and scale the dodgy iron ladder to water my landlords' roof garden. To my left, the World Trade Center winks and shimmers in its oddly comforting way. An enormous bumble bee makes palpitant love to a bending sunflower. I remember this is The Bowery only when I pick up a plastic jerrycan full of water, and it falls to pieces in my hands.

Skid Row, as usual at morning, is like the aftermath of war. The garbage is not merely deep, but trampled and pulverized. A burned-black derelict teeters along the yellow line in the middle of the road, insensible to traffic shrieks. A grizzled ancient, curled in the next doorway, wears a T-shirt inscribed 'Boston Yacht Club'. Not all The Bowery's bums lie prostrate at this hour. Some sit on rickety chairs in attitudes suggesting intense philosophical rumination.

Along Canal Street, the Chinese boys are hammering beds of
crushed ice flat with wooden blocks, arranging huge roseate fish
bodies, dragging out tubs of lobsters with claws tipped scarlet
like courtesans' nails. I avert my eyes from shop window tanks
of carp and turtles, and find myself looking straight into a truck
loaded with live pullets, pheasants, quail and white rabbits.
Chinatown knows no set mealtimes. At barely 9 am, all the
restaurants on Bayard and Lafayette are open and busy.

The only New Yorkers I have ever envied are the old people
one sees in Chinatown, floating through the market uproar on
ebony sticks and little, careful feet. Their faces are as clear and
calm as sleeping babies'. You know that, with such families to
look after them, they cannot have a worry in the world.

My errand is a banal one: to buy stamps and photocopy my
last *Times* article. Chinatown's sub post office, in Doyer Street,
is closed. I must go on to the huge, horrible branch at Church
and Canal. I take the back way across Centre Street, glancing
down to the courthouse where I successfully summonsed my
first New York landlord by hitting him with the summons and
running. I go along Walker Street, a cobbled alleyway like
Victorian Liverpool, where I and someone else lived for six
months, with great difficulty. The plant pots we bought so
hopefully are still up there on the fire escape.

Outside Canal Street Post Office, huge, ugly dogs with idiotic
expressions are tethered like cow ponies to the stair-rail. Inside,
expecting chaos, I find cool emptiness. A black girl clerk dressed
like one of the Poynter Sisters gives me a sheet of airmail
stickers with my stamps, then says, 'I'll get you a folder for
your stamps if you'd care for it."

'Thank you.'

'You're welcome.'

Sometimes, I truly believe I am.

I buy stationery from a discount store, where a fat man
chewing a wet cigar bellows furiously at all three of his assistants
to run around and fetch me carbon paper and clip-fasten en-
velopes. I return along Canal Street, the world's most useful
thoroughfare if you need a sheet of foam rubber or a second-

hand dentist chair. The flea markets are open, the TriBeCa trendies out and strutting. A bundle of rags, that proves to be a man with no legs, lies unregarded in the middle of the pavement.

I turn left up Mott Street, thinking, as always, of Lorenz Hart's words to 'Manhattan' and wishing I'd written them. At Grand Street, Chinatown abruptly becomes Little Italy. Waiting to buy Genoese salami at Di Palo's grocery, I am severely jostled by a moustachioed matriarch. 'Hey!' Mr Di Palo, master sculptor in mozzarella, reproves her. 'You may be my auntie but you still gotta wait in line!'

Crossing back into Chinatown, I buy grapes, outsize greengages and perfect nectarines, all for less than I would pay in Bayswater. I have my *Times* article photocopied at a Chinese newspaper wholesaler's, next to the empty case of the biggest grandfather clock I ever saw.

I return home along Grand, past that magnificent, quite unironic edifice 'The Bowery Savings Bank'. The burned-over derelict is still doing his tightrope act down the middle of the road. Business is booming in the restaurant supply shops and the underground noodle factories. At the rear of my loft, under the propellor fan, I can hear almost none of it. I turn on CBS-FM, sit down at the table and try to think of something to write.

Two blocks east of the Bowery, black boys in satin Bermuda shorts stand on the backs of old farm trucks stacked with watermelons that might have come straight up from Georgia. 'Dollar each, check 'em out,' the boys shout. 'Fine 'n' sweet – jus' like me.'

'. . . all round here used to be real scary,' my friend Kim said. 'It was the big East Side heroin district . . . dealers on the street . . . the dealers' bodyguards . . . people everywhere shooting up. It's all gone since Mayor Koch's Operation Pressure Point. Last winter, the police were here day after day, busting and busting. It cost the City a fortune. But it worked.' She indicated cobbled cross streets, empty but for Chinese housewives tripping home with laden pink grocery bags.

We stopped at the corner of Grand and Essex Street, where Puerto Rican housing 'projects' stretch down to the East River. Essex Street, 20 blocks north, becomes Avenue A, another place one used not to dare frequent alone. Now, Avenue A is long since engulfed by East Village trendies. They are starting to open art galleries even down on Avenue C.

Essex Street at the Bowery end is still in the pre-fashionable state that Kim calls 'funky'. It remains predominantly Hassidic – or, as one haberdasher's signboard proudly proclaims, 'The skullcap center of New York'. Store after store offers supplies and catering for religious festivals and bar-mitzvahs. 'There's Guss Pickles,' Kim said, pointing at a name etched in turquoise glitter. 'And there's a great Jewish deli called Glatt Kosher . . . you should see the lines there before every holiday. If you buy a chicken, you get a free gallon of chicken soup.'

At Essex and Rivington is Bernstein's, New York's first kosher Chinese restaurant, purveying such compromised delicacies as 'sweet and pungent veal'. Inside, a Chinese in a white sailor hat slices pastrami. The Jewish waiters wear skullcaps with scarlet Chinese tassles at the back.

'Have you been to Sammy's Roumanian Restaurant?' Kim asked.

'I passed it in a cab the other night. It looked cheap and cheerful.'

'My God! It's not cheap,' Kim said. "I had a birthday party there . . . because it's really fun. They have a microphone that they pass from table to table and anyone who wants to can sing a song. There was a belly dancer, too. The waiters are identical triplets – three boys with Jewish-Afro haircuts, that you just *can't* tell apart. They kept tricking us into ordering more food. One of them would come up and ask us "Do you want another bottle of vodka?" and we'd say "Okay". Then one of his brothers would say "More vodka?" and we'd say, "Yes, we told you . . ." So we ended up ordering three times what we needed.

"The check, for 30 of us, was 900 dollars. And we didn't even have dinner! Just bottles of vodka and hors d'oeuvres."

'Is there a real Sammy?' I asked.

'Oh, sure. He's Jewish, too, even though he rides around in a big cowboy hat.'

We decided to give Sammy's Roumanian Restaurant a miss. Instead, Kim took me to La Luncheonette, a French bistro founded in the wreck of an old stainless steel soda fountain. We sat and watched Jean-Francois, the owner-chef, cook scallops and swordfish in the open like a short-order cook, but with much more drama.

'Jean Francois started as an actor,' Kim, the omniscient, said. 'In France he met this man who offered him a place in a French theatre group in Washington DC. So Jean Francois sold everything he owned and bought a plane ticket to Washington. When he got there he found that the man who'd hired him had gone to jail for counterfeiting money. Jean Francois couldn't speak a word of English. The only thing he could do was work in a French restaurant. Then he got so disgusted with the way French cooking was in America, he decided to open up on his own . . . I had a birthday party here as well . . .'

She broke off and grimaced as a group of loudly incoherent East Village trendies overran the big window table.

'There'll soon be no real New York left,' Kim said sadly. 'Where will they start to open art galleries next? Brooklyn? Long Island City?'

We walked back up Essex, past Bernstein's kosher Chinese, Guss Pickles and 'The Skullcap center of New York', over the invisible frontier into Chinatown. We walked along Canal Street at its silent eastern end, where the police's 'Jade Squad' seldom goes, and Cadillacs stand all night, in lengths of polished shadow, outside the Chinese speakeasies and gambling dens.

'Next time,' Kim said, 'I *must* take you for dinner at Exterminator Chili. The guys who run it modelled it on a boy's bedroom in the Fifties. It's all boy food – chili, and egg-creams and cookies with milk. It used to be a Chinese coffee shop . . . before that, I think, it was Greek. The same old lady and her daughter have always worked there as waitresses. They *love* the way it is now. They wear great uniforms . . . they get to drink . . . meet funky

people. They can't believe the place can be run by such crazy
guys.'

The store at the corner of Grand and Mott Street announces
itself, thanks to a signwriter's error, as 'Di Palo's Diary Stores'.
One is soon undeceived by the cheeses that throng the window,
lettered all over their waxed skins like medieval parchment; the
huge, streaky hams suspended from ribboned hooks, and the
almost life-size calf, sculpted from mozzarella, squatting back on
its haunches, jovially inviting one to come in.

The entire Di Palo family serves behind the shoulder-high
counter, slicing, weighing and totting up on the thick grease-
proof paper in which one's purchases are wrapped with a care
that disappeared from British High Streets 20 years ago. There
are two Di Palo matriarchs, one fair, one opulently dark, and the
latter's husband, a deep-jowelled, gruffly genial man in a straw
boater. There is a young Di Palo, like his papa but many times
slimmer. There are several Misses Di Palo, black-eyed and
fluffy-haired, at whom I can never look without imagining the
vast protocol necessary for their wooing and winning.

Anyone who enters Di Palo's is instantly involved in the life
of the shop and family. It is, indeed, as pleasant to wait as to be
served, standing under cool fans on the sawdust-strewn floor,
reading the inventory of salamis on offer, enjoying the aesthetics
of Italian packaging, and the constant dialogue. Though many
customers are relatives, scrupulous fairness prevails in the
serving-order. However busy the store, one will be offered a
broad knife, bearing a sliver of cheese to taste, and a small,
savoury corner of Mr or Mrs Di Palo's personality.

The range of cheese extends to Canadian cheddar, even English
Stilton. But the speciality is that wonderful, wet, white rubbery
stuff, spooned from brine and wrapped in damp papers the best of
all hors d'oeuvres with tomato and basil. At morning, you can see
young Di Palo bring out a heated wood crate, with new-made
mozzarellas strung inside like a smoking abacus, to cool on the
sidewalk. Mr Di Palo sculpts in mozzarella – birds, animals, heraldic
devices. 'I was in London,' he said to me, without preamble, one

day. 'Beautiful city . . . only I couldn't find any mozzarella to eat for lunch. I finally bought some in the City of London, and sat down to eat it beside Tower Bridge. It was wonderful!'

Di Palo's tends to throw Little Italy's few other food shops into eclipse. Alleva, at Mulberry and Grand, has nothing like the jollity. You go there for smoked mozzarella, spinach bread – or if you feel taciturn. Opposite is the Little Italy Food Center, a supermarket with an immense, ham-hung deli counter where whole loaves are split and basted with hot sausage and pepper stew for heavy lunches out of doors.

There are precious few such reminders of the genuine Little Italy, in which Sicilian duels used to be fought on parking lots and acappella groups sang at street-corners. Today it is a mainly tourist quarter of tinsely espresso bars and restaurants to avoid. The fetuccini is like knicker elastic, the service disdainful and, if you are specially unfortuanate, men dressed as Swiss Guards barge in with rattling guitars, then hold out their be-ruffed hands aggressively for tips.

Mafia folklore plays its part in the tourist trap. Umberto's Clam House, on Mulberry, has boomed since Joey Gallo was shot there – so has Vincent's Clam Bar, whither the bullet-riddled mobster manager to stagger before dying on the pavement.

Uptown visitors long ago discovered that the best Italian blow-out is to be had at La Luna, a little pink gingham place, just off Canal Street, which still ladles out portions with total disregard for cuisine minceur. The food is stupefying, the welcome variable. As I queued in the porch with some friends recently, a waiter emerged, glared widly at us and groaned '*Jesus*!'

I prefer the less frequented Little Italy, down Mott and Elizabeth Street where, after dark, colloquies of ample women in summer frocks, with errant bodice-straps, sit out on chairs gossiping, and elderly swains, in fitted pink shirts and perma-pressed white bellbottoms, whisper sweet nothings into open ground-floor windows, at lady loves lurking there with the lights out. I am fascinated by the decrepit storefronts, jumbled with plaster madonnas, trucking company showcards and prewar ads for Lucky Strike; and the so innocently named 'social clubs', which scarcely bother to conceal their purpose as gangster job centres.

My favourite excursion from The Bowery has been to eat Vietnamese food in Chinatown, then walk up to the Caffe Roma on Broome Street. It is a cavernous place, painted deep green. At the far end, the Gaggia machine creaks and hisses under an ornate long case wall clock. One sits at marble tables, on ridiculous gilt chairs, drinking the kind of espresso that can have one still awake, planning the rest of one's life, at five o'clock the next morning.

Just round the corner on Mulberry is an ancient, nameless Italian bar with a long green wooden facade somewhat like the old Leoni's restaurant in Soho. Around its walls hang dim oil paintings, several of them showing its proprietor as a god-like young man. He is now a very old man, chewing a fat cigar, with one eye always on the TV ball game, as he pours out your Strega. The bar, I'm told, needed no alteration whatever when used as a location for the film of 'The Godfather'. I only wish I knew the rest of the story.

The luckier Bowery dwellers can scrape up enough small change to buy a wash cloth and window-cleaning aerosol. As cars stop at the lights on Grand Street, they receive an unsolicited windshield valeting. Though most keep their windows firmly wound, an arm will droop out occasionally with a quarter. Any semblance of work seems preferable to straight begging. There is a man out every day among the traffic, wiping windshields with the backs of his bare hands.

The Bowery's dwellers seem anything but menacing. Many of them, indeed, can hardly stand. By noon each day, it is as if some premature holocaust has flung their bundled, inert forms all around, in factory doorways and outside busy banks. One young black man lies among the pedestrians, next to his overturned wheelchair. I pass by with the tunnel vision developed on assignment in kindred cities like Calcutta. But I cannot help noticing the bare ankles of a figure, collapsed beside a fancy

Italian lampshade store. The skin has the colour and texture of thick dark grey velvet.

Like everything else in New York, derelict men keep to their allotted zones. You find them at the junction of Bowery with Grand and Hester and Houston, but seldom even a block to the east or west. They also collect in the lee of the old Court House building on Lafayette, lying in an open air dormitory of fruit-boxes and garbage. From time to time, the police come along and roust them out in the playful spirit of a hayfield coney-hunt.

Destitution levels the races. Everyone has the same scorched-black skin and slow, lurching, slave-manacled walk. Not all, however, wear the uniform of burned-over rags. Some have acquired bizarre outfits, cast off from fortunate lives – Palm Beach plaid coats and pastel flared trousers, high fashion 15 years ago, or baseball caps and sweatshirts inscribed 'Yale' or 'UCLA'. Age is likewise obliterated. You can tell young from old only by the occasional patriarchal white beard.

Among their better-off neighbours, the Chinese show them most compassion. The Peking Dumpling House on Hester Street provides a free tea urn and gives away 10 meals each Sunday. Early in the morning, lines of refugees from the flophouse hotels sit outside the Chinese coffee shops, each with a steaming paper cup and, maybe, a doughnut or Danish. Today I saw a Chinese shopkeeper, bent over a prostrate figure, repeating, 'What you need? What you need?' The Italians by contrast sit, impassive, outside their 'social clubs' or stare at nothing from the idle depths of espresso bars.

Like Harlem, the Bowery used to be somewhere smart New Yorkers went to get their kicks. Sammy's Bowery bar was known as 'The poor man's Stork Club'. Among the books in my loft are collections of photographs by the famous 'Weegee', who was to New York's low life what Bill Brandt was to London's. Here is Sammy's with Sherman Billingsley, owner of the real Stork Club, slumming in silk suit and fedora, and 'Shorty, the Bowery cherub', a diapered dwarf, drinking a toast to New Year, 1945. 'Weegee' could make Skid Row look almost beautiful, too, with sunlight dripping through the slats of the old elevated railway.

The spirit most in evidence among these neglected, humiliated men is still – believe it or not – conviviality. The colloquys on rickety chairs, or squatting along steel manhole covers, strike attitudes of intense rhetorical enjoyment. The lone figure lurching from Al's, the last remaining Bowery bar, raises his empty beer bottle to the health of a real nice guy inside. A tiny, shirtless old man, lying among rubbish outside the AAA Noodle Co, arches up his minute torso towards the sun. 'C'mon over,' someone calls to him from the Hotel Providence. 'There's a whole bunch of guys here. We're talking.'

As I return to 98 Bowery, I find a man in a green baseball cap sitting on the narrow front doorstep. He gets up with such politeness, it is contagious.

'I'll just disturb you a moment,' I say.

He grins and says, 'You gotta be Irish.'

'Almost.'

'I'm Irish,' he says, and draws himself up with visible pride. 'Frank David O'Flynn . . .'

The months of sub-zero temperatures – when men will still go about half-naked – seem far away. There is good humour even among the windshield cleaners on Grand Street. The other day, a blue Impala stopped there, driven by a lone girl. As the wash cloths zeroed in, she looked terrified and buzzed her automatic window shut. The men laughed and sprayed aerosol hearts all over the glass in front of her.